The Poetry of

Seamus Heaney

EDITED BY ELMER ANDREWS

Series editor: Richard Beynon

ICON BOOKS

Published in 1998 by Icon Books Ltd.,
Grange Road, Duxford, Cambridge CB2 4QF
e-mail: icon@mistral.co.uk

Distributed in the UK, Europe, Canada, South Africa and Asia by the
Penguin Group: Penguin Books Ltd., 27 Wrights Lane, London W8 5TZ

Published in Australia in 1998 by Allen & Unwin Pty. Ltd.,
PO Box 8500, 9 Atchison Street, St. Leonards, NSW 2065

Series editor: Richard Beynon
Series devised by: Christopher Cox
Cover design: Christos Kondeatis
Typesetting: Wayzgoose

ISBN 1 84046 017 2

Printed and bound in Great Britain by
Cox & Wyman Ltd., Reading

Contents

sides of the Irish 'cultural debate'. On one hand there are the views of
those (Conor Cruise O'Brien, Ciaran Carson, Edna Longley, Blake
Morrison, George Watson) who are critical of what they see as the
dangerous and debilitating atavisms in Heaney's political poetry, and of
those (Mark Patrick Hederman, Denis Donoghue, Seamus Deane) who
find his mythological and archaeological procedures productive and
impressive. The chapter concludes with a consideration of Heaney's own
views on the relation between poetry and politics.

Gender, Colonialism, Nationalism

This chapter begins by examining Heaney's elaborate sexual myth that
relates gender, colonialism and nationalism. This is followed by exegetical
commentary from Seamus Deane and Jonathan Allison on Heaney's
tropes of sex and marriage. The second half of the chapter is devoted to
feminist critical reaction to Heaney's poetry in recent years, and includes
excerpts from Elizabeth Butler Cullingford's 'Thinking of Her . . . as . . .
Ireland: Yeats, Pearse and Heaney', Patricia Coughlan's '"Bog Queens":
The Representation of Women in John Montague and Seamus Heaney',
and Catherine Byron's *Out of Step: Pursuing Seamus Heaney to Purgatory*.

Powers of Earth and Visions of Air

This chapter concentrates on the major shift in Heaney's poetic outlook
and practice that makes itself increasingly apparent in and after *Field
Work*. A range of interpretative accounts of Heaney's later work charts
this shift and offers an assessment of Heaney's poetic development.
These include Ciaran Carson's sharply evaluative review of *Sweeney
Astray*, Seamus Deane's brilliant account of the 'Antaean'/'Herculean'
tension in Heaney's poetry, Henry Hart's essay on the visionary intensities
of *Seeing Things* and Nicholas Jenkins' review of Heaney's latest volume,
The Spirit Level. The chapter concludes with an excerpt from John Wilson
Foster's study, *The Achievement of Seamus Heaney,* which discusses
Heaney's development in the terms that have been used to structure this
Guide as a whole.

INTRODUCTION

VARIOUS ASPECTS of Heaney's poetry have attracted considerable critical debate from different perspectives. Each of the first four chapters in this Guide identifies and concentrates on a particular aspect, or on closely related aspects, of Heaney's poetry that have proved controversial. Inevitably, though, there is some overlap between the aspects high-lighted in each chapter (for example, questions of gender (chapter four) are intimately bound up with considerations of identity (chapter two) and the arguments about political poetry (chapter three)). In each chapter, the main issues are outlined and explained with reference to both the poetry itself and Heaney's prose comments so that readers will have sufficient contextual information to help them assess the sampling of criticism that is offered. The final chapter is rather more exegetical and descriptive, presenting interpretative accounts of the major development in Heaney's poetry in terms suggested by the chapter title – 'Powers of Earth and Visions of Air'. The title is Seamus Deane's, who used it for his excellent *Times Literary Supplement* review of Heaney's *New Selected Poems*, which is reprinted in this chapter. By considering the evolution of Heaney's vision and poetics up to his most recent volume, *The Spirit Level*, it is hoped the reader will be helped towards discovering for him or herself what Henry James once called 'the figure in the carpet', the pattern of development in Heaney's varied and prolific career.

Some of the most important insights into Heaney's poetry come, of course, from the poet himself who, in his three volumes of prose, seeks, as the American critic and Harvard academic Helen Vendler says, 'to articulate a comprehensive and responsible poetics'.[1] Heaney is his own most severe and penetrating critic and much of what he has to say about other poets says as much about himself as about them. As Chris Agee remarks, in his review of *The Government of the Tongue*, Heaney's criticism of other poets' work 'offers us an opening into the deep values which animate Heaney's progress as a poet.'[2] Much of the other criticism of his work represented in this Guide is rooted in Heaney's own critical and aesthetic vocabulary, which, as Desmond Fennell emphasises, is itself reflective of canonical values: Heaney's prose is read to elucidate the poems and the success or failure of the poems is evaluated by the conformity with the project articulated in the prose; or, more implicitly, the poems are evaluated in terms of a critical orthodoxy that values the New Critical ideal of the 'well-made poem', an orthodoxy to which Heaney himself conforms, and which he thus reinforces, in his own poetic practice and literary criticism.

There is also another kind of criticism represented in this Guide. This is one in which the author creates his/her *own* critical reading that goes beyond not only Heaney's terms (and those canonically sanctioned) but also an evaluative vocabulary centred on appreciation (is the poem a success or a failure?). Thus, we have, for example, David Lloyd's relentless and coldly savage critique of Heaney's poetry from a post-colonial Marxian perspective; Clair Wills' feminist interrogation of Heaney's gender politics; and excerpts from the 'cultural debate' about the controversial intersection between literature and politics that has been conducted by Edna Longley, John Wilson Foster, Mark Patrick Hederman, Seamus Deane and Richard Kearney in the pages of *The Crane Bag*, the Field Day pamphlets and in such stimulating and provocative books as Longley's *Poetry in the Wars*, Deane's *Celtic Revivals*, Richard Kearney's *Transitions: Narratives of Modern Irish Culture* and John Wilson Foster's *The Achievement of Seamus Heaney*. Excerpts from these high-powered contributions to the contemporary 'cultural debate' in Ireland appear alongside a more traditional form of style-based critical appreciation exemplified by John Carey, Christopher Ricks, A. Alvarez and Helen Vendler.

CHAPTER ONE

Heaney and the Anglo-American Canon

WE SHALL begin by considering some important and influential English and American reactions to Heaney's poetry as they appeared in contemporary reviews of individual collections of Heaney's poems and in retrospective assessments of his career as a whole. From these reactions it is possible to deduce Heaney's relation to the Anglo-American canon, and, indeed, follow the process whereby he himself is installed at the very centre of that canon. The material included here will also include discussion of the literary context in which Heaney wrote, and offer comment on Heaney's relation to the English poetic tradition, especially his connection with Wordsworth, Keats and the Romantics, Larkin and the Movement, and with the movements of modernism and post-modernism.

Few writers can boast such an impressive volume of work as Seamus Heaney has produced in the last thirty years: nineteen books of poetry, nine poetry pamphlets, two books of selected poems, one book-length verse translation, three collections of essays, one play, and two anthologies of poetry. And few writers in their lifetime achieve the kind of popularity and reputation that Seamus Heaney has. Rand Brandes, co-author with Michael J. Durkan of a comprehensive bibliography of Heaney materials, *Seamus Heaney: A Reference Guide* (New York: G.K. Hall, 1994), believes 'more critical and media attention has been focused on Heaney and his work than any other contemporary Irish poet and perhaps any other poet in the English-speaking world outside of America in the last thirty years'.[1] Back in the 1970s, Clive James rightly prophesied that 'some people are going to start comparing him with Yeats'. 'The greatest Irish poet since Yeats', Robert Lowell unequivocally announced after reading *North* (1975); 'The one undoubtedly major poet in the English-speaking world',[2] according to John Carey, Merton Professor of Poetry at Oxford University, in 1988. Later, referring to the poems in *Seeing Things* (1991), Carey concluded his *Sunday Times* review with these words: 'Reading these and several other poems, you feel what the first readers of, say,

Keats's odes or Milton's 1645 collection must have felt – the peculiar excitement of watching a new masterwork emerge and take its permanent place in our literature'. To which, Declan Kiberd, Professor of English at University College Dublin, noting Carey's tactful reference to Heaney as an 'English-speaking' poet rather than a 'British' poet (a designation to which Heaney has taken exception) remarks with tongue-in-cheek incredulity: 'But Milton? Keats? "our literature"? Greater love no English critic hath than to write such lines of an Irish poet. You will hunt in vain for a similar plaudit to Yeats in his own lifetime'.[3]

Heaney's attitude to England has always been ambivalent. He made explicit his desire not to be called a 'British' poet in *An Open Letter* (Field Day pamphlet No. 2, 1993) in which he objected to Blake Morrison and Andrew Motion referring to him as 'British' in their anthology *The Penguin Book of Contemporary British Poetry* (1982): 'Be advised! My passport's green. / No glass of ours was ever raised! To toast *The Queen*'. Robert McLiam Wilson was not the only one to be surprised by Heaney's 'uncharacteristically extreme objections' to being included in an anthology of British poetry. In a bitingly critical article, Wilson sarcastically commented that there seemed to be 'some frays, some petty and reductive nationalisms over which a poet finds no need to rise'.[4] John Wilson Foster offered a more understanding view:

■ One suspects the specific pressures on Heaney from his more nationalist colleagues and friends. I hear him talking in this pamphlet less to Motion and Morrison than to his own, and making appropriate anti-colonialist noises, but noises which are not only comfortless but also un-Heaney-like, poetically as well as politically. More than some influential others in Ireland, Heaney knows how tangled are the literary as well as political relations between Ireland and Britain and how unavailable they are to the simplicities of doggerel and pamphlets.[5] □

Despite his desire not to be called a 'British' poet, Heaney has published all his work with the British company Faber & Faber, and has been the recipient of many of the most prestigious British literary awards. The early work especially had an immediate appeal to British readers, including those in the divided community of Northern Ireland, and although he saw himself as 'politicising the terrain' in *Wintering Out* (1972), the poems, as Edna Longley has remarked, 'respect dialect more than dialectic'.[6] His poetry has been largely shaped by the great tradition of English poetry. Early critics were quick to point out the influences of Wordsworth, Hughes and Hopkins as well as the examples of Yeats, Kavanagh and Hewitt closer to home, and Frost in America. Critics of the later work duly noted an ever-widening circle of influence: Hardy, Lowell, Dante, the Eastern European poets such as Zbigniew Herbert,

Czeslaw Milosz, Miroslaw Holub and Osip Mandelstam. Heaney himself has always generously acknowledged the 'British dimension' in his own development, acknowledging a debt even to poets such as Edmund Spenser and Walter Ralegh, who also figure in his poetry as representatives of English colonialism.

Chris Agee interestingly notes that, in his essays on individual poets, Heaney deals with 'exemplary and universal issues in literature' rather than specifically Irish ones; and that 'he has the gift, furthermore, of being both absolutely faithful to the poet under discussion and highly revealing of his own personal stance'.[7] Heaney's criticism of other poets' work, Agee concludes, 'offers us an opening into the deep values which animate Heaney's progress as a poet'. Thus, in his most recent collection of essays, *The Redress of Poetry*, Heaney writes about such diverse poets as Christopher Marlowe, Brian Merriman, John Clare, Oscar Wilde, Dylan Thomas, Yeats, and Elizabeth Bishop. 'In each of the lectures', Helen Vendler comments:

■ Heaney is working out his own relation to possible models. Herbert (the Protestant aristocrat, the Renaissance courtier) could not, in some sense, be further from the boy born to Catholic parents on an Ulster farm. In saluting the extraordinary human depth and linguistic originality of Herbert . . ., Heaney counters the reductive (and ridiculous) notion that one can find ethical and aesthetic sustenance only in writers who resemble oneself in ethnicity and class.[8] □

In the last of his Oxford Lectures of 1995, 'Frontiers of Writing', Heaney explains: 'I wrote about the colour of the passport . . . not in order to expunge the British connection in Britain's Ireland, but to maintain the right to diversity within the border'. He relishes the 'challenge of being in two minds', inviting Northern Protestants to 'make a corresponding effort at two-mindedness, and start to conceive of themselves within – rather than beyond – the Irish element'.[9]

Widely taught in schools and colleges throughout the English-speaking world (and indeed beyond) since his first publication, *Eleven Poems* (1965), Heaney's work has been the subject of over twenty full-length critical studies (books and collections of essays), numerous dissertations and theses, and countless reviews, notices and articles. He won the Somerset Maugham Award in 1967 for *Death of a Naturalist*, the Duff Cooper Memorial Prize in 1975 and the W.H. Smith Award in 1976 for *North*, the Whitbread Award in 1987 for *The Haw Lantern*, the *Sunday Times* prize for excellence in writing in 1988, and, in 1995, the greatest of them all – the Nobel Prize for Literature. A scholar and critic as well as poet, he has scaled the heights of academic success with the appointment to the Boylston Chair of Rhetoric and Oratory at Harvard in 1982, and, in 1989, to the Chair of Poetry at Oxford. It is hard to think how he could have been more thoroughly institutionalised and canonised in Britain and America. In Ireland he is 'Seamus Famous'.

The sources of Heaney's popularity are manifold. In the beginning, at least, the great advantage that his poetry possessed was its accessibility. His Keatsian sensuousness, his gift for recreating the physical actuality of the external world, his primitive trust in the mimetic magic of onomato-poeia and the force of simple visual imagery quickly won him many admirers of all ages. There was a homely, unassuming and reassuring feel to the poetry. It was rooted in rural experience, it celebrated family traditions of silent rural toil and the sturdy strength and restrained speech of a revered pantheon of labourers and craftsmen. In his retro-spective of Heaney's work, 'The Most Sensuous Poet to Use English Since Keats', in the *Sunday Times* (3 April 1988), John Carey, one of Heaney's most enthusiastic admirers, explains the poet's popularity by referring to both his subject matter (the recreating of a vanishing world and way of life) and his way of writing (his avoidance of affectation and obscurity, the vividness and sensuousness of the language):

■ Seamus Heaney's *The Haw Lantern* contains, among other things, a series of poems in memory of his mother, who died in 1984. Heaney remembers how much she distrusted culture, and the swank and affectation that go with it. She used to mispronounce foreign words and names on purpose ("Bertold Breck"), so as not to seem pretentious. "You know all them things", she would say accusingly to her son, and he would find himself, when speaking to her, using bad grammar, as a kind of peace-offering.

Among the factors that have made Heaney into that contradiction in terms, a best-selling poet, is his avoidance of the obscurity endemic in modern poetry since the days of Eliot and Pound – an obscurity designed to keep 'culture aloof from the philistine masses'. His tribute to his mother suggests that this inherent tact in his poetry, its wish not to perplex other people or make them feel inferior, stems partly from family considerations. Like many children of the postwar generation, he had the benefit of an education that estranged him from parents and fore-bears. But at least half of him remained loyal to their unlearned example, and regarded his own bookishness as a kind of treason.

He matters so much as a poet because he never forgets there are other things that matter more. In an interview with John Haffenden, Heaney has commented on this:

'Dan Jacobson said to me once "You feel bloody well guilty about writing", and there is indeed some part of me that is entirely unimpressed by the activity; that doesn't dislike it, but it's the real generations, I suppose, of rural ancestors – not illiterate, but not literary. They, in me, or I, through them, don't give a damn. I don't know whether that's a good thing or a bad thing.'

Good enough it has turned out, to make him at present the one undoubtedly major poet in the English-speaking world.

He was born in 1939, the eldest of nine children of a Roman Catholic farmer and cattle-dealer in Mossbawn, County Derry, Northern Ireland, and the possible inferiority of poetry to farming and cattle-dealing was from the start one of his subjects.

In the now-famous 'Digging', the first poem in his first collection *Death of a Naturalist* (1966), he admires his father's skill in cutting potato-drills with a spade, and worries about the questionable usefulness of his own skill with a pen. But as his poetry developed, concern about the inadequacy of language and poetry became more than a family matter. It deepened and directed his whole poetic effort. He writes, in his early collections, about country crafts – thatching, butter-churning, forging – where creativity retreats from words into silent, traditional operations. It is part of Heaney's paradoxical role as a word-artist suspicious of words that he learnt about these unbookish activities from a book, Estyn Evan's richly-documented *Irish Folk Ways* (1957).

For many of Heaney's readers these country poems are the favourites, and their popularity reflects late-20th-century anxieties. Urbanisation and technology have come to seem destroyers. The primitive lures us. From this angle, the rise in Heaney's reputation and the boom in health foods are sociologically connected.

But it is not just Heaney's wholemeal subject matter that singles him out: it is how he writes. He is the most sensuous poet to use English since Keats. The feel of things comes so vividly into his poems that they seem to be written in something thicker than language – something like mud, for example, which he has, in fact, written about a good deal, and which spreads its darkly glutinous texture through the poetry of his middle years. As a child, he remembers, he loved 'paddling through muck in a deep drain' and fingering slime. Bubbles 'gargling' on stagnant water and the 'warm thick slobber of frog-spawn' fascinated him, in a way that was quite beyond his powers of explanation. Another enthusiasm was old wells, with their mud and rottenness and the rich reek of 'fungus and dank moss'. Writing poetry as an adult satisfies, Heaney insists, the same urges as these early mud-delvings. The mud was his own subconscious, into which poetry sunk a shaft.

Through his musings on mud, the Irish peat bog gradually developed as his central image and obsession. He thinks of it as a great, soft womb, sucking history into itself – flints and arrowheads and muskets.

It is also a deep pollen-bin with centuries of pollen sunk in it, and a sun-bank, storing sunlight since the start of time, and a melting grave and an insatiable bride. [. . .]

So the peat-bog's treasures help Heaney to feel his way down past words to things. The iron-age corpses dug out of peat-bogs (which he first read about in P. V. Glob's *The Bog People*) have inspired some of his greatest poems – 'The Grauballe Man' and 'Bog Queen', for example. It is important that their deaths were violent – they were executed criminals or sacrificial victims. This means that they help Heaney both to distance and to focus the victims of modern Ireland's conflict. As a Northern Irish Roman Catholic, he has known terror and sectarian hatred since childhood.[10] □

Death of a Naturalist and *Door into the Dark* attracted considerable attention from other established and influential critics in Britain such as C. B. Cox, Peter Marsh, Dannie Abse, Elizabeth Jennings and Anthony Thwaite. Christopher Ricks, Professor of English at Cambridge University, co-editor of the influential Oxford journal *Essays in Criticism*, and an Empsonian critic whose studies of Milton, Wordsworth, Tennyson and Keats have earned him the reputation of being one of the most ingenious and sensitive of contemporary literary commentators, admired Heaney's sensuous and evocative power in rendering the places, objects and processes of his Co. Derry childhood. Heaney's second collection, *Door into the Dark* (1969), Ricks declared, consolidated Heaney as 'the poet of muddy-booted blackberry-picking'.[11] Heaney's appeal, Ricks suggested, lay in his concern with 'lasting things', by which he meant 'skills like thatching and salmon-fishing; grievances and injustices like those whose seepage still stains Irish living; the seasons and the hours; the farm-lunch in the field, the scene Horatian . . . '. Ricks emphasised the subtlety and delicacy of Heaney's language, highlighting a new note of 'riddling insidiousness', and a use of myth that takes nothing away from the close observation of actual life. Heaney's poetry, Ricks said, is 'lovingly specific and specifically loving'. 'Lasting Things' – the title Ricks gave his review – reflects a Kavanaghesque Heaney, for it was Kavanagh's belief that a genuinely 'parochial' poetry concerned with the local and the ordinary was universal because it dealt with fundamentals. Heaney satisfied Ricks' poetic ideal of an art that was 'generous' and consoling, that appealed to both the intelligence and the emotions, and that possessed a harmony and unity capable of releasing the reader for a moment from the usual divisions of everyday life.

With the publication of *Wintering Out* in 1972, at the height of the Irish Troubles, the amount of attention afforded to Heaney in both Britain and America grew noticeably. The Irish poet, academic and critic, Brendan Kennelly, addressed the political dimension of *Wintering Out* in his review 'Lines on a Distant Prospect of Long Kesh', but most British and American critics were much more absorbed by Heaney's domestic and rural theme, and by the precise quality of his language. In 1975 the first monograph on Heaney's work appeared, Robert Buttel's *Seamus Heaney*, published by an American academic press (the preponderance of books on Heaney have been written by English or American critics). The same year also saw the publication of *North*, the most problematic of all Heaney's collections. Nevertheless, the book was enthusiastically received and secured his place as an established poet on both sides of the Atlantic. While politics could no longer be overlooked in this volume, the poetry was assessed from strictly New Critical perspectives. A gap opens up between a highly specialised form of critical intelligence and the cultural and political preoccupations that underlie the poetry itself.

Christopher Ricks' review of *Field Work*, which appeared in *The London Review of Books* (8 November 1979), gives some idea of the general approach and tenor of English academic criticism of Heaney in the 1970s. Heaney is seen as a force for civilisation and a source of comfort at a time of emergency, violence and threat. Quoting Heaney's line from Coventry Patmore – 'The end of art is peace' – Ricks sees Heaney's poetry as 'urgently exemplary'. 'Heaney', he ringingly announces, 'is the most trusted poet in our islands'. That trust, he goes on to explain, is built on the integrity of the poet's language, especially when the pressures to bend it to political causes are so great, as they are in Ireland. Ricks' criticism, with its scrupulous attention to textual detail and ingenious unravelling of the finest nuances of literary meaning, represents a traditional Enlightenment rationalism, impatient with theory, expressive of a generous, liberal-minded English intellectualism. Heaney can be 'trusted' for his decency, reasonableness and common human sympathy. Ricks notes the political exacerbations that make themselves felt in the poetry, but his assumption that the work springs from a structure of shared beliefs remains intact. Differences are conveniently ignored.

■ Those of us who have never swallowed an oyster have presumably never lived life to the full. The Augustan poet was not merely mocking the heroic when he said that the man must have had a palate coated o'er with brass who first risked the living morsel down his throat. Seamus Heaney offers 'Oysters' ('Alive and violated') as his opening. Opened at once are the oyster, the mouth, the meal and the book. It is at the start a delicious poem, not least in its play of the obdurate against the liquid:

> Our shells clacked on the plates
> My tongue was a filling estuary
> My palate hung with starlight.

'Clacked', for once, does not rebuke the 'tongue' of other people; 'plates' finds itself soothed out into 'palate', rather like 'oysters' into 'estuary'.

But indignation flickers and though it is appeased, it is not expunged.

> Bivalves: the split bulb
> And philandering sigh of ocean.
> Millions of them ripped and shucked and scattered

We are not to sigh Shucks. For even the happiest recollection is likely to be tinged with snobbery, as if memory were a fine cellar:

> And there we were, toasting friendship,
> Laying down a perfect memory
> In the cool of thatch and crockery.

So, in the end, having next riddled the oysters (they are something of a riddle themselves) as, 'The frond-lipped, brine stung /Nuts of privilege', the *poem* is stung too:

> And was angry that my trust could not repose
> In the clear light, like poetry of freedom
> Leaning in from sea, I ate the day
> Deliberately, that its tang
> Might quicken me all into verb, pure verb.

The anger is real but is headstrong. Instead of the nouns of privilege (property and possessions) there is to be the imaginative activity that is alive only as verb. At least since Ezra Pound this has been a lure for poets, a thrill and a delusion. For as Heaney's last line acknowledges, 'verb' is undissolubly a noun. And the word which matters most is 'trust'.

When we come to close this book which opened with 'Oysters', we have finally contemplated the hideous devouring of a living morsel through all eternity. For the book ends with 'Ugolino', Dante's insatiable avenger, gnawing undyingly and unkillingly upon the head of the man who had starved to death his children and him:

> That sinner eased his mouth up off his meal
> To answer me, and wiped it with the hair
> Left growing on his victim's ravaged skull
> Then said . . .

The eased is cause of wonder, and of horror, like the serviceableness and decorum of that napkin of hair. 'Ugolino' too is in part about trust:

> How my good faith
> Was easy prey to his malignancy . . .

The word 'prey' feels how intimate may be the bonds between trusting and tasting. Both the first and the last poems in this book speak of 'my tongue'.

Field Work is alive with trust (how else would field work be possible?), and it could have been created only by an experienced poet secure in the grounded trust that he is trusted. Heaney is the most trusted poet of our islands. (Larkin is now trusted not to produce bad poems, but not necessarily to produce poems.) *Field Work* is an even better book than *North*, Heaney's last collection, in that it is more profoundly exemplary. One poem is admittedly sceptical of the word 'exemplary' when applied to poets, as is clear from the question which the poet, lodged in the ninth cycle of Hell, puts to his wife when ('Aided and abetted by Virgil's wife') she visits his damnation. About the poets now alive, he asks:

> Whose is the life
> Most dedicated and exemplary?

But Heaney's art is urgently exemplary while being aware that urgency may easily be in collusion with violence and threats. A landscape's peace of nature, a person's peace of mind, a land's peace: 'The end of art is peace' could be, we are told, the motto of the woven harvest bow.

North, by bending itself to deep excavations within the past of Ireland and of elsewhere, achieved a racked dignity in the face of horrors. The poems were truly enlightened. But *Field Work* shows, more variously and with high composure, that there is something more primary than enlightenment. Henry James said of Eugenie de Guerin and her piety, what could not be said of Heaney and his, that she 'was certainly not enlightened'. Yet when James went on, 'But she was better than this – she was light itself,' the respectful directness of this does itself have something of light's unarguable presence. Its presence is not sentimentalised in Heaney's poems. 'I think the candour of the light dismayed us.'

Ungullible trust will always be of value but especially so in Ireland torn by reasonable and unreasonable distrust and mistrust. The resilient strength of these poems is in the equanimity even of their surprise at some blessed moment of everyday trust. So the book's second poem, 'After a Killing', likewise gives us food for thought, but this time the food is not outré like oysters. What hope is there, after a killing? Only this – and if we insist on prefacing it with 'only' we have already sold the pass:

> And today a girl walks in home to us
> Carrying a basket full of new potatoes,
> Three tight green cabbages, and carrots
> With the tops and mould still fresh on them.

Such an ending, in its tender hope, looks cynicism's desperation levelly in the eye. The gait with which the line itself 'walks in home to us' is simply sturdy. There are no exclamations, even of gratitude, just a sense of gratitude. What could be less novel than those new potatoes? Some may think that this is bathos, but the presence within these poems of William Wordsworth (Dorothy and he at one point make a fleeting appearance, grave comic spectres not lightly to be called up for comparison) is a reminder that after the Augustans had derided it there really was discovered to be such a thing as the art of sinking in poetry.

Art practises what it preaches, and it turns into substantial worth what might be unworthy in both of those verbs. Heaney's poems matter because their uncomplacent wisdom of trust is felt upon the pulses, his and ours, and they effect this because they themselves constitute a living relationship of trust between him and us. He trusts you not to snigger at surprising simplicities:

> trusting the gift,
> risking gift's undertow,

says Heaney of a man with a musical gift and it is brought home that there may be as much wisdom in trusting your own gifts as in trusting those who bear gifts.

What saves the poems from cadging is their supple legitimate pre-emption, their conscious bracing and resourceful acknowledgement of what is at stake. Braced to, not against, as in this description of the sunflower as 'braced to its pebble-dashed wall', where even 'dashed' is secure and stable and not destructively hasty. A great deal of mistrust is misconstruction, and like the acrobat half-feigning a faltering Heaney's poems often tremble with the possibilities of misconstruing and misconstruction which they openly provide but which only a predator would pounce upon.

It is there, for instance, in the play of 'mould' against 'fresh':

> and carrots
> With the tops and mould still fresh on them.

After all, one near-fetched sense of the word 'mould' would bring it into contention with 'fresh'. Heaney's sense of the word here (the brown earth not the green mildew) is manifestly unmistakable, but in the force of the line is partly a matter of the other sense's being summoned in order to be gently found preposterous. Nothing can more bring home the innocent freshness of carrots with the earth still on them than the calm rejection – utterly unutterable – of the dingier sense of 'mould'. [. . .]

Heaney's comedy, like all the best comedy, is a matter of trust. So 'The Skunk' is an exquisitely comic love poem, and you have to love your wife most trustingly, and trust in the reciprocity, before you would trust yourself to a comparison of her to a skunk. No offence meant; no offence launched. Then the poem is at once followed by 'Homecomings', where the loved woman is a clay nest and the man a martin. Affectionate, delicate, calmingly dark, and as confidently trusting in its own arc as is the bird in its flights nimbly and repeatedly home, the poem goes out of its way to speak in ways which lend themselves to misconstruction if it weren't that love is a nesting trust. 'Far in, featherbrains, tucked in silence.' For in this sweet evocation of the bird within the nest of the woman's head, nothing could be more remote than the accusation that anyone is feather-brained. How could we appreciate such trustful remoteness except by calling up the sheer ludicrousness of the possibility?

> Mould my shoulders inward to you
> Occlude me
> Be damp clay pouting
> Let me listen under your eaves.

The tucked-in pressure is there in the way in which 'mould' wants to expand into 'shoulders'; and the mouth of the clay nest may be 'pouting', but in the confidence that no other pouting is going on (pure Keats, this). Nothing could be more unmisgivingly an act of loving inclusion than the stern word 'occlusion' here, just as nothing could be less furtive, more openly trusting than the final eavesdropping.

No need of manna when the actual is marvellous, our conversation

> A white tablecloth spread out
> Like a book of manners in the wilderness.

Likewise, the word 'implicated' is consciously innocent in Heaney: implicated, not in wrong-doing, but as the plaiting of the harvest bow. Heaney's resourcefulness is astonishing, not least in that astonishment is not then something which the poems incite. This pacific art has learnt from the poet to whom Heaney offers here an elegy, Robert Lowell, but the effect is altogether different from Lowell's Atlantic astonishments. But then Heaney's trust in other poets is itself part of his art, as in the rueful comfort to be divined within the conclusive line: 'Our island is full of comfortless noises'. Be not afeard, the isle is full of noises . . . And that's true too.[12] □

Another English critic, less impressed by Heaney than Cox or Carey or Ricks, is A. Alvarez. In his controversial review of *Field Work*, 'A Fine Way with the Language' in *The New York Review of Books* (6 March 1980), Alvarez describes Heaney's poetry as 'steady, discreet, reliable, and highly successful'. It has, he says, the right kind of appeal for contemporary English taste. That appeal lies in the poet's 'fine way with the language'. Heaney, Alvarez says, is a poet 'besotted with words', but refined, restrained and operating comfortably in a recognisable tradition. Even though Heaney has acknowledged his debt to Ted Hughes, a great favourite with Alvarez for his anti-genteel iconoclasm, Alvarez doesn't see a Hughesian Heaney so much as a Movement Heaney, an exponent of the 'well-made' poem that is tame, comfortable, orderly and presents no troubling challenge to the reader. In Alvarez's dangerously stereotypical opinion, Heaney's 'fine way with the language' is the mark of his Irishness, but while that famous Irish eloquence and linguistic self-consciousness may have an invigorating effect on English poetry, it has not, Alvarez insists, signalled any real shift in sensibility or outlook.

■ *Field Work* is Seamus Heaney's fifth collection of verse. He published his first in 1966 and since then his output has been steady and discreet. Like his poetry: steady, discreet, reliable, and highly successful. He has won all the prizes and the reviews of his books have been so unanimous in their praise that now the question of his excellence is no longer discussed; the reviewers content themselves with explicating the subtleties of his textures or his references, as if he were some younger Eliot or Yeats.

It is all very peculiar, particularly in England where new voices have a notoriously hard time in being heard. Even more peculiar is the fact that recognition and success happened to Heaney instantaneously. The British jacket of his second book quotes five rave reviews of his first, three of them by university professors. This in itself would be extraordinary for any young poet anywhere. In England, where the divorce is absolute between the academies and what is called in the US 'creative writing', it was more or less unprecedented. Maybe Rupert Brooke did as well, but it didn't happen to Ted Hughes at first, or even to Philip Larkin, however unassailable his status seems now; it still hasn't happened in Britain to Sylvia Plath.

Why, then, was Heaney an exception? Perhaps it has something to do with his being an Irishman. Since Congreve and Sterne there has always been at least one major Irish star on the British literary scene. Yeats and Joyce are long dead; Patrick Kavanagh outlived them but was too patchy and Dublin parochial; the gifted, underrated Thomas Kinsella departed for America, disappeared into the interior, and has scarcely been heard from since. The only obvious and natural contender is Beckett, but he has resited himself to Paris, writes in French as much as English, and is experimental in a radical, forbidding way which many British academics, as well as the Great British Public, find hard to love. Heaney, if nothing else, is far less unsettling. Moreover, he comes from Northern Ireland and has written eloquently about that troubled and troublesome sore on the British conscience. But so, too, has Michael Longley, who comes from the province and is also an excellent poet. Yet his books sell the usual derisory few hundred, while Heaney, like Larkin, numbers his admirers by the thousand. It would be good to believe that craft and restraint can still be so spectacularly rewarded, but I suspect, alas, that his popularity says less about these modest virtues than about contemporary English taste.

Heaney has in abundance a gift which the English distrust in one another but expect of the Irish: a fine way with the language. What in Brendan Behan, for instance, was a brilliant boozy gift of the gab is transformed by Heaney into rich and sonorous rhetoric. He is a man besotted with words and, like all lovers, he wants to display the beauties and range and subtleties of his beloved. Unlike most, however, he disciplines his passion, reining in for better effect. It is an admirable procedure, although there are times when the urge to make a nice noise gets the better of him:

> I dreamt we slept in a moss in Donegal
> On turf banks under blankets, with our faces
> Exposed all night in a wetting drizzle,
> Pallid as the dripping sapling birches.
> Lorenzo and Jessica in a cold climate
> Diarmuid and Grainne waiting to be found.
> Darkly asperged and censed, we were laid out
> like breathing effigies on a raised ground.

The last two tines are purely ornamental; they add nothing except a solemn reverberating, Tennysonian grandeur.

It is something of a miracle for a poet writing at the latter end of the twentieth century to sound so Victorian without, at the same time, sounding merely pompous and second-hand. Heaney's skill in bringing off this difficult balancing act is, I suspect, the clue to his extraordinary popularity. The British have never taken easily or willingly to Modernism. Apart from Joyce and Beckett, the great experimental movement in literature was largely an American concern: Eliot, Pound, Crane, Moore, Stevens, Williams, all of them attempting in their different ways to break the links with English poetry and make it new in distinctly American or cosmopolitan ways. Modernism, in other words, was a literary Declaration of Independence. In contrast, the British adjusted to the times by a process of seepage, gradually adapting the old forms to the rhythms of twentieth century speech: Yeats, Auden, Graves, and so on, down to Larkin. So they are comfortable with Heaney because he himself is comfortably in a recognisable tradition.

He is also a rural poet. Born and brought up in the country and now wisely retired in it from the hurly-burly of literary life. Like Wordsworth, he suggests in one poem; whereupon his wife 'interrupts: "You're not going to compare us two . . . ?"' She's right, of course. Nevertheless, he is squarely in a hallowed tradition running from Crabbe and Clare, through Hardy and Edward Thomas, to excellent contemporary minor poets like Norman Nicholson and the dour R. S. Thomas.

Heaney's position in it, however, is far from countrified. He is an intensely literary writer: his poems on the Irish troubles sound like Yeats, his elegy on Lowell sounds like Lowell; he brings in heroes and heroines with beautiful names from Irish myth, and quotes Wyatt and Dante, whom he also 'imitates' Lowell-fashion. There are, in fact, moments when his literariness turns into downright pedantry. For example, his third collection, *Wintering Out*, contained a four-line poem called 'Nerthus':

> For beauty, say an ash-fork staked in peat,
> Its long grains gathering to the gouged split
>
> A seasoned, unsleeved taker of the weather,
> Where kesh and loaning finger out to heather.

It is a kind of latter-day Imagism, a rhymed and rhythmical celebration of one of the common, unassuming objects of this world in the spirit of William Carlos Williams's love poem to a dish-mop or his red wheelbarrow on which so much depended. The difference is in the title and the last line, which send the conscientious reader scurrying to his reference books. Without, as it happens, much joy. Neither 'kesh' nor 'loaning' figure as such in the biggest Oxford dictionary, although they seem to be dialect variants of words which do: 'kex: an umbelliferous plant with a hollow stalk'; 'loan: an open uncultivated piece of ground near a farmhouse or village.' 'Nerthus' defeats all the encyclopædias on my shelves. No doubt I will be scornfully put in my place either for ignorance or for missing the point. But in a poem as brief, unsubstantial and apparently simple as this, these verbal affectations get in the way; they themselves are ways of missing the point.

Unless, of course, the point is other than what it seems: Heaney is not rural and sturdy and domestic, with his feet planted firmly in the Irish mud, but is instead an ornamentalist, a word collector, a connoisseur of fine language for its own sake,

The exception is *North*, his fourth and best book, which opened with an imposing sequence of poems linking the grim Irish present with its even grimmer past of Norse invasions and ancient feuding. The tone was appropriately stern, but also distanced, the language spare, as though stripped back to its Anglo-Saxon skeleton. For the space of these dozen and a half poems Heaney seemed to have found a theme so absorbing that charm and rhetoric were irrelevant. The poems were as simple, demanding, and irreducible as the archaic trophies from the bog which they celebrated. And like an archaeo-logist, he pared away the extraneous matter and kept himself decently in the background.

That reticence and self-containment have largely gone from *Field Work*. He is back with the seductions of fine language, the verbal showman's charming sleights of hand. Consider, for example, the first stanza of 'Oysters,' the opening poem of the book:

Our shells clacked on the plates.
My tongue was a filling estuary
My palate hung with starlight
As I tasted the salty Pleiades
Orion dipped his foot into the water.

First there is a verbal discovery, 'clacked,' the right and precise word to set the scene; then a precise evocation of the seawater taste of the creatures 'My tongue was a filling estuary'; after that, Heaney takes off into graceful, expanding variations on the same theme. In other words, the poem does not advance into unknown territory, it circles elegantly around on itself until it ends where it began, with language: 'I ate the day / Deliberately, that its tang / Might quicken me into verb, pure verb.' This is a twentieth century expression of a nineteenth century preoccupation, old aestheticism and new linguistics, Gautier filtered through Barthes.

Heaney's real strength and originality are not, I think, in his flashy rhetorical pieces, or in the poems where he takes on the big themes that are unavoidable for a serious poet living in Northern Ireland. They are, instead, in modest, perfect little poems like 'Homecomings,' or the short sequence which gives this book its title, or the closing stanzas of 'The Skunk'.

[. . .] It is, however, precisely these reassuring qualities which have been seized on by his champions as proof of the fact that in Heaney Britain has, at last, another major poet. This seems to me grossly disproportionate both to the fragility of the verse and also to Heaney's own modest intentions. After all, he does not often come on like Yeats reincarnated and much of his excellence depends on his knowing his own range and keeping rigorously to it, no more, no less.

In the circumstances, his current reputation amounts, I think, to a double betrayal: it lumbers him with expectations which he may not fulfil and which might even sink him, if he were less resilient; at the same time, it reinforces the British audience in their comfortable prejudice that poetry, give or take a few quirks of style, has not changed essentially in the last hundred years. If Heaney really is the best we can do, then the whole troubled exploratory thrust of modern poetry has been a diversion from the right true way. Eliot and his contemporaries, Lowell and his, Plath and hers had it all wrong: to try to make clearings of sense and discipline and style in the untamed, unfettered darkness was to mistake morbidity for inspiration. It was, in the end, mere melodrama, understandable perhaps in the Americans who lack a tradition in these matters, but inexcusable in the British.

These as I understand them, are the implications of Heaney's abrupt elevation into the pantheon of British poetry. Few well-established critics care to cope with work outside a correspondingly established tradition and even fewer, in the words of the margarine advertisement, can tell Stork from butter. But their current dedication to safety, sweetness, and light seems, at this late stage of the game, a curiously depressing refusal of everything that is mysterious and renewing in poetry. They remind me of Ophelia in her madness:

> Thought and affliction, passion, hell itself,
> She turns to favor and to prettiness.[13] □

Blake Morrison, in his book, *Seamus Heaney* (1982), while acknowledging that Heaney himself, somewhat in the manner of Robert Frost, has cultivated a self-image of relaxed, traditional craftsman in his interviews and lectures, nevertheless objects to Alvarez's denigration of Heaney as a 'safe', unchallenging kind of poet:

■ One does not have to look too deeply into Heaney's work, however, to see that it is rather less comforting and comfortable than has been supposed. Far from being 'whole', it is tense, torn, divided against itself; far from being straightforward, it is layered with often obscure allusions; far from being archaic, it registers the tremors and turmoils of its age, forcing traditional forms to accept the challenge of harsh, intractable material.[14] □

As well as identifying a Wordsworthian Heaney who wrote about traditional labourers and craftsmen, Morrison also sees a poet shaped by 'the modes of post-war Anglo-American poetry' exemplified by Larkin, Gunn, Wilbur, Roethke, Hughes, Plath, Lowell and Berryman. More controversial was his discovery of a post-modernist Heaney:

■ Moreover, Heaney's preoccupation with language and with questions of authorial control makes him part of a still larger modern intellectual movement which has emphasized that language is not a transparent medium by means of which a writer says what he intends to, but rather something self-generating, infinitely productive, exceeding us as individuals. Heaney's belief that the poet does not so much master language as surrender to it might look like a Romantic theory of 'inspiration', but it also bears surprising resemblances to recent structuralist discourse, some of which he is certainly acquainted with. There is the shared notion of language working through the medium of the author rather than the author through language.[15] □

Morrison identifies in Heaney's poetry a concern with poetry itself, and a tendency (which, Morrison claims, Heaney shares with Beckett) 'to weigh inarticulacy against articulation, to acknowledge the claims of silence as well as those of speech'.[16] Heaney's 'sense of belonging to a silent ancestry' of inarticulate farming stock, Morrison says, made him distrustful of words. But there were other reasons. As Catholics living in Northern Ireland, there were political and religious factors that lay behind the silence of Heaney's people. Morrison alludes to the motto that used to be popular amongst Ulster Catholics: 'Whatever you say, say nothing'. This silent ancestry, Morrison believes, shaped Heaney's art. Referring to Heaney's portraits of various traders, labourers and craftsmen that fill his first two books, Morrison notes how, unlike Heaney himself, these figures are 'lacking in speech'. While acknowledging the validity of Morrison's comments about Heaney's 'mediation between speech and silence', it is still hard to see this early Heaney as a postmodern poet.

Morrison, along with Andrew Motion, returns to Alvarez and Heaney in the Introduction to their *Penguin Book of Contemporary British Poetry* (1982). Here they assert that Heaney does represent something significantly new in English poetry, hailing him as 'the most important new poet of the last fifteen years, and the one we very deliberately put first in our anthology'.[17] Alvarez, in his influential *The New Poetry* (1965), had dismissed the Movement poets such as Larkin, Thom Gunn, John

Wain, Donald Davie and Kingsley Amis as monotonous and mundane. Morrison and Motion present Heaney as the key figure in a movement away from the Movement. Their 'new poets' are introduced in Heaney's phrase (from the poem 'Exposure') as 'inner émigrés' – detached but fascinated observers, situated at a sufficient distance from their world to enable them to make the familiar strange again. The anthropological Heaney meets Craig Raine's Martian invader. And, indeed, Heaney powerfully exemplifies Morrison and Motion's 'new poet' who has 'a preference for metaphor and poetic bizzarrerie to metonymy and plain speech'[18] in poems such as 'Bog Queen' where, identifying himself with the long-dead denizens of the bog's darkness, Heaney sees the human form merge with the landscape: 'I lay waiting / on the gravel bottom, / my brain darkening, / a jar of spawn / fermenting underground / dreams of Baltic amber. / Bruised berries under my nails, / the vital hoard reducing / in the crock of the pelvis. / My diadem grew carious, / gemstones dropped / in the peat floe / like the bearings of history'.

Heaney also exemplifies another aspect of Morrison and Motion's 'new poet'. In their view, the distance that exists between the poet and his world produces, within these new liberating and defamiliarising perspectives, a poetry of 'greater imaginative freedom and linguistic daring', a poetry that reasserts 'the primacy of the imagination . . . as a potential source of tenderness and renewal'.[19] Thus, Morrison and Motion do not see contemporary poetry collapsing into the obliqueness and obscurity of a private language. Rather, they see the new poetry's indeterminate and enigmatic quality, its alienating devices and secret symbolism contributing, not to a post-modern apocalypse, but to a process of reconstituting the very grounds of faith and hope. This is clearly the case with Heaney: post-modern scepticism is never allowed to obliterate the poet's faith in poetry's powers of 'redress'.

Writing in 1982, Morrison's discovery of a post-modern Heaney was somewhat controversial. Certainly, John Carey, in his review of Morrison's study, *Seamus Heaney*, thought so. However, Morrison may have been prophetic. Heaney's later work, especially *The Haw Lantern*, contains more compelling evidence of a post-modern Heaney. For in *The Haw Lantern* he explores in a direct and explicit manner his uneasy relation with the linguistic, discursive and ideological systems in which he is caught. Writing about Heaney's early work, John Carey emphasised the way it concentrates on 'objects and textures' because they cannot let you down as people do. But then words become suspect too. Ironically, Carey notes, this most sensuous of poets is ultimately engaged in 'a quest for silence', a 'bright nowhere' beyond 'the stain of words'. The longing for silence, says Carey, 'spells a recoil from politics'. Language, which had been such a wonderful resource and consolation for the awareness of loss and death, is now handled in *The Haw Lantern* (1987) with a typically post-modern self-consciousness. The excerpt below is from Carey's review of *The Haw Lantern* entitled 'The Stain of Words', which appeared in the *Sunday Times* (21 June 1987).

■ If all previous literature vanished, Muldoon's poetry would instantly suffocate. Heaney's you feel would amble on unconcerned. His new poems warn against the imperialism of language – the greed with which it steals from life – and strive to return us from words to things. A world rid of the stain of words is paradoxically the dream of this greatest of living poets in the English tongue. His opening poem, Alphabets, traces the child's gradual seduction by signs – the shadow rabbit his father makes on the wall; the forked stick teacher calls Y. Eventually signs replace things altogether, and the astronaut, through his capsule's window, sees all he has sprung from as an 'aqueous, lucent O'. The poems that follow celebrate sign-destroyers. The Stone Grinder is about an artisan who prepares and reprepares stones for lithography, effacing the marks of cartographers and print-makers and restoring the clean stone, 'a ripple perfected in stillness'.

Poems, being words, necessarily recede from truth, as Heaney admits. They are like hailstones, caught and dissolving in the hand, 'the melt of the real thing smarting into its absence'. But falser than poets are the system-builders – politicians who surround innocent, meaningless things with the fierce possessiveness of rival doctrines. Heaney recalls how, in his boyhood, sermons about the Mammon of iniquity would make the coins in his pocket redden 'like stovelids' – turned to hell's oven by the deceit of words.

He imagines absconding from language in a series of poems about fictional countries. The Republic of Conscience is a quiet backwater where seawater forms the basis of all inks and pigments. In the Land of the Unspoken, a bar of platinum is kept as the standard measurement, and Heaney wills himself to enter its wordless core, 'slumbering at the very hub of systems'. [. . .]

Silence and emptiness have been Heaney's themes before. But they resurface in this volume, enriched by bereavements, which give vacancy a new value. In one poem for a dead friend, the impulse towards nothingness is symbolised by an arrow, shot through the sockets of a row of axeheads, 'perfectly aimed towards the vacant centre'. Commemorating his mother, he thinks of a chestnut tree that was cut down, leaving 'a bright nowhere' on the spot where it stood. The ideal object he selects in his title poem is silent and diminished. The wintry haw hanging on the thorn offers tough, unspectacular integrity for us all to measure ourselves against. This pecked berry, Heaney imagines, was the lantern Diogenes took when he went through the marketplace seeking a true man.[20] □

John Bayley, Professor of English Literature at Oxford University, and author of *The Romantic Survival* (1957) and *The Characters of Love* (1961), has also written sympathetically and perceptively on Heaney in an essay, 'Living In and Living Out: The Poet's Location for the Poetry', which appeared in the spring 1989 special Heaney edition of *Agenda*, and is reprinted below. Bayley's criticism is founded on the values of love and charity towards human beings, and a regard for an impersonal and therefore truly liberating literary style that does not draw attention to itself but provides a neutral space in which the reader can 'manoeuvre on his own'. Bayley sees in Heaney a poet who avoids the excesses of Romantic egotism and the Romantic's preference for the ideal over the real. Taking the (post)modernist awareness of the disjunction between the word and the world as his starting point, Bayley quotes Blanchot – 'la négation est liée au langage' – and shows how, in Heaney's case, this awareness of 'death and separation' implicit in language produces a characteristically elegiac poetry. Hence, the note of 'diffidence' and 'apology' about the power of words in Heaney's poetry, which makes it so different from the magisterial Yeats's. This self-consciousness about language, Bayley argues, is the mark of the Modernist, the writer who, instead of willing himself into the centre of the poetry, detaches himself from the kind of central emotional obsession that takes over the Romantic.

■ Maurice Blanchot, the most pretentious if also at times the most suggestive of poet-type critics, has observed that *la négation est liée au langage*. A word is the memorial to what it signifies. Death is implicit in the distinction between sign and self. Clever, eh? Well, striking at least. But where the morale of contemporary poetry is concerned it may be rather more than that. Everyone has remarked on the apparent inability of poetry to assert its speech with authority over the great horrors of our age. An awareness among poets similar to Blanchot's, however much less conscious and formulated, may be the reason? Defeatism about language is in the air, and of all users of the language, poets are most sensitive to it. They are also sensitive to critics, the only audience they can rely on. And many critics – George Steiner for one – have told them that their art is no longer capable of responding to what is happening around them in life.

All they can pronounce is an elegy, in words which cannot convey the true matter of what they signify, but only raise a consciously inadequate memorial to it. Persons of intelligence and discernment may also feel thoroughly inhibited today about putting headstones and epitaphs in churches and churchyards; and this signifies the same defeatism that poets feel. Restraint and good taste are the only hope: their very inadequacy argues the only way we have now of being sincere. Just a name and a date and the right sort of stone. There is a striking parallel here with the inhibitions in a poet's words. We do not live any more with and among the dead, as if they were still alive, because we are aware that what we say about them only recognises extinction by drawing attention to our own survival.

Seamus Heaney is a poet whose consciousness of these things has become his chief strength as a poet. His poetry is continually aware that it does not live in its own area of discourse, but only visits it. His poetry is a pilgrimage to its own subject, like the journey of the pilgrims in 'Station Island'. Afterwards it returns to real life for breakfast. And yet Heaney has converted what might in this item sound like weakness and inadequacy into a source – a source for poetry – of honesty and strength. The essential flavour of his poetry is one of diffidence, a quality as distant as possible from the overbearing and energetic stance of Yeats, and perhaps deliberately so. Yeats's whole ego was devoted to living in his poetry: so much so that when he tells us 'Once out of nature I shall never take / My bodily form from any natural thing/ But such a form as Grecian goldsmiths make' he persuades us, at any rate momentarily, that this is a genuine desire and ambition, and that he has every expectation of finding it fulfilled. To live in his verse was for Yeats an act of the will, but for many poets of our time and during the last century – one could cite such otherwise contrasting figures as Emily Dickinson and A.E. Housman, Philip Larkin and Paul Celan – it seems the most natural thing in the world.

Natural how? And in what ways that Heaney, for example, is not? There is always in Heaney's poetry, I think, as, in its very different way, in Geoffrey Hill's, a note of apology. Both poets seem to have taken sober and rational thought about what might be said against them and their poetry; and they seem to have taken it, in a sense, before the poetry itself has been written. Such an effect, in the context of their own special skill and personality, is oddly impressive. The meeting with the ghosts of earlier poets and writers in 'Station Island' is an echo of Dante, amongst other echoes, including those from 'Little Gidding': but what makes it especially typical of Heaney is the note of withdrawal, the true humility which sets aside the man writing from the poetry he writes. The recognition of death and separation is implicit in the distinction between the words of the poetry and the poet himself. Analogously the modern stone in the churchyard, or the new tablet on the church wall, do not identify with their subject but seem to say: this is the proper and decent thing to do, though death is not a subject about which anything now can be said. Heaney's poetry has strange delicacy, as well as humility, in suggesting that poetry nowadays has to be written about things like patriotism, affection, belief itself about which there is in fact no longer anything to say.

Such a tone is most literally and truthfully elegiac in its practical demonstration that, in Blanchot's words, negation is tied in with language. An age which feels this, and a poet of the age who expresses it, however unconsciously, have absorbed the first lesson of Modernism, which was: think before you write; study before you do so. Since you cannot be spontaneous, do not attempt to imitate or to cultivate spontaneity. Do not live, or affect to live, in 'poetry', but in the house of learning, from which the good poetry of this age must proceed. Write notes on it, or in it; and think with T. S. Eliot rather than feeling with Harold Monro.

The message has been learnt to the third or fourth generation: a Geoffrey Hill or a Seamus Heaney have come to take it for granted. Not so Philip Larkin, who was in silent, or sometimes not so silent, reaction against the Modernist assumption. He lived over the shop, lived in the poems that came to him, in the same sense that A. E. Housman had done. Death was a holy terror to him, not a subject for historic reverie in verse, and there being 'nothing to say' is itself a matter of the starkest import. The fact of death that accompanies us through life, and makes life 'slow dying', means nothing – or everything.

And saying so to some
Means nothing, to others it leaves
Nothing to be said.

The cousin's ghost, who speaks with such care and precision to Heaney in 'Station Island', may forfeit in so doing this kind of immediacy, but through him the poetry gains in denseness and delicacy of reference. Heaney's individuality is of a strangely passive sort, as if he were urged in different directions by external forces that the poetry keeps in equilibrium by a wise passiveness, rather than by an adroit or wary control. This gives the poetry its special quality, but the poet pays a price for his neutrality in seeming at the side of what he writes. Like most poets in the Modernist tradition his sense, and learning, and skill detach him from the kind of central emotional obsession that wells up in the verse of a Larkin or Housman. Hence in Heaney the tone of gentleness, of unassertiveness, and of something wistful too, as of a poetry apologising for its own civilised qualities.

None of that savagery which is cultivated by Yeats or by Sylvia Plath, who will themselves into the centre of their poetry as a personal obsession. Other non-Modernist poets – Housman and Larkin again, or Dickinson, or Marianne Moore – seem to live in it without effort, as their native environment. In a brilliant but bewildering piece in *Essays in Criticism* (January 1987), from which I have borrowed some of my examples, John Kerrigan shows a puzzling lack of awareness of the surely basic difference between poets like the Modernists, who live outside their sophisticated, referential, and highly group-conscious verse, and those who live inside it with the confidence born of total solitariness. There are giant figures who can do both, as Eliot does in 'The Waste Land', a poem related as much to Dante and to Pound on the one hand as to Housman or Burns on the other; but Heaney, like Hill, is surely a poet whose readability comes from the precision with which both chart their own difficulties in approaching from outside the poetic area.

Once there, there is, in a curious way, nothing to be said: the effect of the poetry lies in the mode of approach and the mode of uncertainty. Kerrigan's essay on 'Knowing the Dead' . . . assumes concord and indivisibility between such an extraordinary poem as Celan's *Engführung – Lies nicht mehr-schau! Schau nicht mehr geh!* – with its absolute existence in the primitive terror brought by the vertiginous unmeaning of the Holocaust, and the thoughtful elegies of poets who live well outside such areas of recall and of memory. It is the basic difference, if you like, between Romanticism – the spontaneous overflowing of powerful feelings – and the much wider, more perennial notion of poetry as the *Sprachgefühl* of civilisation, the repository of intelligence, perception, personality, in its highest linguistic form. The distinction was made by Housman when he claimed that poetry was different from the things the poet was saying, the things *in* poetry. The difference is clear and obvious in Wordsworth, and at the other end of the scale it is equally obvious in such a poet as John Betjeman: whose 'total' and atavistic voice, overflowing about Leamington Spa or Miss Joan Hunter-Dunn, is quite different from his expository, pseudo-Augustan, pseudo-Victorian tones. Heaney is one of the very few poets – indeed perhaps the only poet writing in English today – whose poetry seems able *in itself* to take cognizance of the distinction, and to give such an awareness continuous and unique expression. And this is a very remarkable achievement.[21] □

Heaney's awareness of death and separation was, of course, more than a matter of the nature of language in general. Loss is very much the condition of his poetry, which concerns itself with dying rural crafts, the disappearance of an old language, the death of friends and acquaintances, the erosion of a magical, folkloric, pagan sense of the world. The first volume, *Death of a Naturalist*, is a *recherche du temps perdu*, its title indicating the preoccupation with loss – a lost time, a lost childhood, a lost intimacy with the natural world. Succeeding chapters in this Guide will present and discuss the critical arguments for seeing Heaney's poetics of loss and absence as expressive of a peculiarly Hibernicised version of the (post) modern condition.

In America, Heaney's success was no doubt in part due to the fact that he reminded Americans of Robert Frost and the rural theme in poetry. His teaching in American universities (guest lecturer at the University of California at Berkeley in 1970–1; one of a series of temporary successors to Robert Lowell at Harvard in 1979; Boylston Professor of Rhetoric and Oratory at Harvard in 1984) and his frequent readings, lectures and media appearances also helped to ensure his popularity among the American poetry-reading public. He found a powerful champion in the person of his Harvard colleague Professor Helen Vendler, who took the title for one of her books on modern poetry (*The Music of What Happens*, 1988) from one of Heaney's poems ('Song'), and to whom Heaney dedicated his latest volume *The Spirit Level*. Vendler represents what some consider to be a virtual critical orthodoxy in the American academy. At a time when it seemed as if poetry was in danger of being swamped by theory, she emphasised the value of an 'aesthetic criticism' that focused on the poetry itself rather than on the 'statement' it makes.

■ The aim of a properly aesthetic criticism, then, is not primarily to reveal the meaning of an art work or disclose (or argue for or against) the ideological values of an art work. The aim of an aesthetic criticism is to describe the art work in such a way that it cannot be confused with any other art work (not an easy task), and to infer from its elements the aesthetic that might generate this unique configuration. (Ideological criticism is not interested in the uniqueness of the work of art, always wishing to conflate it with other works sharing its values.)[22] □

The excerpt below from Vendler's essay on Heaney in *The Music of What Happens* represents this kind of criticism, which emphasises 'aesthetic value' over 'civic value' or 'ethical values'. By listening in to the music of Heaney's verse, she analyses the 'aesthetic claim' made by poems such as 'Churning Day' and 'The Diviner'; she demonstrates Heaney's Keatsian 'sensuous responsiveness' and talent for exploiting between words the 'binding secret' that depends on 'the cooperation of mind and feeling and ear'; she probes his experiments with local vocabulary and speech, and his Gaelicisation of the English language. Vendler doesn't see, as Alvarez does, a poet 'besotted with words' but finds, instead, self-correcting 'astringency' that checks any tendency towards 'linguistic revel'. Heaney's poems – 'mammalian, amphibious, vegetative' – are the kind that wins Vendler's strongest approval.

■ At first, Heaney aggrandized and consecrated his infant world. It is a silent world (his eight siblings are nowhere in the poetry), and it is pregnant with import. The child hiding from his family in the hollow of a willow tree is an oracle who can hear and speak for mute earth; he is its *genius loci*:

> small mouth and ear
> in a woody cleft,
> lobe and larynx
> of the mossy places.

The child is half Ariel, half an innocent Caliban, living with flowers and frogs as though he spoke their language. He watches, in absorptive stillness, the activities on the farm, digging, thatching, churning, plowing. In the poems he writes later, he makes all the farm processes analogous to the process of writing, as if he could understand or justify the writing of verse only by seeing it as a form of sublime agriculture. The pen is a spade he will dig with; like the thatcher, he will ruminate and measure, then finally stitch all together 'into a sloped honeycomb, a stubble patch'; he will turn his verses as the farmer turns his plow round furrow ends; he will lay up poems on his shelves as they coagulate, like butter from a churning:

> Out came the four crocks, spilled their heavy lip
> of cream, their white insides, into the sterile churn . . .
> Their short stroke quickened, suddenly
> a yellow curd was weighting the churned up white,
> heavy and rich, coagulated sunlight
> that they fished, dripping, in a wide tin strainer,
> heaped up like gilded gravel in the bowl.

The aesthetic claim made by a poem like this is that the passage of life can indeed be tallied in a narrative, and that the physical processes of life exquisitely resemble the mental ones, with a fluid sliding of import between them. Fluid signals pass in these earlier poems between the human and the natural as well; the poet is a diviner, feeling in his responsive blood the spring water 'broadcasting! Through a green hazel its secret stations.' The early world seems perpetual and inexhaustible; as Heaney says of a cow in calf, 'her cud and her milk, her heats and her calves / keep coming and going,' and her lowing falls as naturally in the poem as her fertility.

On the other hand, the poverty of every child's restricted early life appears in Heaney as rural restriction – famine, bigotry, and decline. His elegies for a lost terrain are paradoxically rich and stinted at once. It is not, for instance, an easy eye in Heaney that watches, first as seed potatoes are halved and buried in furrows called drills and, later, as the potato crop is harvested and stored. The Keatsian harvest is corrected by a harsh history, and an inherited English amplitude of style is roughened, shortened, and darkened:

> Flint-white, purple. They lie scattered
> like inflated pebbles. Native
> to the black hutch of clay
> where the halved seed shot and clotted
> these knobbed and slit-eyed tubers seem
> the petrified hearts of drills. Split
> by the spade, they show white as cream
> To be piled in pits; live skulls, blind-eyed . . .

[. . .] Heaney is the sort of poet who, because he is so accomplished in each stage, is begrudged his new departures; we want more of what so pleased us earlier. In his lobe and larynx there seemed to lie the greatest natural talent since Keats for creating between words that 'binding secret' (as Heaney has called it) which, although it depends in part on sound, depends even more on the intellectual and emotional consent between two words – a consent surprising and, in retrospect, seemingly inevitable, that rises from an arduous cooperation of mind and feeling and ear.

[. . .] The eye that after early circumscription looked outward to the shore and downward under the ocean and inward to writing now looks farther down. Below the level of agriculture, below even the silt where the eel swims, there lies Heaney's most fertile level – the primitive and slippery ground where memory and creation lie side by side.

For Heaney, the recesses of recollection and imagination alike find their symbol in the landscape of central Ireland – the peat bog, in which successive cultures have left their sunken traces:

> Every layer they strip
> Seems camped on before.
> The bogholes might be Atlantic seepage.
> The wet centre is bottomless.

No longer possessing the child's confidence in narrative cohesiveness or in the easy single correspondences of emblematic agriculture, or even the eel's confidence in its biological purposiveness, Heaney enters the quicksand, where deepening strata offer no sure footing but a source of treasure at once untouched, fearful, deathly, and rich. The poems grow slow, layered, reflective, deep; the hasty faith of youth in clearly defined forms vanishes in favor of a murkier interrogation of the wet center, and the poems move less straightforwardly ahead. Instead, they tend to send ripples outward from an original disturbance. A primitive goddess in whose honor bodies and gold were deposited in the bog presides over these poems. She is still agricultural, and in that sense linked to the early farm, but she is pre-Christian, and she belongs not to retrospection but to introspection.

Heaney's irreproachable sequence of bog poems appeared in *Wintering Out* (1972) and in *North* (1975). They brought him to public attention, not only because the poems were so accomplished and unfaltering but because they took on political and historical force in the relation – sometimes indirect and sometimes pointed – that they bore to the undeclared war in Ulster.

[. . .] The bog poems represent Heaney's coming to grips with an intractable element deep both in personal life (insofar as the bog and its contents represent the unconscious) and in history. They lift him free from a superficial piety that would put either sectarian or national names to the Ulster killings, and they enable a hymn to the 'ruminant ground,' which as it digests 'mollusc and seed-pod' is an 'embalmer/of votive goods/and sabred fugitives.' In words that can stand beside Whitman's 'This Compost,' Heaney undergoes the tireless cyclic processes of the ground:

> The mothers of autumn
> sour and sink
> ferments of husk and leaf
>
> deepen their ochres.
> Mosses come to a head,
> heather unseeds,
> brackens deposit
>
> their bronze.

This is a poetry of verbs, where each living form gives up its being in its own singular way. Each figure of decay subsides into another grain in the peat, until all living vegetation is seen to be 'a windfall composing/the floor it rots into.' The poet, kin to the plants, is only another stem in the expanse of bracken and mosses:

> I grew out of all this
> like a weeping willow
> inclined to
> the appetites of gravity.

He remarks dissolution and change by tasting things as they grow sour, feeling them sink in himself, losing part of himself bubbling in the acrid changes of fermentation.

[. . .] In the elegies of *Field Work*, one friend is recalled whose 'candid forehead stopped/A pointblank teatime bullet'; another was blown up in a pub, 'his cornered outfaced stare/Blinding in the flash.' In each of these poems, Heaney refuses the easy climax of placing death at the end; instead, he puts it squarely in the center, flanked early and late – by life, on the one hand, and memory, on the other. The poems refuse accusation in favor of a steadily widening pool of reflection, question, and recollection. The whole of *Field Work* poses aesthetic questions as well. 'You are stained, stained/to perfection,' it cries out at one pitch of conviction; at another, it envisages a possible poise 'between the tree in leaf and the bare tree'; at yet another, it allows for original rural pieties as well as for a later ambition toward a crystalline arrangement of language, while wanting to make room for a poetry foreign to each:

There are the mud-flowers of dialect
And the immortelles of perfect pitch
And that moment when the bird sings very close
To the music of what happens.

Writing down 'the music of what happens' entails for Heaney poems with a new language and new structures, poems drawing on poets as various as Dante, Marvell, and Wyatt. Heaney wants his social voice to make its way into his poetry, joining that voice of secret brooding in which he first found a poetic self. As Keats said of Milton, he wishes to devote himself rather to the ardors than the pleasures of verse; the attempt seems to be a necessity for every ambitious poet.[23] □

At home, in a wildly controversial pamphlet, *Whatever You Say, Say Nothing: Why Seamus Heaney is No. 1* (1991), Desmond Fennell launched a blistering attack on the Anglo-American influence on Heaney's poetry, particularly the influence of Helen Vendler, whom he designated the 'queen' of 'the American poetry establishment'.[24] Fennell charges Heaney with pandering to Anglo-American taste and expectations by specialising in the short, well-made, allusive lyric that lends itself well to the kind of practical criticism that prevails in the Anglo-American academy, and is particularly suited to public reading on tours and media events. During the 1980s, according to Fennell, 'Heaney adopted Vendler's view of poetry, and developed it, and this has been influencing both his poetry and his apologia for it'.[25]

■ 'A private musing addressed, painfully, to the self, and expressed in active language'. That seems to be the core notion of really good poetry which runs through Vendler's discourse. And it seems to me that we have here another instance of justification after the event. Certain persons, by getting their verses published, rank as poets; and some of these, judged very good or the best by the academic-poetic complex, are producing quantities of verse which mean little or nothing to ordinary literate people: they are obviously not speaking to them, nor trying to. *Ergo*, poetry, at its best, is not public speech, but private musing addressed to the self. As a delivered product, it is *published* private musing. Since the verse in question was, presumably, written for publication, this is a fiction; but it is a useful fiction because it explains everything. No one expects somebody's musing to himself to mean much to others; it has its private syntax, its own unique and personal way of connecting meanings and words. Logically, moreover, if a number of poets are at it, it needs Vendlers, hundreds of them, to interpret it and 'teach' it. In short, the poet *par excellence* becomes a sort of ruminating, groaning shaman, delivering oracles which his academic acolytes interpret to the students within the temple and the heedless multitude beyond the gates.

Heaney qualified in Vendler's terms, and he worked to qualify better. Obviously he had the 'active language' and the 'pain'. For the rest, it was a matter of how you conceptualised and described poetry which, though published to wide audiences, said nothing about general matters, and therefore cancelled itself as genuine public speech. For Vendler it was musing directed to the self, and, as such, poetry at its best. Quite early in his career, Heaney had hinted in his poem 'Thatcher' that poetry was a work of rumination and measuring. Neil Corcoran, in his book, finds in some poems in *Wintering Out* and *North* that 'the poet's "I" is detached from ordinary social circumstance, withdrawn to solipsistic meditation, ruminatively entranced . . .' The fact is that much of Heaney's poetry in the 70s could be regarded as private musing or meditation with any intrusive general views censored out – rather than as public speech which, in the County Derry manner, 'said nothing'. But Heaney, with long Irish and English traditions of poetry as public speech behind him, had hesitated to commit himself to the 'private meditation' concept. Now, in response to Vendler's high valuation of such poetry, he did so, and the result can be noticed in the increased self-absorption and indifference to readers in *Station Island* and *The Haw Lantern*. Significantly, the first blurb of a Heaney collection to describe his work as 'meditative' is that of *Station Island*. Since then he has been consciously not speaking to us, even to 'say nothing'.[26] □

Fennell finds Heaney's poetry politically evasive (there is a particular allusion to Heaney's silence 'during the long agony of the Long Kesh hunger strike'),[27] tied to the forces of consumer capitalism, and expressive of his people's 'say-nothing' mentality. McLeish's 'A poem should not mean / But be', in Fennell's view, prepared the way for Heaney's success in both England and America. It meant in Heaney's case that his poetry never had any real vision or quotable philosophy. Heaney, Fennell says, 'avoids speaking about the world', and seeks to perform a 'social good' through resorting to a 'mystical' answer to the Irish Troubles: 'At its core is the Vendler idea of the poet as ruminating, world-reflecting shaman; but developed, and given a socially beneficial dimension'.[28]

Fennell represents the opposite kind of criticism from that which matters most to Vendler. As an ideological polemic, Fennell's criticism brackets the question of aesthetic success. This kind of criticism is useful as cultural history or sociology, but useless in accounting for the aesthetic power of the poetry. Fennell shows no interest in the uniqueness of the poetry (or individual poem), which is precisely Vendler's starting point and abiding concern. Fennell wants poetry to say something, to have an easily extractable or paraphrasable meaning, and in that respect finds Heaney badly wanting: Vendler believes 'one cannot write properly, or even meaningfully, on an art work to which one has not responded aesthetically'.[29] The general outline of Fennell's critique of Heaney's work and reputation in his pamphlet *Whatever You Say, Say Nothing* appeared in an *Irish Times* article (30 March 1991), entitled 'The Heaney Phenomenon', the full text of which is reproduced below:

■ Everyone is agreed that Seamus Heaney is a good poet, but people you talk to in Dublin – literate people, poetry lovers – have been worried for some time by what they call the Heaney Phenomenon. It exists 'out there in the world', in Britain, America, Australia, and by overspill in Ireland. 'The best Irish poet (or poet simply) since Yeats', 'the leading poet writing in English', professor of poetry in Harvard and Oxford, all those prizes, lectures and honorary degrees in foreign parts, and the legend of Seamus touring England in a Faber and Faber helicopter.

In Ireland we buy more poetry books than in any other English-speaking country. We believe we know what good poetry is, what is great poetry, and that we are capable of judging and ranking poets accurately, particularly our own. We think Heaney is good but many of us think he is not *that* good; not another Yeats, nor even, indisputably, the best contemporary Irish poet. So there is a disparity between the work and the reputation, and this is worrying for several reasons.

The reputation was made without consulting us. Its excessive nature, and the hype attending it, make poetry seem like pop culture. And it is wrong – wrong for poetry, poets, and the future of the art – to tenant the top storey rashly; it should be kept vacant, even for a century, until it can be properly and deservedly filled. Lower the ceiling frivolously and it may be lowered for good.

This matter has been simmering, and I think it is time to thrash it out. Perplexity about the Heaney Phenomenon has disabled us critically – induced a paralysis of critical discourse. Except for rare articles, years apart, we avoid overall critical writing about Irish poetry, let alone poetry generally, because such criticism, done seriously, would entail dealing with the Heaney Phenomenon; and that, to be blunt, intimidates us.

So there is a poetry jungle rampant in which anyone who manages to get a publisher to print his or her verses is called a poet, reviewed benignly and interviewed reverently. The general books on modern Irish poetry are being written in America. Of the nine books about Heaney's work that now exist, only one, by Elmer Andrews of the University of Ulster, is by an Irish author, and it was published in London. Apart from reviews of Heaney's books and two or three short critical essays, the Republic of Ireland has been lockjawed about the most famous contemporary Irish poet.

I think we owe ourselves a connected critical discourse which would re-appropriate Heaney and accord him his due place. I will set the ball rolling by saying briefly why he is not a major poet and by suggesting how and why the Heaney Phenomenon occurred.

He began very well, and made us all happy, with his rustic nostalgia, strong images, vigorous and exact language, tenderness, toughness, and chiselled finish. But, from the late 70s onwards, and especially with his two collections in the 80s, he has not grown stronger, widened his scope or dug deeper. Under the influence of his Dante readings and the American scene, he has veered away from his central talent and towards literature rather than life. Robert Lowell, Joseph Brodsky, and the critic and Harvard colleague Helen Vendler, have not – to name a few – been good for him.

Great poetry illuminates the world. It does this by making true, quotable statements about matters of common experience and general concern, or by presenting images of particular subjects in such a manner that they have universal meaning. It is therefore rich in word and in meaning.

Heaney's poetry takes its motto 'Whatever you say, say nothing' from his Northern Catholic background. It makes no quotable statements about general matters and, except in two or three instances, its images of particular and private subjects convey these and nothing more. In his later poetry, partly because the language ignores its audience and sometimes because the subject is obscure, what he is saying is often difficult to penetrate. In short, his poetry – like much good but minor poetry – is poor in word and meaning and says nothing of general relevance. That is one of the reasons why, apart from a few well-turned phrases, no one quotes Heaney.

The other reason is that his poetry is not, in the ordinary sense of the word, *musical*. Much of it gives verbal pleasure, but the pleasure comes from the aptness of words and phrases, from subtle but irregular sound-relationships, and – for Eng. Lit. academics – from the frequent use of archaic and dialect words. It seldom adds up to the rhythm and melody which, combined with illuminating content, makes people memorise poetry and quote it for its wisdom or delight.

Despite these limitations, Heaney ranks, transatlantically, as a major poet, the equal of Yeats. Not every American and British critic agrees, but that is the consensus of the overlapping fraternity of academics, poets and critics who make up the academic-poetic complex in both countries. It was this complex, through its own publications and its links with the general media that created the Heaney Phenomenon.

It originated with the London critics and the American East Coast academics and spread from there. When you consider the concrete circumstances of Heaney's early career, his good luck and his extra-poetic skills, and when you read in London or East Coast publications why, and for what, he has been appreciated there, his exaggerated reputation becomes understandable. Understandable, but as literary judgement, still false.

The Northern Ireland factor was at the root of it. For a good poet in Ireland or Britain in the late 1960s and early 1970s, the *best* formula for fame was to be from Northern Ireland and to publish in London. In the 1960s the London critics were hailing the 'Northern Ireland poets' as the fresh hope of British poetry. In the 1970s the violence put Northern Ireland in the headlines transatlantically. London looked to new hopefuls, in particular their leader, Seamus Heaney, to produce war poetry. When, in 1975, he produced a book of it in *North* it was a huge media success and made him top poet in Britain. That reputation went with it when it appeared in New York.

To get to the top today in poetry, transatlantically, it is necessary to be successful first in London. Poetic reputations travel easily from London westwards, less easily in the opposite direction. It is also necessary to write only or mainly lyrics, short poems. Most contemporary criticism treats 'poetry' as meaning simply lyrics; and they are the most suitable kinds of poetry for poetry-readings, TV interviews, radio and the printed media. Heaney fulfilled both these conditions.

The London critics and the East Coast academics found in his poetry many values that were not strictly literary but, rather, fashionable ideological and moral values in literary guise. So, poetry's 'nothing-saying' quality and its low yield of 'meaning' turned out to be advantages. The London critic, Blake Morrison, writes of *North* 'His poetry was valuable insofar as it could not be seen to be making statements: poetry, after all, should not mean but be'. East Coast literary puritanism appreciated the chaste, astringent diction; the avoidance of excessive pleasure taken or given: the guilty soul-searching. Liberal critics and academics admired the avoidance of commitment, and empathised with a sensitive soul confronted with terrorist violence.

Robert Lowell, after reading *North*, coined 'the best Irish poet since Yeats'. Up to his death, Lowell was the favourite poet of the American academy and particularly of Helen Vendler, queen of US poetry criticism. Heaney, learning from, among others, Lowell and Vendler, accommodated his poetry even more to American academic taste. Vendler, in turn, has championed him.

Last, but not least, Heaney, unlike many poets, has taken his poetic career seriously as a career, and has managed it accordingly. Responding agilely to 'market forces', he has avoided provoking antagonism, aimed at the most prestigious academic posts, and been an assiduous and charming communicator about himself and his work.[30] □

CHAPTER TWO

Place, Identity, Language

THE QUESTION of identity crucially involves consideration of the tension between the sense of individual freedom on one hand and, on the other hand, the demands of tradition, the past, place, religion, the tribe, society. The question is particularly acute for the poet, and even more acute for the poet writing in a time of war and continually under pressure to 'say something', to take sides. In *Preoccupations*, his first volume of essays, Heaney indicates the 'two often contradictory demands' under which the Irish poet has laboured: 'To be faithful to the collective historical experience and to be true to the recognitions of the emerging self'. He opens his collection of essays with the transcript of a 1978 BBC Radio 4 talk entitled 'Mossbawn' (the name of the family farm in Co. Derry where he grew up), in which he emphasises rootedness in a sacred, feminine landscape. His concept of origins is symbolised by the pump in the yard, the sound of which he associates with the Greek word *omphalos*, 'the centre of the world':

■ I would begin with the Greek word, *omphalos*, meaning the navel, and hence the stone that marked the centre of the world, and repeat it, *omphalos, omphalos, omphalos*, until its blunt and falling music becomes the music of somebody pumping water at the pump outside our back door . . . I remember, too, men coming to sink the shaft of the pump and digging through that seam of sand down into the bronze riches of the gravel, that soon began to puddle with the spring water. That pump marked an original descent into earth, sand, gravel, water. It centred and staked the imagination, made its foundation the foundation of the *omphalos* itself.[1] □

But powerful forces of modernity were also at work. Heaney was one of many beneficiaries of the 1947 Education Act, which opened up secondary education to all, and produced an emergent, upwardly mobile class of middle-class Northern Catholics capable of challenging the Ulster

40

Protestant hegemony (the 'Ministry of Fear') as well as question the traditional values of the family, the farm, the tribe. In 'Belfast', another early piece that was collected in *Preoccupations*, Heaney explains:

■ One half of one's sensibility is in a cast of mind that comes from belonging to a place, an ancestry, a history, a culture, whatever one wants to call it. But consciousness and quarrels with the self are the result of what Lawrence called 'the voices of my education'.[2] □

This double vision is also the theme of his later essay in *Preoccupations*, 'The Sense of Place':

■ I think there are two ways in which a place is known and cherished, two ways which may be complementary but which are just as likely to be antipathetic. One is lived, illiterate and unconscious, the other learned, literate and conscious. In the literary sensibility, both are likely to co-exist in a conscious and unconscious tension.[3] □

As John Carey indicates, this tension was at first a family matter. The poet feels uneasy about the way university education and poetic vocation have estranged him from his family and forebears. A part of him wants poetry to compensate for his treason. His favourite tropes are those that emphasise a continuity or correspondence between the work of labourer or craftsmen and that of the poet. One of his earliest poems, the much-anthologised 'Digging', expresses pious devotion to inheritance, asserting continuity with the past, family, community; the desire for attachment and acceptance; a sense of guilt for departing from tradition. Standing at the head of his first collection and retained as the opening poem in both the *Selected Poems* and the *New Selected Poems*, 'Digging' is clearly intended to have the force of a manifesto. At the same time, it is clear from the first book that he also cherishes an ideal of freedom: 'Follower', another much-loved early poem that is often considered alongside 'Digging', highlights the way family relationships can be a burden as well as sustaining. Here, old ways and old allegiances prevent free movement and personal development. In order to realise his own will to imaginative freedom, his own identity, the poet must distance himself from, and turn to advantage, the influence of the father, the 'strong precursor'. Taken together, these two early poems constitute a thematic paradigm for all Heaney's work to come.

In 'An Open Letter' (1983) Heaney declares: 'My *patria*, my deep design / To be at home / In my own place within / The proper name'. The lines acknowledge a Heideggerean feeling of 'not-being-at-home' in the world, but also a powerful and persistent nostalgia for a primordial home, a commitment to a project of poetic recuperation of the feeling of being-at-home. The critical problem arising here is that this 'design' can betray the poet into unreality. Writing, as well as being a potentially detribalising and therefore guilt-inducing activity, may also be elaborate rhetorical self-delusion. Heaney himself is aware of the problem – that the identity he seeks to affirm may be mere wishful thinking, the product of a falsified history, 'pap for the dispossessed'.

The dialectic of emplacement and displacement has been the focus of some of the most intense, often theoretically charged, commentary on Heaney's writing. This chapter presents a range of views – some in direct opposition to each other – of Heaney's relationship with place, the past, community. We shall begin with David Lloyd and Clair Wills, who focus on the Heideggerean, Antaean strain in the poetry and deconstruct Heaney's images of unity as unhelpful mystifications of Irish identity.

Heaney's popularity on both sides of the Atlantic, Lloyd believes, owes much to the way he has articulated his sense of Irish identity. Traditionally, Lloyd argues, literary culture in Ireland has served to resolve the problems of subjective and political identity:

■ The political function of aesthetics and culture is not only to suggest the possibility of transcending conflict, but to do so by excluding (or integrating) difference, whether historically produced or metaphysically conceived, in so far as it represents a threat to an image of unity whose role is finally hegemonic.[4] □

Lloyd objects to the ways in which Heaney uses language to 'perform the rituals of synthesis and identity' in disregard of historical reality. Heaney, Lloyd argues, reduces history to myth, leaving only 'the timelessness of repeated fundamental acts'. Focusing on the 'place-name poems' and the 'bog poems', Lloyd charges Heaney with subordinating ethics to aesthetics: by giving himself over to 'the establishment of myths' and the aesthetic ideal of the 'well-made poem', Heaney, in Lloyd's view, is unable to critique traditional concepts of national identity or interrogate the nature and function of acts of violence. The excerpt below is from Lloyd's essay '"Pap for the Dispossessed": Seamus Heaney and the Poetics of Identity'.[5]

■ 'And when we look for the history of our sensibilities I am con-vinced as Professor J.C. Beckett was convinced about the history of Ireland generally, that it is to what he called the stable element, the land itself, that we must look for continuity.'

Heaney, 'The Sense of Place', *Preoccupations*

Since his earliest volumes, Seamus Heaney's writings have rehearsed all the figures of the family romance of identity, doubled, more often than not, by a more or less explicit affirmation of a sexual structure in the worker's or the writer's relation to a land or place already given as feminine. A certain sexual knowingness accounts in part for the winsome quality of such poems as 'Digging', 'Rites of Spring' and 'Undine' in the early volumes (*DN*, pp.13–14; *DD*, pp.25–26). The winsomeness and the knowingness are compacted by the neatness with which the slight *frissons* produced by the raised spectres of patricide, rape or seduction are stilled by denouements which stress the felicities of analogy or cure the implied violence of labour and sexuality with a warm and humanising morality. That such knowledge be so easily borne and contained makes it merely thematic, and renders suspect the strenuousness of that agon which Harold Bloom seems to identify in Heaney's work as the effort to evade 'his central trope, *the vowel of the earth*'.[6] Bloom here identifies quite correctly a crucial theme in Heaney's work, and one which indeed organises his preoccupations with the establishment of poetic identity. The relevant question, however, is whether that 'agon' ever proceeds beyond thematic concerns, and, further, whether it could do so without rupturing the whole edifice within which the identity of the poet, his voice, is installed. [. . .]

'Digging' holds out the prospect of a return to origins and the consolatory myth of a knowledge which is innocent and without disruptive effect. The gesture is almost entirely formal, much as the ideology of nineteenth-century nationalists – whose concerns Heaney largely shares – was formal or aesthetic, composing the identity of the subject in the knowing of objects the very knowing of which is an act of self-production. This description holds for the writer's relation to the communal past as well as to his subjective past: in the final analysis, the two are given as identical. Knowledge can never truly be the knowledge of difference: instead, returned to that from which the subject was separated by knowledge, the subject poses his objects (perceived or produced) as synecdoches of continuity:

> poetry as divination, poetry as revelation of the self to the self, as restoration of the culture to itself; poems as elements of continuity, with the aura and authenticity of archaeological finds, where the buried shard has an importance that is not diminished by the importance of the buried city; poetry as a dig, a dig for finds that end up being plants.[7]

Poetry as divination, poetry as dig: in both these formulations Heaney resorts to metaphors which seek to bypass the problematic relation of writing to identity on several fronts. Firstly, the objectification of the subject that writing enacts is redeemed either through the fiction of immediate self-presence, or in the form of the significant moment as synecdoche for the whole temporal sequence which composes the identity of the subject as a seamless continuum. Secondly, the predicament of a literary culture as a specialised mode of labour is that it is set over against non-cultural labour, yet Heaney's writing continually rests in the untested assumption that a return is possible through writing back to the 'illiterate' culture from which it stems and with which, most importantly, it remains at all times continuous. No irreparable break appears in the subject's relation to his history by accession to culture, nor is culture itself anything but a refined expression of an ideal community of which the writer is a part. Thirdly, not focused here, but important, given that the 'touchstone' in this context is Wordsworth, is the specific relation of an 'Irish identity' to the English literary – and political – establishment, which provides not only the language, but the very terms within which the question of identity is posed and resolved, the terms for which it is the question to be posed and resolved. For it is not simply the verse form, the melody, or whatnot, that the poet takes over;[8] it is the aesthetic and, in so far as that category may be said to subsume the others, the ethical and political formulations that the Romantic and imperial tradition or culture supplies. [. . .]

Place, identity and language mesh in Heaney, as in nationalism, since language is seen primarily as naming, and because naming performs a cultural reterritorialisation by replacing the contingent continuities of a historical community with an ideal register of continuity in which the name (of place or of object) operates symbolically as the commonplace communicating between actual and ideal continua. The name always serves likeness, never difference. Hence poems on the names of places must of their nature be rendered as gifts, involving no labour on the part of the poet, who would, by enacting division, disrupt the immediacy of the relation of culture to pre-culture:

> I had a great sense of release as they were being written, a joy and a devil-may-careness, and that convinced me that one could be faithful to the nature of the English language – for in some senses these poems are erotic mouth-music by and out of the anglo-saxon [*sic*] tongue – and, at the same time, be faithful to one's own non-English origin, for me that is County Derry.[9]

The formulation renovates the concerns, even the rhetoric, of early nationalist critics. Thus the name 'Anahorish' resides as a metonym for the ancient Gaelic culture that is to be tapped, leading 'past the literary mists of Celtic twilight into that civilization whose demise was effected by soldiers and administrators like Spenser and Davies'.[10] 'Anahorish', 'place of clear water', is at once a place-name and the name of a place-name poem in *Wintering Out* (*WO*, p. 16). The name as title already assures both continuity between subject and predicate and the continuity of the poet's identity, since titular possession of this original place which is itself a source guarantees the continuity of the writing subject with his displaced former identity:

> Anahorish
> My 'place of clear water',
> the first hill in the world
> where springs washed into
> the shiny grass . . .

The writer's subjective origin doubles the Edenic and absolute origin, the untroubled clarity of his medium allowing immediacy of access to the place and moment of original creation which its own act of creation would seem to repeat and symbolise, knowledge cleansed and redeemed to graceful polish. The poem itself becomes the adequate vocable in which the rift between the Gaelic word and its English equivalent is sealed in smooth, unbroken ground, speech of the landscape:

> Anahorish, soft gradient
> of consonant, vowel-meadow.

The rhetoric of identity is compacted not only in these metaphors, representative again of Heaney's metaphors of identity. In the two sentences that compose the first and most substantial part of the poem, no main verbs appear to fracture the illusion of identity and presence. The name itself asserts the continuity of presence as an 'after-image of lamps', while in the last sentence those lamps appear to illuminate genii of the place – 'those mound-dwellers' – a qualification which expels history, leaving only the timelessness of repeated, fundamental acts. Their movement unites, as it were, the visible with the invisible, while the exceptional moment of fracturing is regained as a metaphor for access to the source and the prospect of renewed growth:

> With pails and barrows
> those mound-dwellers
> go waist-deep in mist
> to break the light ice
> at wells and dunghills.

What is dissembled in such writing is that the apparent innocence, the ahistoricity, of the subject's relation to place is in fact preceded by an act of appropriation or repossession. 'Anahorish' provides an image of the transcendental unity of the subject, and correspondingly of history, exactly in so far as it is represented – far from innocently – as a property of the subject. The lush and somewhat indulgent sentiment of the poems of place in *Wintering Out* ('Anahorish', 'Toome', 'Broagh', and 'A New Song') can be ascribed to that foreclosed surety of the subject's relation to place, mediated as it is by a language which seeks to naturalise its appropriative function.

'Erotic mouth-music': it is indeed the seduction of these poems to open a regressive path through orality beyond the institution of difference in history and in writing. Hence perception of difference, through difference, which is in fact fundamental to their logic of identity, has to be suppressed. Difference is of course registered throughout Heaney's work, at all those points of division and dispossession that have already been observed. Those divisions are, furthermore, embraced within sexual difference, which comes to provide for political, national and cultural difference a matrix of the most elementary, dualistic kind: 'I suppose the feminine element for me involves the matter of Ireland, and the masculine strain is drawn from the involvement with English literature.'[11] This difference, however, is posed as the context for a resolution beyond conflict, in the poem as in relation to the land, which is at once pre-existent and integrating:

> I have always listened for poems, they come sometimes like bodies come out of a bog, almost complete, seeming to have been laid down long ago, surfacing with a touch of mystery. They certainly involve craft and determination, but chance and instinct have a role in the thing too. I think the process is a kind of somnambulistic encounter between masculine will and intelligence and female clusters of image and emotion.[12]

> It is this feeling, assenting, equable marriage between the geographical country and the country of the mind, whether that country of the mind takes its tone unconsciously from a shared oral inherited culture, or from a consciously savoured literary culture, or from both, it is this marriage that constitutes the sense of place in its richest possible manifestation.[13]

For all their rigid, dualistic schematisation, which is only the more rigid for its pretension to be instinctual and unsystematic, and for all the inanity of the content of that dualism – oral, feminine, unconscious image and emotion versus cultured, masculine, conscious will and intelligence – such formulations acutely register the form of integration which is projected. Non-differentiation lies in the matter which precedes all difference, and in the product which is the end of difference, the aesthetic object, the poem. Culture repeats primary cultivation, its savour is oral, racy of the soil. Masculine and feminine marry likewise in the moment in which the poem is forged out of their difference, reproducing a unity of word and flesh which was always assumed to pre-exist that difference.

Only when special and explanatory status of a serious kind is pleaded for this consolatory myth do contradiction and difference return, to use a Heaneyish notion, with a vengeance. This is precisely what occurs within the series of bog poems which commences with 'The Tollund Man' in *Wintering Out*, and is extended through *North*. The origin of these poems in P. V. Glob's *The Bog People* is doubtless familiar, but it is as well to reproduce Heaney's own account:

> It [Glob's book] was chiefly concerned with preserved bodies of men and women found in the bog of Jutland, naked, strangled or with their throats cut, disposed under the peat since early Iron Age times. The author, P.V. Glob, argues convincingly that a number of these, and in particular the Tollund Man, whose head is now preserved near Aarhus in the museum at Silkeburg, were ritual sacrifices to the Mother Goddess, the Goddess of the ground who needed new bridegrooms each winter to bed with her in her sacred place, in the bog, to ensure the renewal and fertility of the territory in the spring. Taken in relation to the tradition of Irish martyrdom for that cause whose icon is Cathleen Ni Houlihan, this is more than an archaic barbarous rite: it is an archetypal pattern. And the unforgettable photographs of those victims blended in my mind with photographs of atrocities, past and present, in the long rites of Irish political and religious struggles.[14]

Heaney here posits a still operative psychic continuity between the sacrificial practices of an Iron Age people and the 'bankrupt psychology of the Irishmen and Ulstermen who do the killing'.[15] This is effectively to reduce history to myth, furnishing an aesthetic resolution to conflicts that are constituted in quite specific historical junctures by rendering disparate events as symbolic moments expressive of an underlying continuity of identity. Not surprisingly, the aesthetic which supports that identity here doubles the aesthetic politics of nationalism which finds its intensest symbolism in martyrdom. [. . .]

Contradiction returns where the myth that has most effectively served the goal of integration by obviating the state's need for overt coercion comes into conflict with those 'civilised values' which it underwrites. For both Unionists and nationalists in Ireland, in ways which agree in form but differ in specific content, concepts of racial identity asserted since the nineteenth century have performed such an integrative function in the service of domination, at the cost of institutionalising certain differences. That the interests served by these myths should have come into conflict at various periods, of which the current 'Troubles' are only the latest instance, does not affect the correspondence that subsists between the ideologies which continue to mask the class interests they subserve. It is an aspect of the petit-bourgeois nature of terrorist ideology – despite the socialist rhetoric it affects – that it should seek by symbolic acts of violence to forge integration within boundaries already set by a dominant hegemony. What is at stake is not so much the practice of violence – which has long been institutionalised in the bourgeois state – as its aestheticisation in the name of a freedom which is expressed in terms of national or racial integration. This aesthetic frame serves to deflect attention from the interests of domination which the nation state expresses both as idea and as entity.

The aestheticisation of violence is underwritten in Heaney's recourse to racial archetypes as a means 'to grant the religious intensity of the violence its deplorable authenticity and complexity'.[16] In locating the source of violence beyond even sectarian division, Heaney renders it symbolic of a fundamental identity of the Irish race, as 'authentic'. Interrogation of the nature and function of acts of violence in the specific context of the current Troubles is thus foreclosed, and history foreshortened into the eternal resurgence of the same Celtic genius. That this thinking should come into conflict with 'the perspectives of humane reason'[17] is, within the poetry that results from such a position, only an apparent contradiction, in so far as the function of reason is given over to the establishment of myths. The unpleasantness of such poetry lies in the manner in which contradictions between the ethical and aesthetic elements in the writing are easily resolved by the subjugation of the former to the latter in the interests of producing the 'well-made poem'. Contempt for 'connivance in civilized outrage' is unexamined in that frequently cited poem 'Punishment' (N, pp. 37–38), where the 'artful voyeurism' of the poem is supposedly criticised as the safe stance of the remote – and lustful – 'civilized' observer, but yet is smuggled back in as the unspoken and unacknowledged condition for the understanding of the 'exactness' of 'tribal, intimate revenge':

> I can feel the tug
> of the halter at the nape
> of her neck, the wind
> on her naked front.

It blows her nipples
to amber beads,
it shakes the frail rigging
of her ribs.

I can see her drowned
body in the bog,
the weighing stone,
the floating rods and boughs.

Under which at first
she was a barked sapling
that is dug up
oak-bone, brain-firkin . . .

My poor scapegoat,

I almost love you
but would have cast, I know,
the stones of silence.
I am the artful voyeur

of your brain's exposed
and darkened combs
your muscles' webbing
and all your numbered bones:

I who have stood dumb
when your betraying sisters,
cauled in tar,
wept by the railings,

who would connive
in civilized outrage
yet understand the exact
and tribal, intimate revenge.

The epithet 'tribal' cannot, in this context, be immanently questioned,
since it is at once sustained by and compacts the metaphor of tribal
rites which organises the whole poem, and which is at once its pretext
and its subject matter. Neither the justness of the identification of the
metaphor – the execution of an adulteress by Glob's Iron Age people –
with the actual violence which it supposedly illuminates – the tarring
and feathering of two Catholic 'betraying sisters' – nor the immediacy
of the observer's access to knowledge of his object ('I can feel . . . I can
see . . . ') is ever subjected to a questioning which would imperil the
quasi-syllogistic structure of the poem. Voyeurism is criticised merely

49

as a pose, never for its function in purveying the intimate knowledge of violence by which it is supposedly judged. As so often in Heaney's work, the sexual drive of knowing is challenged, acknowledged, and let pass without further interrogation, condemning the stance but nevertheless exploiting the material it purveys. Thus a pose of ethical self-query allows the condemnation of enlightened response – reduced in any case to paralytic 'civilized outrage' as if this were the only available alternative – while the supposedly irrational is endowed as if by default with the features of enlightenment – exactitude, intimacy of knowledge – in order to compact an understanding already presupposed in the selection and elaboration of the metaphor. The terms of the dilemma are entirely false, but the poem rehearses with striking fidelity the propensity of bourgeois thought to put 'reason' to the service of representing irrationality as the emotional substratum of identifications which, given as at once natural and logical, are in fact in themselves thoroughly irrational. □

Clair Wills, in her sophisticated, theoretically informed book, *Improprieties: Politics and Sexuality in Northern Irish Poetry* (1993), explores the links between gender, identity and language. She shows how Heaney, in taking over the traditional symbolism of the motherland in his account of the roots of the Troubles, sets up a conflict between an original femininity and a colonial masculinity: an 'indigenous territorial numen' has had her sovereignty temporarily usurped by 'a new male cult' of imperial power. Referring to Heaney's poem 'Act of Union', Wills comments:

■ The Act of Union becomes a struggle between primitive, landed, situated femininity and rational, social, organized masculinity which creates the inhabitants of the bastard province of Northern Ireland.[18] □

Wills objects to this kind of thinking, first because of 'the effacement of the materiality of the woman's body', and secondly because of 'the elision of history which the use of such mythic metaphors demands':

■ The desecration of the motherland signals a fall into history, into the discontinuities of modernity. The feminine becomes the sign of secure national identity, the body of the woman is both the site where a breach in national continuity and tradition has been effected (the result of the rape) but also the place where that breach may be healed, through a return 'home' from linguistic exile.[19]

Focusing on Heaney's dinnshenchas or 'place-name' poems, she shows how, through their use of the trope of the motherland, such poems present a mythic version of history in which the loss of the Gaelic language signifies exile from a true cultural and emotional home. This effort of returning 'home', of cultural repossession, in Wills' view, tends to involve a denial of history. History, she reminds us, 'is not singular and indivisible – it is not the ground of a unified identity'.[20]

■ In *Preoccupations*, Heaney describes the roots of the Troubles in terms of a battle between history and myth:

> To some extent the enmity can be viewed as a struggle between the cults and devotees of a god and a goddess. There is an indigenous territorial numen, a tutelar of the whole island, call her Mother Ireland, Cathleen Ni Houlihan, the poor old woman, the Shan van Vocht, whatever; and her sovereignty has been temporarily usurped or infringed by a new male cult whose founding fathers were Cromwell, William of Orange, Edward Carson, and whose godhead is incarnate in a Rex or Caesar resident in a palace in London. What we have is the tail end of a struggle in a province between territorial piety and imperial power.[21]

The struggle here is between a mythic motherland and a historical masculinity. As David Trotter has argued, the conflict within the realm of culture is referred to a supposedly self-evident and immutable distinction in the realm of gender.[22] Heaney issues a refusal of history as he draws up usurping historical characters, Cromwell and William of Orange, against a mythological deity above and beyond history, as if to suggest that history itself, in the shape of male imperialism, were the intruder. So, as in 'Act of Union' where the land is opposed to the arbitrary kingdom, there is a distinction between the authority of creation which, god given, is invested in the land, and the law of society set up by human and political means. In linguistic terms Heaney sets the self-confirming mother tongue against the patriarchal symbolic order. It is not simply that there are two languages, Irish and English, but that there are two species of language; one natural, rooted in the soil, connected to the living power of speech, the other arbitrary, male, alien. The entry of the arbitrary into language, like the entry of the imperial male into Ireland, thus taints the very life of the language, and with it the 'spirit' of the nation. The Irish nation impresses its past in words, language becomes the repository of the nation's genius, the site of the nation's heritage, as the 'truth' of the oppressed culture inheres in its territory, or the language which embodies it. In taking issue with this tendency I do not wish to argue that language is not the site of history, but rather that history is not singular and indivisible – it is not the ground of a unified identity. Heaney is being only partly ironic when he complains about his inclusion in the *Penguin Anthology of British Poetry*: 'Names were not for negotiation / Right names were the first foundation / For telling truth'. Some names, he implies, come closer to the truth of an identity than others.

Heaney's interest in the connection between land and language in *Wintering Out* divides into two areas – that of pronunciation and that of etymology. In 'Fodder' and 'Anahorish' he employs phonetic terminology to investigate the regional distinctiveness of accent; he establishes a distinctive regional identity, and at the same time reveals the difference which such identity implies. And in 'The Other Side' that difference is not merely geographical but religious, as the Puritan neighbour dismisses with 'the tongue of a chosen people'. Language segregates, isolates the nation in its nationhood; however, in 'Broagh' Heaney shows how language use also works to bring different strands of the community together. Because of their inability to pronounce the place-name English outsiders are set against the Northern Irish, both Protestant and Catholic, whose shared accent draws them together: 'That last *gh* strangers found difficult to manage'.

Apart from pronunciation, one of the central themes of *Wintering Out* is the etymology of place-names; but unlike the poems which emphasize shared speech, Heaney's historical/etymological investigations tend to deny the possibilities for a national language to work in an inclusive manner, because of the nature of the history which the language is deemed to represent. Language and soil are both rich in historical evidence, poems have 'the aura and authenticity of archaeological finds'.[23] In his review of *Field Work*, Terry Eagleton argues that Heaney 'textualises' nature, allows it to be read, at the same time recognizing that language is in some sense material.[24] This 'materiality' is seen as linked to a view of history inhering in the land, which Eagleton casts as a defining feature of much Northern Irish poetry. He finds a radical, anti-imperialist commitment in the theme of 'disinterring' history and tradition which runs through Heaney's 'Bog' poems, Montague's *The Dead Kingdom*, and some of Longley's and Mahon's work. For Eagleton, radical or revolutionary thought, in the manner of Walter Benjamin, reverses what he terms the ruling-class 'denial of history' by rewriting the present in terms of a past that refuses to die:

> Much recent Irish writing has been 'political' less in its explicit declarations and allegiances than in this ceaseless nurturing of historical traces, this disinterring of concealed geological strata stacked beneath a surface which mistakes itself for all there is.[25]

Eagleton is undoubtedly correct in terming this archaeological unearthing a positive project. However, as in Benjamin's theory, the historical find needs to be placed in a significant relation to contemporary events, rather than merely offered as an explanation for them. The danger is that Heaney's finds will comprise merely the remnants of history, not its living force. So in the place-name poems in *Wintering Out* he disinters an epic past from layers of bog which have preserved moments of time pure and intact. In 'Toome' the 'blastings' of mouthing the word parallel blastings into the subsoil:

> prospecting what new
> in a hundred centuries'
> loam, flints, musket balls,
> fragmented ware,
> tores and fish-bones
> till I am sleeved in
>
> alluvial mud that shelves
> suddenly under
> bogwater and tributaries,
> and elvers tail my hair.

The word 'Toome' derives from the Irish *tuaim* (Latin *tumulus*), and of course it is not without connections to the English 'tomb'; it is inside this grave mound that Heaney finds his buried history. The history is one of imperialist advance, new objects are the relics of war.[26] So the word is valuable because it is a symbol of dispossession, but the poem does not place that symbol in a significant relation to the present. The problem with the poem is that both word and find become museum pieces, mere curiosities to be visited and contemplated in isolation. □

In Wills' view, Heaney is simply recycling the dominant nationalist discourse in constructing a poetic out of an opposition between 'femininity, nature and continuity on the one hand, and masculinity, culture and discontinuity on the other'. Her special interest is in the work of several other Northern Ireland writers, particularly Tom Paulin, Medbh McGuckian and Paul Muldoon, who 'distance themselves from the dominant paradigm by figuring the feminine and the home as fragmented and discontinuous, a source of impropriety (both in the sense of indiscretion and non-possession) which affects Irish cultural tradition as a whole'.[27] Where some critics (Conor Cruise O'Brien, Edna Longley) are opposed to the use of myth for political ends (see pages 81–4 and 93–103), Wills (along with Richard Kearney, Mark Patrick Hederman and Elizabeth Butler Cullingford, see pages 54–64, 103–8 and 126–7) believes that it is possible to critique the political implications of specific myths without rejecting the notion of political poetry altogether. By focusing on the 'improper' elements of Paulin's, McGuckian's and Muldoon's poetry – the refusal of a sense of home, the disruption of 'traditional' poetic form, and the sexual narratives told – Wills argues that theirs is the kind of work (unlike Heaney's) that offers a radical challenge to the dominant discourse on matters of place, identity and language. Their poetry, Wills claims, 'cannot be understood without a redefinition of the relationship between poetry and politics'.[28]

Robert Welch vigorously disputes Lloyd's and Wills' view of the poet's profound passivity before the tribal *mythos*. Welch insists that Heaney's relation with tradition and the past is not one of passive submission or passionate intensity, but a search for 'a balanced psychic freedom' within 'a sense of larger cultural archetypes or entities'. To explain Heaney's concept of identity, Welch, in his essay 'A rich young man leaving everything behind him: Poetic Freedom in Seamus Heaney' adopts a Jungian model of self-individuation, and emphasises Heaney's concern with the constructed nature of identity. Heaney, says Welch, is one of 'Bogland's pioneers: they are not reciters of the litanies handed out by schools, courts or churches. They work'.[29] Thus, Welch opposes those critics such as Lloyd and Edna Longley (see pages 42–50 and 93–103) who accuse Heaney of simply and unquestioningly repeating old myths, and emphasises the dynamic of self-definition in his work.

■ It is sometimes argued that Heaney's transactions with the tribal are merely a fascination with the myth-kitty, and that by indulging this he is opportunistically identifying with the stereotypes of Irish cultural nationalism. Such a view seems to me wholly to miss the point, which can be stated simply: Heaney is engaged upon a cultural and tribal exploration; he is testing out his cultural inheritance to see where the significant deposits are located; but he is not engaged upon a mindless submission to the old tradition or the goddess or whatever, Heaney is interested in individuation, in the way that Jung explained it, as being a holding-in-balance of the sense of the self with the sense of larger cultural archetypes or entities. Again, it should be said, Heaney is concerned with balance rather than passionate intensity for its own sake; the *lucidus Ordo* rather than the savage god. This enterprise is difficult and needs to be pursued with caution, intelligence and the utmost precision. In this area of psychic and cultural excavation blunders are extremely dangerous and presumption may literally be mortal.[30] □

Richard Kearney, Timothy Kearney, Alistair Davies and Stan Smith also take issue with Lloyd's and Wills' construction of Heaney as a traditional 'revivalist' writer, committed to the 'backward look' and preoccupied with images of mythology, archaeology, etymology and anthropology in an effort to reclaim forgotten origins, a sacred homeland, a lost identity. Instead, these critics focus on Heaney's own notion that identity is best found in 'displacement', and present a more modern, even postmodern, Heaney. Richard Kearney's study of Heaney, 'Heaney and Homecoming', is to be found in his book *Transitions*, the title reflecting Kearney's concern with a culture in transition and the 'essentially conflictual nature of contemporary Irish experience'.[31] Writers such as Heaney, the playwright Brian Friel and the novelist John Banville exemplify for Kearney the tension in modern Irish culture between 'revivalism and modernism', between the 'pull of tradition' and an impulse towards creative freedom.[32] These writers, according to Kearney, are engaged in a common project of shaping the new through a 'translation' or reformulation of the old. Thus, Kearney sees Heaney as being involved in a radical revision of traditional notions of history, identity and language: language is no longer a transparent means for representing a preordained identity, but the means whereby we construct an identity for ourselves. Tradition is not sacred and inviolable, but must be continually revised and worked upon to ensure relevance for the present and the future. There may be no possibility of recovering a pure origin, but by engaging interpretatively and creatively with the past in an effort to produce a less alienated future with which we can assuage the angst of 'homelessness' and lostness, Kearney aims to show that for Heaney identity is constructed out of a dialectic between 'the opposing claims of home and homelessness'.[33] As an émigré of the imagination, Heaney is, in Kearney's analysis, both inside and outside his culture, feeling 'lost' and 'unhappy' even while 'at home'. The chosen emblems of Heaney's 'journeywork', Kearney notes, 'are, accordingly, Terminus (the god of boundaries), Sweeney Astray (the displaced, wandering king) and Janus (the double-faced god who looks simultaneously backward to the myths of indigenous culture and forward to the horizons of the future)'.[34] In adducing the poet's preoccupation with thresholds and pilgrimage and the crossing of frontiers, Kearney emphasises what Heaney himself calls in one of his Oxford lectures ('Frontiers of Writing') the 'challenge to be in two minds'. Kearney's study is reproduced with cuts below.[35]

■ Seamus Heaney is often hailed as Ireland's greatest poet since Yeats. While such praise generally adverts to Heaney's remarkable sense of craft, his verbal and formal dexterity, it frequently betrays another kind of evaluation: one concerned less with Ireland's greatest *poet* than with *Ireland*'s greatest poet. Here the emphasis falls on the typically and traditionally Irish quality of Heaney's writing. He is enlisted as the poet of the *patria*, a home bird, an excavator of the national landscape devoted to the recovery of natural pieties.

Heaney's primary inspiration, we are told, is one of place; his quintessentially Irish vocation, the sacramental naming of a homeland. Hence the preoccupation with images of mythology, archaeology and genealogy, of returning to forgotten origins. This revivalist reading conforms to the paradigm of the 'backward look' which, Frank O'Connor has argued, typifies Irish literature.

This orthodox view would have us believe that while other contemporary Irish poets embraced the more modernist idioms of existential angst or the crisis of language, Heaney remained faithful to the primacy of the provincial. He didn't need to take his tune from current trends in Continental or Anglo-American poetry; for he had discovered the cosmos, as it were, in his own backyard. Mahon, Montague, Longley and Kinsella engaged in metaphysical meditations about the problematic rapport between self, language and history. Durcan and Bolger composed biting satires about urban bourgeois hypocrisy and the ravages of advanced industrial capitalism. But Heaney stuck to the home patch. He resisted the modernist impulse and remained, inalienably, 'one of our own'. A true revivalist.

Some commentators have offered a more ideological interpretation of the nostalgia for lost traditions which is said to exemplify the 'native' strain of Irish literature. The harking back to an abandoned, or at least threatened, organic life-style still in harmony with all that is best in the national heritage, has been seen as an attempt to reconstruct a cultural unison which would overcome, by overlooking, the actual social divisions which torment modern Irish society. As one critic remarked: 'An emergent Catholic capitalist class espoused a myth of natural pious austerity in opposition to the profane forces of modernity, while the Anglo-Irish déracinés sought harmony with nature and a people characterised by wild, irrational, asocial energies'. Viewed in such an ideological perspective, Heaney's poetic efforts to bring Irish culture 'home' to itself, might be dismissed as a conservative return to antiquated mythologies of 'tradition' and 'nature'.

By focussing on the central theme of 'homecoming' in Heaney I propose to show how it involves a complex conflict of sensibility which has little or nothing to do with insular notions of parochial *pietas*. I will analyse Heaney's preoccupation with 'homecoming' less in standard formal terms than *in philosophical* terms. My aim is to demonstrate that Heaney's treatment of 'homecoming' involves an unresolved dialectic between the opposing claims of home and homelessness. The revivalist reading of his work could do with some debunking. It is time to prise Heaney free from stereotypes.

First, it should be noted that Heaney's poems are not in fact primarily about place at all; they are about *transit*, that is, about transitions from one place to another. One need only look to the titles of some of his major works to see just how fundamental this notion of poetry as transitional act is: *Wintering Out, Door into the Dark, Field Work, Sweeney Astray, Station Island*. One of the central reasons for Heaney's preference for journey over sojourn, for exodus over abode, is, I suggest, a fidelity to the nature *of language* itself. Far from subscribing to the traditional view that language is a transparent means of representing some identity which precedes language – call it *self, nation, home* or whatever – Heaney's poetry espouses the view that it is language which perpetually constructs and deconstructs our given notions of identity. As such, poetic language is always on the move, vacillating between opposing viewpoints, looking in at least two directions at once.

Heaney has been criticized for refusing to adopt a clear political position, for not nailing his colours to the mast, particularly with regard to the 'national question' (i.e. his attitude to his native North). One Irish politician described him as an 'artful dodger' who displays 'all the skills of the crafty tightrope walker . . . sidestepping and skipping his slippery way out of trouble. Bemoaning the fact that his work is a 'job of literary journeywork', this same critic admonishes him to 'seek a less ambivalent position'. The point is, however, that Heaney is a poet, not a party politician. He does not deny that his work has political connotations – for that would be to deny that it is concerned with life as it is lived. But this does not mean that he is compelled to subscribe to a definitive ideological standpoint. His refusal to be fixed, to be *placed* in any single perspective is no more than a recognition that poetry's primary fidelity is to language as an interminable metamorphosis of conflicting identities. Heaney himself states his position on language as dual or multiple perspective in the following passage from *Preoccupations*: 'When I called my second book *Door into the Dark* I intended to gesture towards this idea of poetry as a point of entry into the buried life of the feelings or as a point of exit for it. Words themselves are doors: Janus is to a certain extent their deity, looking back to a ramification of the roots and associations and forward to a clarification of sense and meaning . . . In *Door into the Dark* there are a number of poems that arise out of the almost unnameable energies that, for me, hovered over certain bits of language . . .[36] The poet's commitment to an aesthetic of endless migration is clear. [. . .]

Heaney's commitment to the ambivalence of poetic language is, I believe, manifest in his exploration of the pivotal motif of 'homecoming'.

Whereas in the early works, Heaney usually talks of home in terms of a personal quest for self-identity, in his later collections – and particularly *North* or *Station Island* – he begins to interpret homecoming more in terms of a linguistic search for historical identity. As he himself remarks in *Preoccupations*, words cease to be fingerprints recording the unique signature of the poet and become 'bearers of history'. But if Heaney insists that one of the tasks of the poet is to recover a sense of belonging to a shared past – 'an ancestry, a history, a culture' – he construes this task as a *project* rather than a *possession*, as an exploration of language rather than some triumphalist revival of a lost national identity.

Poetry, in short, comes to express the sense of 'home' less as a literal (i.e. geographical, political or personal) property than as a metaphorical preoccupation. Home is something that cannot be taken for granted as present. It must be sought after precisely because it is *absent*. For Heaney, homecoming is never the actuality of an event but the possibility of an advent.

At this point it may be useful to look at some poems in Heaney's collection *North* which deal explicitly with this theme. In a poem entitled 'Homecomings', Heaney would seem to be affirming the experience of home as a *positive* goal. He meditates upon the 'homing' manoeuvrings of a sandmartin as it circles back to its nest:

> At the worn mouth of the hole
> Flight after flight after flight
> The swoop of its wings
> Gloved and kissed home.

The poet sees this instinctual, almost atavistic, homecoming of the sandmartin as an analogy for his own aspiration to return to an originating womb of earth where he may regain a sense of prenatal silence, unity and belonging:

> A glottal stillness. An eardrum.
> Far in, featherbrains tucked in silence,
> A silence of water lipping the bank
>
> Mould my shoulders inward to you.
> Occlude me.
> Be damp clay pouting.
> Let me listen under your eaves.

This experience recalls the opening passage from *Preoccupations* where Heaney invokes the image of the *omphalos* as a hidden underground well of childhood memory. 'I would begin', he writes, 'with the Greek word, *omphalos*, meaning the navel, and hence the stone that marked the centre of the world, and repeat it, *omphalos, omphalos, omphalos*, until its blunt and falling music becomes the music of somebody pumping water at the pump outside our back door . . . th[e] pump marked an original descent into earth, sand, gravel, water. It centred and staked the imagination, made its foundations the foundation of the *omphalos* itself'. [37] [. . .]

In one of the first of his bog poems – the last poem of *Door into the Dark* – Heaney describes how a great elk and a morsel of butter were recovered from Irish bogs, having been preserved for centuries in the dark and watery peat. The poem concludes with the following image of an interminable excavation for a vanished *omphalos*:

> Our pioneers keep striking
> Inwards and downwards,
>
> Every layer they strip
> Seems camped on before.
> The bogholes might be Atlantic seepage
> The wet centre is bottomless.

[. . .]

Heaney informs us in *Preoccupations* that one of the main sources of his 'bog' motif was Glob's *The Bog People* (a work he first read in translation in 1969, which was 'appositely, the year the killing started' in Ulster). Heaney is under no illusions about the potentially terrifying consequences of the 'quest for home' when this degenerates – as it so easily can – into tribal fanaticism. He offers the following account of how, on reading Glob's work, the various emblems of the 'northern' (Nordic) sacrificial practices came together with the contemporary realities of the 'northern' (Ulster) conflict:

> It was chiefly concerned with preserved bodies of men and women found in the bogs of Jutland, naked, strangled or with their throats cut, disposed under the peat since early Iron Age times. The author, P. V. Glob, argues convincingly that a number of these, and in particular the Tollund Man, whose head is now preserved near Aarhus in the museum at Silkeburg, were ritual sacrifices to the Mother Goddess, the Goddess of the ground who needed new bridegrooms each winter to bed with her in her sacred place, in the bog, to ensure the renewal and fertility of the territory in the spring. Taken in relation to the tradition of Irish political martyrdom for that cause whose icon is Cathleen Ni Houlihan, this is more than an archaic barbarous rite: it is an

archetypal pattern. And the unforgettable photographs of these victims blended in my mind with photographs of atrocities, past and present, in the long rites of Irish political and religious struggles.[38]

While recognizing the fecundity of this material for the poetic imagination, Heaney admits its dangers for political reality. The temptation to fudge the dividing line between a figurative and literal interpretation of this cult is strenuously resisted. Heaney states his critical reservations on this score when he comments on his attitude to 'The Tollund Man', another of his bog poems: 'When I wrote this poem, I had a completely new sensation, one of fear. It was a vow to go on a pilgrimage and I felt as it came to me . . . that unless I was deeply in earnest about what I was saying, I was simply invoking dangers for myself'.[39] This mention of fear is significant not only in its reference to the traditionally mystic attitude to the sublime of holy as *fascinans et tremendum*, but more directly still in its bearing on the experience of the *Unhomely* (see appendix). In 'Tollund Man', Heaney counterpoints the ritual act of returning home with a critical scruple of exile and distance. The poet describes an imaginary pilgrimage northwards to pay homage to an ancestor recovered from a bog still intact after thousands of years and attired in his sacrificial garb of cap, noose and girdle. But it is significant that the northern bog is not in fact in Ulster but in Jutland – and the ancestor in question is not an Irishman but a Tollund man. In other words, Heaney is returning to a home away from home: an *unheimlich* home.

The Tollund victim is described as a 'bridegroom to the goddess', the suggestion being that he has been sacrificed to the earth deity so that she might be sexually regenerated and he preserved in her 'cradling dark' for posterity. In this image of the sanctified scapegoat from the far north, Heaney finds an 'objective correlative' for the near north of his own homeland in Ulster. And the security which the sentiment of home-coming might normally confer is thus offset by a careful awareness of uncanny estrangement. 'Out there in Jutland', Heaney confesses, 'In the old man-killing parishes / I feel lost, / unhappy and at home'.

Heaney does not ignore the disobliging implications of such death rites for his native North. In the 'Grauballe Man', he concedes that the perfected memory of the sacrificial bog-victim remains haunted by the present Ulster reality of 'each hooded victim / Slashed and dumped': the poet's response thus hangs in the 'scales with beauty and atrocity'. And elsewhere, in a poem called 'Funeral Rites', Heaney compares the 'slow triumph' of the funeral procession towards the mounds of the ancestral Boyne Valley (considered in Irish legend to be the mystical

PLACE, IDENTITY, LANGUAGE

centre or *omphalos* of the earth) to the ominous winding of a serpent. A similar note of caution is struck in the title poem of *North* which recounts how the poet had to travel to the 'unmagical' Nordic lands of Iceland and Greenland before he could hear again the voices of his own Viking ancestry in Ireland – 'Ocean deafened voices/Warning me, lifted again/In violence and epiphany'. He imagines the swinging tongue of a Viking longship speaking to him 'buoyant with hindsight' of revenge, of 'hatreds and behind backs . . . memory incubating the spilled blood'. So that while beckoning the poet to 'lie down in the word-hoard' of his *literary* heritage, this ancestral voice simultaneously warns against a cyclical repetition of past atrocities at the *literal* level of political blood-letting.

Heaney remains mindful of the fact that a culture's 'great first sleep of homecoming' is also a death and a forgetting. The act of poetic remembering must always observe a delicate balance between the opposite risks of belonging to a home and being exiled from this home. To resolve this paradox by opting in absolute fashion for either extreme would be to betray the dual fidelity of his poetry.

It is altogether fitting, finally, that this paradox should find both historical and linguistic correlatives in Heaney's own predicament. Historically, Heaney is aware that the British plantation of Gaelic Ulster in the seventeenth century resulted in the displacement of the Irish language by English (an historical event which received more recent expression in this century with the drawing of a border across the map of Ireland). Part of Heaney's ambivalent predicament is due, consequently, to his maintenance of a notion of himself 'as Irish in a province that insists that it is British'.[40] And this double consciousness is operative at the level of his poetic language where two tongues engage in conflictual dialogue. As Heaney emblematically remarks: 'I think of the personal and Irish pieties as vowels, and the literary awareness nourished on English as consonants.'[41]

The very words of Heaney's poems bear witness to this aesthetic of dual residence, to a poetic scruple of tireless migration. □

Kearney concludes:

■ This poetic paradox of 'homecoming' is powerfully sustained in Heaney's later work. In *Station Island* (1984), a collection which takes its name from the northern place of pilgrimage, Lough Derg, Heaney returns to an exploration of the homing instincts of religious and political reverence. Here, perhaps more explicitly than in any previous work, Heaney self-consciously interprets the fascination with 'home' as a need for tradition, community, memory, mythology, the collective unconscious. In the long title sequence, the poet is assailed by several

accusing voices from his past – usually victims of the bloody carnage
in his native Ulster. These 'ancestral' ghosts address him in dream or
reverie as he rehearses the ritual stations of Lough Derg. Here is a
privileged place and time for recollection, for coming to terms with
what Joyce's Stephen Dedalus called the 'nightmare of history' – the
'revivalist claims' of motherland and mother church. And here, more
than anywhere, is the poet privy to the hauntings of his 'migrant
solitude'.

The sequence opens with the poet's alter-ego, Sweeney, shouting
at him to 'stay clear of all processions'. But the poet persists on the
'drugged path' of tribal ceremony; he embraces the 'murmur of the
crowds', the pious solidarity of the living and the dead. The poet's visitor
from beyond the grave is Carleton, another Irish writer who had
experienced 'gun butts cracking on the door' and whose rejection of
both 'hard-mouthed Ribbonmen and Orange bigots' (tribal northern
gangs) had 'mucked the byre of their politics'. The poet confesses that
he himself has 'no mettle for the angry role' of ancestral revenge; yet
he is compelled by Carleton's counsel to 'remember everything and
keep (his) head'.

For Heaney, however, as for Hugh in Friel's play *Translations*, 'to
remember everything is a form of madness'. In the first instance,
remembrance is racked with guilt – and particularly the poet's guilt
about his lack of direct political involvement with the sufferings of his
tribe. One visitation from an assassinated childhood friend provokes
the poet to seek forgiveness for 'the way (he) has lived indifferent'.
And another murder victim, a second cousin, chides the pilgrim for
consorting with effete fellow-poets when he first heard the news of
his death:

> I accuse directly, but indirectly, you
> Who now atone perhaps upon this bed
> For the way you whitewashed ugliness . . .
> And saccharined my death with morning dew.

Faced with this litany of ancestral accusations, the author drifts
towards repentance. But he also realises that his primary commitment
as a poet is to the exploration of the buried truths of *language* – which
mediates, records and structures our experience – rather than to the
immediate exigencies of political legislation or reprisal. 'As if the
eddy could reform the pool'. The buried truths of language are
revealed by poetry to the degree that (1) the poet takes the step back
from our familiar use of words as means/end strategies and (2) listens
in silence to what language is saying in and through us. The poem is
in this way a response, before all else, to the silent voices of language

itself. This is what modern thinkers such as Heidegger, Lévi-Strauss and Lacan have taught us. As the latter remarked: 'The subject is spoken rather than speaking. . . . It was certainly the Word that was in the beginning, and we live in its creation, but it is because the symbol has made him man'.[42] Heaney makes this point about his own work when he declares that 'the creative mind is astraddle silence',[43] an echo perhaps of Beckett's pregnant statement that 'silence is our mother-tongue'.

The final visitation in the Lough Derg sequence of *Station Island* is Joyce's ghost. Joyce, like Carleton, serves as a *literary* conscience. But unlike Carleton's revivalist exhortation to remember everything, he recommends the modernist commitment to writing itself – to 'signatures' of the writer's own frequency. Joyce warns the poet that the obsession with collective guilt and tribal grievance is a mistake:

> That subject people stuff is a cod's game . . .
> You lose more of yourself than you redeem
> Doing the decent thing.
> Keep at a tangent.
> When they make the circle wide, it's time to swim
> Out on your own and fill the element
> With signatures of your own frequency . . .
> Elver-gleams in the dark of the whole sea.

Significantly, the figure of Sweeney Astray – the exiled wandering bard of Irish legend and the subject of a verse translation by Heaney from the Gaelic *Buile Suibhne* – returns in the third section of the book as symbol of the dissenting and disinherited poet. Sweeney's migratory impulses confirm the Joycean plea. But one of the main strengths of *Station Island* is the refusal to choose between Heaney and Sweeney – between the guilt-ridden pilgrim of history and the carefree émigré of the imagination. As the Janus-faced author remarks early in the collection (citing Milosz):

> I was stretched
> between contemplation
> of a motionless point
> and the command to participate
> actively in history.

Heaney's ultimate fidelity to the ambiguity of opposing demands, and to the inner manoeuvrings of poetic language which sustain such demands, his refusal of any single place or position which would permit the illusion of a final solution, is proof of his tireless transiting between revivalism and modernism. Whether Heaney's continuing 'journeywork' will lead him closer to the radicalist modernism of Joyce or the revivalist modernism of Yeats remains an open question. Perhaps he will succeed in forging a post-modernist synthesis somewhere between the two – what we might call a poetics of perpetual detour? As he observes in a poem called 'Terminus', (*The Haw Lantern*, 1987), dedicated to the god of boundaries and borders:

> Two buckets were easier carried than one.
> I grew up in between. □

For some critics, the poet's sense of displacement produces an even more fundamentally alienated persona than Kearney recognises. For Timothy Kearney, another *Crane Bag* writer, Heaney's identification with 'the figure of the victim', his position on the margins of community and politics, his 'stance of indirection', his 'divided loyalties' and his refusal 'to be seduced by a single answer' make him a poet particularly sensitive to the post-modern 'crisis of alienation'. Where Richard Kearney emphasises the production of a new communal consciousness and the opening up of new horizons of meaning, Timothy Kearney focuses on the intensities of 'unresolved conflict' between individual and community. The excerpt below is from Timothy Kearney's essay, 'The Poetry of the North: A Post-Modernist Perspective', which was originally published in *The Crane Bag* (1979).[44]

■ When we come to consider the main body of poetry which has been written in the province of Ulster since Yeats, we cannot omit consideration of this feature of all Post-Modernist literature – the alienation of the individual from his community. Arnold's belief in the stability of a homogeneous culture as the basic dynamic for literary endeavour has been replaced in our own age by the instability of heterogeneous culture. And these poets provide perfect illustration of the thesis. Whatever cultural discrepancies one wishes to highlight as the watermark of this crisis of community in the poetry of the North (the crisis of national identity, the conflict of religious sectarianism, the severance of city and country, or the tension between the parochial and the cosmopolitan), this discrepancy between the individual and his social orbit of value underlies them all. The real identity crisis in the poetry of the North is not specifically national or religious or provincial, but communal. It turns on the conflict of the individual endeavouring to find community in the cultural force-field of these intractable tensions. In other words the crisis issues not only from the question 'To which community can I best belong?', but also from the more searching question 'Can I belong to any community at all?'.

. . . Seamus Heaney has frequently been hailed, and not without reason, as the connoisseur *par excellence* of the Catholic communal consciousness. Denis Donoghue has shown how his transcendence of self has allowed him a natural continuity with his landscape. Thus a poem like 'The Diviner' is seen as a parable of the vital connection between man and nature; or a poem like 'Belderg' is cited to illustrate the same theme where an archaeological discovery is described in human terms. By the same reading, the lines 'Processional stooping through the turf/Recurs mindlessly as Autumn' are focussed upon in the poem 'At a Potato Digging'. For they hint at that communal satisfaction and ease where action, in Montague's phrase, has been wrung to ritual. But the Earth-Godess with which these workers so gracefully liaise has another face which is overlooked in this reading. For the irony of this poem lies in the fact that the workers spilling their libations of cold tea and crusts, fail to discern that the ground on which they lie is 'faithless', that in less prosperous times she is the 'bitch earth', 'the black mother', 'the famine god' whose centuries of homage

> Toughen the muscles behind their humbled knees,
> Make a seasonal altar of the sod.

In other words, not only is she the provider of plenty but also the per-petrator of sacrifice, the creator of victims. And it is precisely the figure of the victim which receives most of Heaney's imaginative generosity. From the 4-year-old victim of 'Mid-term Break' to the distraught mother of 'Elegy to an Unborn Child' to the sequestered defective of 'Byechild' to the 'poor scapegoat' of 'Punishment' – the pattern is con-sistent. Attendant upon it has been the delineation of the poet himself as one whose natural habitat is the margin. In the opening poem of his first collection, 'Digging', the poet contemplates his exclusion from the community of his grandfather and father as potent men of action – 'I have no spade to follow men like them' – and finds his surrogate in his pen. In the closing poem of *Exposure* he still inhabits the periphery, this time of his province's political troubles:

> I am neither internee nor informer;
> An inner émigré, grown long-haired
> And thoughtful; a wood-kern
> Escaped from the massacre.

But it is not simply a case of cancelling one interpretation against the other. The evidence for reading Heaney's poetry as the expression of a communal consciousness is commensurate with that which supports our seeing it as an articulation of an outsider's sympathy for his fellows. And this is precisely the point. For any poet to risk the communal incarnation of his experience today is at the same time to risk confronting the strain between communal and individual values which lurks at the heart of that endeavour. And exactly how much poetic integrity is required in order to endure that discrepancy, we have already seen.

But this, it appears to me, is exactly where Heaney's most characteristic and intense poetry is located. In *Wintering Out* we saw its classical expression in 'The Tollund Man'. Caught between the sacrificial demands of his allegiance to the soil of Ireland 'our Holy ground' and the loss of human life which that of necessity entails, he chooses a stance of indirection.

Though this may appear, *pace* Terence Brown,[45] as a form of indecision. This stance attends with compunction to both:

> Out there in Jutland
> In the old man-killing parishes
> I will feel lost,
> Unhappy and at home.

In *North* the poem 'Punishment' illustrates the poet doggedly confronting the same strain. His communal comprehension of his tribe's ritual codes is combined with his recognition of the cost this entails:

> Who would connive
> In civilized outrage,
> Yet understand the exact
> And tribal, intimate revenge.

In his most recent volume *Fieldwork*, this theme is seen to have developed in a most interesting direction. The poet's voice is his own throughout, his primary allegiance no longer being to his mythological muse but to his domestic one. His Sybil is no longer the volatile Earth-godess of Irish history but the young girl in 'Triptych', one of the 'smalleyed survivor flowers' of his country's troubles. She is apotheosised as she

> walks in home to us
> Carrying a basket full of new potatoes
> Three tight green cabbages, and carrots
> With the tops and mould still fresh on them.

But rather than retreating from his communal responsibilities into the private and protective arms of his new-found muse, he has her answer the question confronting his community, 'what will become of us?' And her answer, characteristically, is one of indirection.

Heaney recently said that he was tiring of his door into the dark and was now searching for a door into the light, the light of Dante's virtues of wisdom and truth beyond the satisfactions of the purely aesthetic impulse. In his ostensible switch of allegiance from the 'bitch earth' to his 'pined-for, unmolested orchid' Heaney has effected this change of direction. It is not by chance that many of these poems with their quality of intense and exact description which is at once revelation, their sense of enacting a desultory itinerary which suddenly corners into order, are reminiscent of those in *Death of a Naturalist*. For of his first four volumes that is the one which exhibits the poet at his most individual, peering at his reflection in the dark bottom of wells, rhyming to see himself 'to set the darkness echoing'. But now this self, no longer content to brood introspectively on the dark depths of its own imagination, has directed its gaze outward to the light of its community, individually considered.

[. . .]

The achievement of the Northern poets lies in the sensitivity of their response to the Post-Modernist crisis of alienation. They have insisted on realizing their experience in communal terms. As that experience is one of unresolved conflict, the task of attendance is difficult. The main temptations are twofold. Firstly, the seductiveness of the Yeatsian vision of culture, of setting oneself up as the vatic spokesman of one's tribe. This tribal tone has not been absent in the poetry of the North: when it has occasionally surfaced in the poetry of Montague and Heaney its effect has been detrimental. Secondly, the temptation to flee from such intense cultural confusion into an introverted lyrical cul-de-sac. Here the bugbear is the English *Bien Fait* tradition. Content with producing well-made commentaries on Britain's ordinary universe, it has sacrificed much. Its suburban domesticity risks an atrophy of feeling. Without the nourishment of myth or atavism it has lost imaginative vitality. The early poetry of Michael Longley bears the taint of this influence.

But at their most characteristic moments, these poets have endured the discrepancies inflicted by their culture. They have not allowed the violence of their feelings to dissipate their imaginative energies, but have contained it in the formal restraint of their verse. Rather than being limited by the colonial peculiarities of their culture, their verse has been enriched by them.[46] For, seen in the Post-Modernist perspective we have outlined, the communal expression of their alienation as something specifically Northern is the register of something universal. They have shown that in engaging their cultural peculiarities they are capable of transcending them. And it is in the measure that they realized this capacity that their poetry has been significant. □

An interesting account of Heaney as a post-modernist is Alistair Davies' essay, 'Seamus Heaney: From Revivalism to Postmodernism' (in *British Poetry from the 1950s to the 1990s: Politics and Art,* 1997), which examines the evolution of both Heaney's poetic and the criticism it has attracted. The essay was to some extent written as a reply to Richard Kearney. Davies acknowledges Richard Kearney's anti-revivalist impulse, but shares with Timothy Kearney a sense of a much more radically marginalised and 'dispersed' persona. Where Richard Kearney saw Heaney as an exponent of Heideggerean post-modernism ('Heaney's ambivalent attitude to homecoming expressed as a double-movement of attraction and revulsion, intense questing and sceptical questioning – bears a certain resemblance to Martin Heidegger's notion of the poet's 'search for Being as a dialectical movement towards "home" through the "unhomely"'),[47] Davies argues that Heaney's post-modernism after *Station Island* is more Barthesian than Heideggerean. With special reference to 'Station Island', Davies shows Heaney's relation to Roland Barthes' notion of the text as irreducibly plural, an endless play of signifiers that constantly elude any single centre, essence or meaning. The excerpt from 'Seamus Heaney: From Revivalism to Postmodernism' that is given below begins with Davies' remarks on Kearney's revisionist rereading of Heaney.[48]

■ The reasons for rereading Heaney in this way are clear. The poet, aware of the inevitability of 'homelessness', not only puts under question the revivalist myths upon which all nationalist traditions are based but also makes available from that questioning the possibility of a more authentic, and more plural community:

> Balor will die
> and Byrthnoth and Sitting Bull.
> ('Hercules and Antaeus')

Yet this rereading may entail less of a reversal than Kearney believes, for it shares with the revivalist tradition the same assumption about the poet's function. In each case, the poet puts into words and thereby gives substance to the idea of a community. 'The word alone gives being to the thing,' Heidegger stated in 'The Nature of Language',[49] and this notion underlay the answer he gave to the question: 'What are poets for?' Their function in the derelict present, he suggested, was to construct through language no less than 'a house of Being'. The attractiveness of Heidegger's view of the function of the poet lies precisely in the fact that it grants poetry a cultural centrality which, even in contemporary 'high culture', it no longer possesses. By considering Heaney as a figure founding a world, the critic not only obscures the marginal social and cultural conditions within which he produces, but also the marginal social and cultural conditions out of which he writes.

We might think that Heaney's ironic self-representation in 'Singing School 6, Exposure', 'weighing and weighing' amidst the turmoil of Northern Ireland 'my responsible *tristia*', involves the very acknowledgement of the marginality of the poet. The poet can make nothing happen. He may well complain that the language and the forms in which he writes are not his own, but then the native 'guttural muse' was, he had conceded in 'Traditions' in *Wintering Out* 'bulled long ago' by the invaders' alliterative tradition. Is he not the poet of the play of their differences, possessing and possessed by both? His technical innovations within the lyric form might be seen as a subtle form of resistance to the English lyric tradition, but they could not undermine its massive authority nor its admirable commitment to the spirit of ambiguity and of necessary delay. Was he not destined, like the manumitted slave he describes in 'Freedman', to a career made up of biting the hand that *fed him*?

Yet this irony reflects less the ineffectuality of all poets within a particular historical situation than his failure, on account of the immobility engendered by divided affiliations, to give adequate voice to something which remains central to him and to his fellow kin – the spirit of place violated by the invasion of the English and the imposition of their cultural forms:

Iambic drums
Of English beat the woods where her poets
Sink like Onan.

('Ocean's Love to Ireland')

His irony is the product of self-enfeeblement, and even though he can seek compensation for this by identifying with the Viking warriors of the North or envisage the overthrow of England's political and cultural forms through an apocalyptic combination of natural and linguistic forces, this last dream, as we can see in *Wintering Out*, is significantly set in train by a Wordsworthian encounter not with a Highland lass but with a Gaelic-speaking girl from Derrygarve:

But now our river tongues must rise
From licking deep in native haunts
To flood, with vowelling embrace,
Demesnes staked out in consonants.

('A New Song')

69

Heaney's irony appears the Rousseauite-Wordsworthian confession of an artificial man who has lost his naturalness and his natural strength by the very act of writing, by creating images of the self to circulate within urban and urbane society. He is haunted by the loss of his power over that primal song which in turn binds utterance and place, place and the community which inhabits it. By enclosing his career within one continuous process of perpetual detour, a Heideggerean reading of Heaney not only draws our attention away from such politico-sexual self-figurations but also obscures the degree to which he begins to dismantle them in his recent work. The publication of *Station Island* (1984) marks, I believe, a profound transformation. This judgement might seem too assertive for a volume which Helen Vendler found on its appearance a 'verbally firm and assured but psychologically beset and uncertain mid-life recapitulation'.[50] There is certainly a mid-life recapitulation in the central Dantesque sequence, 'Station Island', from which the volume takes its title. Here the poet-speaker imagines a series of encounters with the dead – with Irish writers, William Carleton and James Joyce, and with friends and relatives, some killed in the sectarian violence in Northern Ireland – during a pilgrimage on Station Island, or St Patrick's Purgatory, a small island in Lough Derg, Co. Donegal, which has been a place of pilgrimage for Irish Catholics since medieval times. He had, in his youth, undertaken the pilgrimage three times; now, in imagination and in middle age, he seems, in the phrase of his clerical interlocutor in canto IV, to be there 'taking the last look'. He is, it is true, saying farewell, but not with the uncertainty Vendler describes. He is saying farewell because, like the disillusioned priest, he is a man who realises that the choice of his vocation was not 'freely chosen but convention'. The poem is Heaney's belated renunciation: I will not serve. He can no longer function as the kind of poet his background demands, providing what he mocks the priest for providing:

> 'You gave too much relief, you raised a siege
> the world had laid against their kitchen grottoes
> hung with holy pictures and crucifixes.'
>
> ('Station Island, IV')

This leave-taking is more, however, than a rejection of old habits on the way to a more fulfilling new life. This would be to concede too much to the spiritual significance of the pilgrimage itself and to the embodiment of the idea of pilgrimage, in different but distinctive forms, in the poetry of the middle way of Yeats, Kavanagh and Eliot, the intertextual ghosts of Heaney's own rite of passage. His leave-taking involves the much more fundamental rejection of the social, cultural and religious conventions by which the poet has been bound because he recognises that they are not freely chosen but the constricting codes and discourses of a social majority. The fact that they have taken their precise form under siege and in response to the oppression of the colonialism of the plantation does not make them any less codes articulated by power. The very feelings of dispossession make the need for their enforcement all the more acute. The more capitalism follows its tendency to 'decode' and 'de-territorialise', Felix Guattari usefully reminds us, 'the more it seeks to awaken or re-awaken artificial territorialities and residual encodings, thus moving to counteract its own tendency'.[51]

We might find an explanation for this radical change in the fact that Heaney had been displaced by education, by travel, by the very success of his career as a poet and academic. The journey from being a pupil at Anahorish School to the Boylston Professorship of Rhetoric and Oratory at Harvard is certainly as far and as dislocating as those traversed by other poets of his generation – I think of Tony Harrison and Douglas Dunn – who have reflected upon the ambiguous nature of the opportunities offered to them as working-class children by the Butler Education Act of 1944:

> Everywhere being nowhere,
> who can prove
> one place more than another?
> ('The Birthplace')

We might find an explanation for this in *Field Work* (1979), in the failure to find an affinity with the newly-acquisitive South in which he had made his home:

> My people think money
> And talk weather. Oil-rigs lull their future
> On single acquisitive stems.
> ('Triptych, II. Sibyl')

No longer preoccupied with the dispossession of his native realm he is, like Joseph Brodsky or Czeslaw Milosz, liberated in the space of exile, between worlds, in 'my free state of image and allusion' ('Sandstone Keepsake'). Empowered by the shade of James Joyce, the most exuberant exile of them all, he writes 'for the joy of it' ('Station Island, XII').

Such an explanation. I think, simplifies the nature and the consequences of the transformation described in *Station Island*. The poet who had in his earlier work employed the perspectives of the anthropologist, captivated by the strength of myth and ritual, now writes as a semiologist analysing the hidden means by which and the oppressive ends to which myth and ritual function in the family, in Catholicism, in the educational system, in nationalist culture, and in the larger social system of divisions and hierarchy:

> 'I hate how quick I was to know my place.
> I hate where I was born, hate everything
> That made me biddable and unforthcoming,'
> ('Station Island, IX')

With such knowledge of their determining effect, he explores the ways in which codes and discourses, including literature itself, operate in order to make the subject biddable and he includes in his interrogation of the social and cultural production of subjectivity both the lyric and the autobiographical poem. There is, however, no possibility of finding some pure and originary point of consciousness which preexists the imposition of such codes and discourses. 'Master, what must I do to be saved? The rich young man's question to Christ is not only at the heart of the pilgrimage: it is echoed in the last of the 25 lyrics in the first section of the volume and in the last of the 20 Sweeney poems in the third and final section of the volume. For Heaney, the answer lies not in divestment but in dissonance in juxtaposition, in unsettling codes and discourses by disclosing their artificiality. He cannot reclaim reality: it is always prefigured. He can however, delight in the variety of modes by which he can recover it, embellishing that reality in the very act of constituting it. In the first poem of the volume, 'The Underground', he recalls a moment on his honeymoon, racing through the underground to arrive on time for a concert at the Albert Hall, but he complicates that moment by redescribing it through the perspectives of a Pan, a Hansel or an Orpheus. Each perspective carries its own enriching implication, but together they function to unsettle the notion of poetic authority. The poem does not offer us the satisfying shelter of Heidegger's 'house of Being', but it does give us a pleasurable awareness of the artifice of all poetic constructions.

With *Station Island*, Heaney becomes a postmodern poet, not in the sense defined by Heideggerean hermeneutics, but in the sense defined by Roland Barthes in his own postmodernist exercise in autobiography, *Roland Barthes by Roland Barthes*, by means of the concept of 'diffraction'.

> This is why, when we speak today of a divided subject, it is never to acknowledge his simple contradictions, his double postulations, etc.; it is a diffraction which is intended, a dispersion of

energy in which there remains neither a central core nor a structure of meaning: I am not contradictory, I am dispersed.[52]

Within the volume as a whole, we confront a multitude of selves, each one, as we can see from the opening poem, enunciated within specific scenes of language or explicitly defined by the processes of displacement and resistance. In an earlier poem in *Field Work*, 'In Memoriam Francis Ledwidge', on the nationalist poet killed fighting in France in 1917 in the British army, Heaney had found in the circumstances of his death all the strains of Irish culture criss-crossed in 'useless equilibrium'. In this volume, there is no such sense of immobilising contradiction. He places himself beyond the preordination of social, cultural and religious binaries which ensures that each Irish identity is shaped and reduced by a repudiated Other and he finds an appropriate persona in the sceptical and myriad Sweeney.

[. . .] After *Station Island*, Heaney's writing occupies a new kind of cultural context and relies upon a new kind of reading. For the poet, analysing and enacting the construction of the subject through various cultural codes, is concerned to establish by this the concept of an infinitely dispersed subject existing in a verbal space in which no one code or discourse is dominant. In his succeeding volume, *The Haw Lantern* (1987), this leads Heaney, with a considerable levy on recent deconstructionist and reader-response theory, to play (perhaps most notably in 'Parable Island' and 'From the Canton of Expectation') not only with language but also with the expectations of the reader.

Yet, as with Barthes, Heaney's aim is to write from the margin in order to share with his readers a more multiple and less constrained subjectivity. He contests the codes which trap him within social, tribal, professional or familial expectations; but, at the same he does not envisage a position where these will be abolished. As the shade of James Joyce advises in the final canto of 'Station Island':

'You lose more of yourself than you redeem
doing the decent thing. Keep at a tangent.'
                                                ('Station Island, XII')

Heaney is, in Barthes' phrase, 'like an intermittent outsider' who can 'enter into or emerge from the burdensome sociality, depending on my mood – of insertion or of distance.'[53] He writes not for a community in which he would be subject to Barthes' oppressive 'spirit of likelihood' but for that dispersed audience which shares and understands his own intermittent position. □

Other critics have developed Davies' recognition of the poet's displacement into 'a verbal space in which no one code or discourse is
dominant'. The process of the poet's displacement from origins, from the
local collective, from a traditional, folkloric ethos and magical world
view, is ultimately seen to involve a displacement into the linguistic, discursive and ideological systems in which he is inscribed. His prolonged
self-interrogation in 'Exposure' and in 'Station Island' and *The Haw
Lantern* extends to a questioning of the nature of language itself. At
times, emphasising the conditions of loss, difference and absence out of
which any poetry is written, he longs to return to a pre-verbal state at
'the hub of systems' ('From the Land of the Unspoken'); at other times
he celebrates the uniqueness, the miracle, the 'perfection' of art
('Hailstones') which, by virtue of that mysterious configuration, aesthetic
form, can outlast the societies, philosophies and religious beliefs from
which it sprang, thereby transcending the given 'systems'. What
becomes ever more apparent is a profound ambivalence about the
nature of language: on one hand a corrosive post-modern scepticism,
informed by recent critical theory, concerning subjectivity, identity and
representation, and, on the other hand, a persistent faith in the power of
language to forge meaning and identity.

In 'Alphabets', the first poem in *The Haw Lantern*, Heaney rehearses
the process of his own inscription in an established order propagated
through the educational system and enacted in writing. At first the child
experiments with a simple mimetic form of expression ('he draws smoke
with chalk the whole first week'), then reaches the stage when he is
introduced to the sign systems on which meaning will increasingly come
to depend ('Then draws the forked stick they call a Y./This is writing.')
The authoritarian aspect of this whole process of socialisation is stressed:
'there is a right / Way to hold the pen and a wrong way'; there is 'copying
out', and then the first attempts at writing English that are 'Marked
correct'. Gradually, the whole external world is interpreted in terms of
symbols. Symbols are interpreted in terms of other symbols: 'A globe in
the window tilts like a coloured 0'. The poem is firmly rooted in the
poet's first childhood world of rural Mossbawn. In Part 1, the new chiro-
graphic symbols the child learns are described in term of familiar objects:
the letter Y is a forked stick, the figure 2 is a swan's neck and back, lines
of script are like briars, capitals are orchards in full bloom. Ireland and
the larger world are encoded in a complex field of languages, literatures
and educational institutions. From the primary school Heaney attended
in Anahorish he passes to the lecture platform at Harvard where he
alludes to Shakespeare, Graves (the name an ominous reminder of the
loss as well as gain that comes with progress) and the vast world beyond
his parochial origins that language has opened up to him. His first language
of English is supplemented by Latin and by Irish. As the learning process

continues, Heaney's origins are replaced by modern forms of progress. A radical change occurs, signalled by the phrase that opens Part III: 'The globe has spun'. The school has been flattened, and the loss of the old rural childhood world is described in linguistic terms rather than, as before, the other way round: now a potato pit has a 'delta face', a horseshoe is an 'omega', balers drop bales 'like printouts', and stooked sheaves 'made lambdas' in the fields. The poem tells of a rite of passage, of the death of a naturalist and the education of a symbolist, of the displacement of the child embedded in a natural, rural, residually pagan first world and his reconstruction in a modern symbolic, technological world. The process involves anxiety and loss, but it also proclaims power and joy: 'Declensions sang in the air like a hosanna', and the poet luxuriates in 'a new calligraphy that felt like home' (in contrast to the earlier 'toils of his calligraphy' in 'Viking Dublin'). At the end, the image of the flying astronaut intimates a sense of spaciousness and freedom from the earthly home, yet the focus of the astronaut's attention remains 'all he has sprung from', and it is to that which he must return.

This double view of language as both powerfully liberating and treacherously limited is the focus of Patrick Crotty's stimulating review of Heaney's *New Selected Poems*, which first appeared in *The Irish Review* (1990). Here, Crotty discusses the 'caution and distrust' that he believes characterise Heaney's visions, and which Crotty relates to the poet's 'contradictory apprehensions of the nature of poetic language':[54]

■ A troubled sense that experience is betrayed when given a verbal formulation – an uttered thought being a lie, as Fyodor Tyutchev put it – can be found as early as *Door into the Dark*'s 'The Peninsula'. The opposite view, however, is at first predominant. The onomatopoeic robustness which so impressed reviewers of *Death of a Naturalist* and *Door into the Dark* testifies to belief that words can sing very close indeed to the music of what happens. An ever deeper faith in the jurisdiction of language underlies the attempt in *Wintering Out* and *North* to repossess the past by reactivating the word-hoard. And yet *Wintering Out* has a sort of fifth column of poems – 'Limbo', 'Bye-Child' and the greatly undervalued 'Westering' – in which Heaney is haunted by intimations of 'lunar distances' intervening between reality and its representations.

In the more recent work those distances are everywhere honoured. The mimetic exertions of the earlier books give way to gestures towards, walkings round, and evocation of spaces, clearings, centres, nowheres – a range of loci which though situated beyond utterance are understood to be its authorisation and guarantor. The pivotal moment in the career is enacted when Heaney, as protagonist of 'Station Island', seeks absolution through his translation of a poem by St John of the Cross on the 'eternal fountain whose non-existent source is all source's source and origin'. In the act of translating he is himself translated and the 'poetry of inner freedom' of 'Sweeney Redivivus' and *The Haw Lantern* made possible.

So shriven, so lightened are these later works that it might seem as if Ariel has cast out the Caliban who revelled in the slap and squelch of the early volumes, or, to use the poet's own metaphor, as if 'sky-born' Hercules has finally triumphed over Antaeus the 'mould-hugger'. Yet Heaney's progress is not nearly as fractured as such tropes suggest. Whether rendered in terms of dying rural crafts in the first two collectiones; of the 'disappeared' of history in *Wintering Out* and *North*; of the poet's own departed in *Field Work*; of a ghostly procession of mentors and lost contemporaries in 'Station Island'; or of the whole world of experience streaming into nothingness ('the melt of the real thing smarting into its absence') as he shores the dismayed eloquence of *The Haw Lantern* against its ruins, vanishings are a central concern of all his work . . .

Yet, if outcry against the transience of the good – that ancient, perennial business of the lyric – is Heaney's business too, he is no warbler over the irretrievable. Poetry's attraction for him lies rather in its promise of loss redeemed. The promise is fulfilled, dazzlingly, in the first four collections as vanishing crafts are reconstituted in the consoling analogues of language and the dead worked to perfection in the matrix of the imagination. By *Field Work*, though, the young poet's intoxication with the possibilities of his art has given way to troubled brooding on the distance between the realms in which loss and its redemption have their being. The analogues no longer console. 'A Postcard from North Antrim's' tender, absurd injunction to the murdered Sean Armstrong to get up from his blood on the floor emphasises the fictive status of the lyric's repossessions – a status of which the ever more self-conscious poetry of the subsequent decade never loses sight. □

Crotty probes 'the distance between' the realms in which loss and its redemption have their being: Stan Smith takes up this idea in his essay 'The Distance Between' (in *The Chosen Ground*, ed. Neil Corcoran, 1992). Smith argues that poem and speaker are constructed in that intercalated 'distance . . . between' of which Heaney speaks in an interview: 'there is a bemused, abstracted distance intervening between the sweetening energy of the original place and the consciousness that's getting back to it, looking for sweetness'.[55] Displacement, Smith argues, is 'the necessary ground upon which to find one's place'.[56] Language, he says, is both the 'site of perpetual return home' and the 'place of necessary exile'.[57]

■ Kavanagh's landscapes, Heaney says, are 'hallowed by associations that come from growing up and thinking oneself in and back into the place'.[58] Heaney's own most Kavanaghish poem is probably 'The Old Team' in *The Haw Lantern*, but even here the real places 'Have, in your absence, grown historical', part of a history which is a repertoire of antagonistic stories. The title of *Field Work* had pointed the way to these later developments, poised equivocally between the local – the real fields and hedges of this sequence, from which the particular poetic talent emerged – and the larger field of meanings within which that life now finds itself, which, as indicated in a poem such as 'A Postcard from North Antrim', is always elsewhere. 'A Postcard from Iceland' in *The Haw Lantern* reads like an ironic postscript to Auden's and MacNeice's *Letters from Iceland*. Auden may have had his Ulster travelling companion in mind when he wrote in the opening poem to that volume, 'North means to all: reject!'. Certainly Heaney seemed to be recalling this when, in the title poem of his own *North*, he 'faced the unmagical/invitations of Iceland', foremost of which is the invitation to encompass by going beyond, rejecting his native culture as Auden did in casting from Iceland a cold anthropologist's eye on Englishness. Heaney's island parables (including 'Station Island' and 'Parable Island' itself), all test and transcend the limits of Irish insularity, the better to return to and interpret it – to rediscover, thinking in and back into the place, 'How usual that waft and pressure felt/When the inner palm of water found my palm.'

It is from outside the field that the pattern of forces can best be understood, rather than simply suffered. That identity is best found in displacement, in both the literal and the psychoanalytic sense, is the point of the important lecture on *Place and Displacement* Heaney delivered at Dove Cottage in 1984, seeing in the uprootedness of the returning native Wordsworth, a displaced person, *persona non grata* in his own country, a model for all subsequent poetic displacements:

> The good place where Wordsworth's nurture happened and to which his habitual feelings are most naturally attuned has become . . . the wrong place. He is displaced from his own affections by a vision of the good that is located elsewhere. His political, utopian aspirations deracinate him from the beloved actuality of his surroundings so that his instinctive being and his appetitive intelligence are knocked out of alignment. He feels like a traitor among those he knows and loves.[59]

Recent Northern Irish poetry, he says, reveals the same double displacement. The way to cope with 'the strain of being in two places at once, of needing to accommodate two opposing conditions of truthfulness simultaneously'[60] is not despair, however, but Jung's strategy of finding a displaced perspective in which the suffering individual can outgrow particularist allegiance while managing to 'keep faith with . . . origins, stretched between politics and transcendence . . . displaced from a confidence in a single position by his disposition to be affected by all positions, negatively rather than positively capable . . .'[61]

The echo of Keats's 'negative capability' as an answer to Wordsworth's 'egotistical sublime' indicates the way out Heaney was to find from the Northern Irish deadlock from *Field Work* onwards. It is in the 'lyric stance', in language as itself a site of displacement, 'the whispering gallery of absence', 'the voice from beyond'[62] that the writer can seek the hopeful imaginary resolution of real conflicts. Heaney's poetry has pursued language as political metaphor and metonymy through to its source, to a recognition of language as both place of necessary exile and site of perpetual return home. *Station Island* is the product of such a recognition, a volume full of departures and returns. Displacement is here seen not as exile but as freedom, whether in the wide-blue-yonder of America or the poetically licensed other worlds of Dante's *Divine Comedy*. The loving fidelity of the émigré who, like Wordsworth, is necessarily now just 'visiting' that which he's left behind provides the motive force for the volume, and a poem such as the ironically entitled 'Away from it All' catches some of the complexities of such a position. In *The Haw Lantern* Heaney goes a step further, beyond the margins altogether, to deconstruct those blarney-laden tales of nativity, decentring and redefining a self-regarding Irishness. In the words of the title poem, it is not enough to husk in 'a small light for small people'. The modest wish to 'keep/the wick of self-respect from dying out,/not having to blind them with illumination' is too limited, too easy an ambition. Now 'it takes the roaming shape of Diogenes/with his lantern, seeking one just man' to be the true measure of this field, scrutinising with a gaze which makes 'you flinch . . ./its blood-prick that you wish would test and clear you.' The terror of being tested, assessed, and the anxious yearning for clearance, run through most of the poems in the volume. The gaze that 'scans you, then moves on' here brings to bear both a moral and a poetic measure. 'Parable Island' tells us that there are no authenticating origins, only a plethora of story-tellings which push the origin further back into an original emptiness, scrawled over with too much meaning. It is in this area of dense secondary signification, where script dissembles an original emptiness, that Ireland 'begins'. □

The 'parable poems' in *The Haw Lantern*, Smith believes,

■ by calling our attention to the process of analogy making . . . emphasise that meaning is a linguistic act, subject to choice and capriciousness, and not a natural event. 'Parable Island' is the clearest exploration of such a process. Stressing in the idea of parable the gratuitous and deliberate drawing of analogies between one narrative and another, it offers a metanarrative in the parable-making act itself.[63] □

Heaney's language of displacement, Smith argues, is designed to make us see things in a new way; it enacts, through writing itself, the process of self-definition. In this analysis, identity depends not on the return to forgotten origins but on the poet's negotiations with a range of discourses out of which he constructs 'not just a writing, but a self'.[64] Smith concludes his essay with a reference to the ending of the last poem in *Station Island*, 'On the Road':

■ Contemplating a prehistoric 'dried-up source' in the last poem of *Station Island*, Heaney speaks of keeping a stone-faced vigil 'For my book of changes', 'until the long dumbfounded / spirit broke cover / to raise a dust / In the font of exhaustion'. Neil Corcoran[65] sees this as a holy water font, and so it is. But it is also the font of print itself, which is where all new texts find their origins. Here, in the punning metaphoric overlaying of particular life and printed page, Heaney figures forth that relation between place and displacement which is the very ground of his writing.[66] □

CHAPTER THREE

Poetry and Politics

HEANEY'S TREATMENT of violence in *North* made it the most controversial of all his books of poetry, before and since. The pressure
was on him to speak for his people, the oppressed Catholic minority of
the province. His move from war-torn Belfast to the rural peace of Co.
Wicklow in 1972, three years before the publication of *North*, was
regarded by some as a rejection and a betrayal. Some critics felt that in
the poetry that followed, instead of confronting the contemporary situation,
he had sought to avoid it and allowed his aesthetic sense to mask the
horror of actual violence. The young Ulster novelist, Robert McLiam
Wilson, himself from a Catholic nationalist background, asks:

■ Can there be any real doubt that he has largely avoided writing a
great deal about political violence in Northern Ireland? . . . 'Bog
Queen' doesn't really pass muster as an investigation of modern
Northern Ireland . . . Anyone who's actually read Seamus Heaney's
work can only conclude that, in the main, he has left out that unpoetic
stuff, that very actual mess.[1] □

Eoghan Harris, a one-time member of the 'Official' IRA and now an
apologist of the Unionist position, echoes these criticisms. Writing in the
Sunday Times on Heaney's Nobel laureateship in 1997, he stated:

■ I am not sure that his poetry has much to say to modern Ireland. It
comes from haunts of coot and fern. It deals with pre-Christian people
who put bodies in Danish bogs, not post-Christian people who put
them in binliners. It is literally bogged down in the past.[2] □

Others were disturbed by what they took to be Heaney's alignment with
'Catholic', 'Nationalist' and 'Republican' attitudes and his lack of interest
in exploring the minds and lives of his Ulster Protestant neighbours. Are
not the few portraits of Protestants that Heaney gives us in poems such

as 'Docker' and 'The Other Side' examples of a dangerous Catholic stereotyping? In the poem 'Exposure', Heaney describes himself as 'neither internee nor informer/An inner émigré . . . escaped from the massacre', to which the poet James Simmons replies:

■ What massacre? With some lamentable exceptions, you only get interned if you are sympathetic to the IRA. The bravest of his tribe are informing on killers for the common good.[3] □

Simmons, the original 'Honest Ulsterman' and the first editor of the magazine of that name, accuses Heaney of either endorsing a tribal position or making vague gestures towards the inevitability of carnage.

North reopened the old question of the proper relation between poetry and politics. Conor Cruise O'Brien concentrated on the political implications of Heaney's poetry in his seminal review of *North*, 'A Slow North-East Wind', (in *The Listener*, 25 September 1975), which was based on ideas he had developed in another important article in *New Review* in the same year:

■ The area where literature and politics overlap has, then, to be regarded with some suspicion. It is suffused with romanticism, which in politics tends in the direction of fascism . . .

I have come to suspect the relation between literature and politics, certainly the tragic heroic relation. Ours is a small country, much afflicted by ballads, and by persons shooting and bombing their way to a place in the ballads to be. I have heard Yeats's line 'A terrible beauty is born' used to glorify, or better to bedizen, the sordid horrors which the Provisional IRA and their competitors have brought to the streets of Belfast. In these conditions one develops – or at any rate I have developed – a resistance to romanticism, an aversion to the ballad form, a horror of the manic passages in the poetry of Yeats, and a tendency to see the influence of literature over politics, in the tragic heroic mode, as a contagion to be eradicated where possible.[4] □

For O'Brien, Heaney's poetry has also been affected by the 'contagion' of politics. Not only does Heaney engage in a morally dangerous aestheticisation and mythicisation of violence in *North*, but in adopting an ahistorical approach to the contemporary situation, produces, in O'Brien's opinion, a 'bleak' and 'pessimistic' analysis born out of a kind of tragic fatalism: 'Heaney's relation to a deeper tragedy is fixed and pre-ordained; the poet is on intimate terms with doom'. The full text of O'Brien's review of *North*, 'A Slow North-East Wind', is reprinted below:[5]

■ The pigskin's scourged until his knuckles bleed.
The air is pounding like a stethoscope.
                    ('Orange Drums, Tyrone, 1966')

I had the uncanny feeling, reading these poems, of listening to the thing itself, the actual substance of historical agony and dissolution, the tragedy of a people in a place: the Catholics of Northern Ireland. Yes, the Catholics: there is no equivalent Protestant voice. Poetry is as unfair as history, though in a different way. Seamus Heaney takes his distances – archaeology, Berkeley, love-hate of the English language, *Spain*, County Wicklow (not the least distant) – but his Derry is always with him, the ash, somehow, now standing out even more on the forehead.

A prehistoric body, dug out of a bog 'bruised like a forceps baby', leads to and merges with the image of a girl chained to a railing, shaved and tarred, with the poet as silent witness:

> My poor scapegoat,
> I almost love you
> but would have cast, I know
> the stones of silence . . .
>
> I who have stood dumb
> when your betraying sisters,
> cauled in tar,
> wept by the railings,
>
> who would connive
> in civilized outrage
> yet understand the exact
> and tribal, intimate revenge.
>   ('Punishment')

'Betraying' . . . 'exact' . . . 'revenge' . . . The poet here appears as part of his people's assumption that, since the girl has been punished by the IRA, she must indeed be guilty: a double assumption – that she did in fact, inform on the IRA and that informing on the IRA is a crime. The IRA – nowhere directly referred to – are Furies with an 'understood' role and place in the tribe. It is the word 'exact' that hurts most: Seamus Heaney has so greatly earned the right to use this word that to see him use it as he does here opens up a sort of chasm. But then, of course, that is what he is about. The word 'exact' fits the situation as it is felt to be: and it is because it fits, and because other situations, among the rival population, turn on similarly oiled pivots, that hope succumbs. I have read many pessimistic analyses of 'Northern Ireland', but none that has the bleak conclusiveness of these poems.

In a poem with the finely ironic title, 'Act of Union', Heaney has 'the man' addressing a woman pregnant by him, with the metaphor of England addressing Ireland.

[. . .]

The terms of the metaphor are surprising. After all, it is not just the 'obstinate fifth column' engendered by England – the Ulster Protestants – who wield parasitical and ignorant little fists; and most Ulster Protestants would be genuinely bewildered at the thought that it was they, rather than their enemies, who were beating at borders, or threatening England.

It is true that the act of impregnation can be thought of as producing the total situation in Northern Ireland, a fifth column relative to both England and Ireland: the poem is rich enough. (Elsewhere, Seamus Heaney writes of the Catholics as 'in a wooden horse', 'besieged within the siege'.) In a sense, the poet here is deliberately envisaging the matter mainly as 'the man' feels the woman (Ireland, the Catholics of Ireland, within the metaphor) feels it to be; and in relation to these feelings he is never likely to be wrong. In any case, there is a kind of balance at which Seamus Heaney is not aiming. He mocks at one of the protective Ulster clichés in 'Whatever You Say, Say Nothing': '"One side's as bad as the other," never worse.' His upbringing and experience have given him some cogent reasons to feel that one side is worse than the other, and his poems have to reflect this.

[. . .]

Seamus Heaney is being compared with Yeats, and this is unavoidable, since his unmistakable emergence as the most important Irish poet since Yeats. Yet to call them both 'Irish poets' would be more misleading than illuminating, unless the Protean nature of 'Irishness' is remembered. It would be wrong to say that 'Southern Protestant' and 'Northern Catholic' have nothing in common, but to state what they do have in common, which they do not have in common with the British, would be an enterprise requiring delicate discriminations within the concept of 'Irishness'. One such common characteristic is an uneasy but fruitful relation to the English language, a tendency to use language in surprising ways, yet without individualist eccentricity.

Seamus Heaney's writing is modest, often conversational, apparently easy, low-pitched, companionably ironic, ominous, alert, accurate and surprising. An Irish reader is not automatically reminded of Yeats by this cluster of characteristics, yet an English reader may perhaps see resemblances that are there but overlooked by the Irish – resemblances coming, perhaps from certain common rhythms and hesitations of Irish speech and non-speech. One may, of course, be reminded, by 'the subject-matter' of Yeats's 1916 poems and of 'Nineteen Hundred and Nineteen' and 'Meditation in Time of Civil War'. Again, I am more struck with the differences than the resemblances. Yeats was free to try, and did splendidly try, or try on, different relationships to the tragedy: Heaney's relation to a deeper tragedy is fixed and pre-ordained; the poet is on intimate terms with doom, and speaks its language wryly and succinctly:

> I am neither internee nor informer;
> An inner émigré, grown long-haired
> And thoughtful: a wood-kerne
> Escaped from the massacre. . .

As I read and re-read *North*, I was reminded, not so much of any other Irish poet, as of one of Rudyard Kipling's most chilling fairy-stories, 'Cold Iron'. It is a story in which bright and tender hopes are snuffed out by ineluctable destiny, the hand of Thor. And the way in which Thor makes his presence felt is always 'a slow north-east wind'. □

Ciaran Carson, poet and Arts officer with the Arts Council of Northern Ireland, in his influential *Honest Ulsterman* review of *North*, '"Escaped from the Massacre"?' (1975), criticises Heaney in similar terms, charging him with having become 'a laureate of violence – a mythmaker, an anthropologist of ritual killing, an apologist for "the situation", in the last resort, a mystifier'. Carson objects to Heaney's conflation of past and present, Iron Age ritual slaughter and the contemporary Troubles, charging Heaney with 'falsifying issues . . . applying wrong notions of history instead of seeing what's before your eyes'. Heaney's cyclical notion of history is one that, according to Carson, implies that the killing is somehow normal and understandable, pre-ordained and unavoidable:

■ Badly reproduced on the literary pages, beside the reviews, Edward McGuire's portrait of Seamus Heaney is blurred and ambivalent; it appears both as an advertisement and as a record of literary achievement. Idealized almost to the point of caricature (the foreshortened legs, the hen-toed boots, the squat fingers resting on the table, the open book) – it seems to forestall criticism; the poet seems to have acquired the status of myth, of institution. One can hardly resist the suspicion that *North* itself, as a work of art, has succumbed to this notion; Heaney seems to have moved – unwillingly, perhaps – from being a writer with the gift of precision, to become the laureate of violence – a mythmaker, an anthropologist of ritual killing, an apologist for 'the situation', in the last resort, a mystifier. It makes *North* a curiously uneven book. Its division into two parts seems to reflect some basic dilemma, between the need to be precise, and the desire to abstract, to create a superstructure of myth and symbol.

The first few lines of section III of 'Kinship' for example, can hardly be faulted for their accuracy and sense of reality. [. . .] But then something goes wrong. Not content to leave well enough alone, Heaney finds it necessary to explain, to justify the lines in terms of his myth. The spade is no longer a spade, it becomes elevated to the status of a deity:

'And now they have twinned
that obelisk:

among the stones,
under a bearded cairn
a love-nest is disturbed,
catkin and bog-cotton tremble

as they raise up
the cloven oak-limb.
I stand at the edge of centuries
facing a goddess.'

The two methods are not compatible. One gains its poetry by embodiment of a specific, personal situation; the other has degenerated into a messy historical and religious surmise – a kind of Golden Bough activity, in which the real difference between our society and that of Jutland in some vague past are glossed over for the sake of the parallels of ritual. Being killed for adultery (for example) is one thing; being tarred and feathered is another, and the comparison sometimes leads Heaney to some rather odd historical and emotional conclusions. In 'Punishment' he seems to be offering his 'understanding' of the situation almost as a consolation:

'I who have stood dumb
when your betraying sisters,
cauled in tar,
wept by the railings,

who would connive
in civilized outrage
yet understand the exact
and tribal, intimate revenge.'

It is as if he is saying, suffering like this is natural; these things have always happened; they happened then, they happen now, and that is sufficient ground for understanding and absolution. It is as if there never were and never will be any political consequences of such acts; they have been removed to the realm of sex, death and inevitability. So, when he writes 'Act of Union' Ireland's relationship with England is sentimentalized into something as natural as a good fuck – being something that has always happened, everywhere, there is no longer any need to explain; it is like a mystery of the Catholic Church, ritualized and mystified into a willing ignorance.

For all that, some of the bog poems do succeed – 'Strange Fruit', for example, refuses to fall into the glib analyses which characterize too many of the poems. It does not posture in its own 'understanding' of death; Heaney says quite honestly that he doesn't know:

'Murdered, forgotten, nameless, terrible
beheaded girl, outstaring axe
And beatification, outstaring
What had begun to feel like reverence.'

The same honesty of observation comes across again in – for instance – Part 1 of 'Funeral Rites.' This time it is a visual honesty: this, we feel, is what a corpse looks like:

'They had been laid out
in tainted rooms,
their eyelids glistening,
their dough-white hands
shackled in rosary beads.

Their puffed knuckles
had unwrinkled, the nails
were darkened, the wrists
obediently sloped.'

Yet, the rest of the poem seems to suggest that Heaney doubts the worth of his own simplicity; all too soon, we are back in the world of megalithic doorways and charming, noble barbarity. The poem ends with Gunnar looking beautiful and dead, chanting – inevitably – verses about honour, and staring at the moon.

Gunnar seems to be a sort of relative to Shakespeare, Hercules and Raleigh (to name but a few who figure in the Madame Tussaud's Gallery of Greats), and there is at times a temptation to think that Heaney is trying to emulate Eliot, or Yeats, or both, in a quest for importance. Certainly, the references are sometimes verbal Cornflakes; sometimes, as in 'The Seed-Cutters', the apostrophe works perfectly; we realise how Breughel's realism, his faithfulness to minutiae, are akin to Heaney's, and what could have been portentousness takes on a kind of humility. I think this is one of the best poems in the book.

[. . .]

The second half of *North* is a kind of Pyrrhic victory: it doesn't quite hang together, either by itself, or as the other side of the mythical coin. Poems like 'Whatever you say, say nothing' are not improved by age or by their inclusion in the Great Work, and the good bits in 'Singing School' are almost but not quite obscured by the bad bits. And yet, in an odd way, there is more humanity and honesty in this section than in the acres of bogland in Part I; one gets the impression of someone involved in writing, of trying to come to terms with himself, instead of churning it out like Bord na Mona. 'Singing School', for all its faults, has an air of going somewhere; in its tentative precision, it continues where *Wintering Out* left off, and 'Exposure', the last poem in the book rates with 'Mossbawn' as one of the real successes of *North*.

No-one really escapes from the massacre, of course – the only way you can do that is by falsifying issues, by applying wrong notions of history instead of seeing what's before your eyes, or by taking blurbs at their face value (as many reviewers seem to have done). Everyone was anxious that *North* should be a great book; when it turned out that it wasn't, it was treated as one anyway, and made into an Ulster '75 Exhibition of the Good that can come out of Troubled Times. Heaney is too good and too sensible a poet to turn into Faber's answer to Georgie Best.[6] □

David Lloyd, in another influential article, '"Pap for the Dispossessed": Seamus Heaney and the Poetics of Identity' (see pages 42–50), develops Carson's point. Lloyd objects to Heaney's attempt 'to reduce history to myth, furnishing an aesthetic resolution to conflicts constituted in quite specific historical junctures by rendering disparate events as symbolic moments expressive of an underlying continuity of identity'. Maurice Harmon, the late Associate Professor of Anglo-Irish Literature and Drama at University College, Dublin, and editor of the *Irish University Review*, also indicated an escape from history and violence into myth and ritual, and a flight from personal feelings to communal response:

■ The metaphor of ceremony permeates *North*, a collection deeply concerned with the violence of Northern Ireland. The poems do not confront that violence. They do not speak of individual pain or individual outrage. Instead Heaney adopts a communal response. Whatever personal feelings he has about death and suffering are deflected into large, ceremonial gestures.[7] □

David Cairns and Shaun Richards, in their important study of cultural politics in *Writing Ireland: Colonialism, Nationalism and Culture*, see Heaney's mythicising as a demoralising form of 'historical determinism' that denies historical process and renders political action redundant and irrelevant:

■ An historical determinism seems to result from too deep a digging in which the modern desire to engage actively in the historical process is rendered impotent by the very completeness of intellectual understanding.[8] □

Denis Donoghue, Professor of English Literature at University College, Dublin until 1980, and currently Henry James Professor of English Letters at New York University, does not share any of these critics' reservations about Heaney's attempt to escape from time into levels of action and consciousness below history and politics. In a lecture entitled 'The Literature of Trouble' given at Princeton University, an abridged version of which was published in *Hibernia* (1978), and the full text included in Donoghue's collection of essays, *We Irish* (1986), he argues that Heaney's mythic approach to the Troubles allows him to place them in larger perspectives. Myth, Donoghue believes, provides the poet with an aesthetic distance that enables him to express more than mere outrage, and to 'release the reader's mind from the immediacy of his experience' so that he can be restored to a sense of 'the universality of human life'. Far from being a falsification or evasion of history, Donoghue believes that this 'turning away from the terminology of time' may be 'a prudent as well as a consoling thing to do'.

■ That poetry makes nothing happen is normally a tolerable fact; but there are occasions on which a poet feels that he must respond to one act with another similar in character and force.

Even in a quieter poet, like Heaney, there are moments of impatience. One of his Northern poems is called 'Whatever you say, say nothing,' a satirical piece, not one of his better poems but a minor essay in observation. His theme is the Northern habit of keeping one's counsel, saying nothing, intoning the clichés of communication for safety's sake. Heaney recites many of the currencies of such conversation, but at one point he breaks through them into an apparently direct speech of his own:

Christ, it's near time that some small leak was sprung
In the great dykes the Dutchman made
To dam the dangerous tide that followed Seamus.
Yet for all this art and sedentary trade
I am incapable.

'This sedentary trade' is a phrase from Yeats's poem 'The Tower,' and Heaney's use of it brings him in under Yeats's shadow for the moment, the theme being the poet's general predicament, the gap between writing and action. But the reference to incapacity comes immediately after an outburst of political rhetoric; it's nearly time, Heaney says, the Unionist structures were undermined, and he goes back to the Dutchman William's victory over James at the Boyne in 1690 and the Orange Ascendancy in force in the North since that day. Heaney is more patient than Kinsella and Friel, but there are moments in him, too, when he chafes under the constraints of his trade. Not surprising in an Irish poet. Is it not significant, for instance, that Yeats normally used 'violent' as a word of praise, especially when he surrounded it with words of strong heroic cast.

'Some violent bitter man, some powerful man': the power takes the harm out of the violence and the bitterness. 'To show how violent great hearts can lose . . .'; greatness and violence are kin. And in 'Cuchulain Comforted' there is that line, 'Violent and famous, strode among the dead.' Indeed, I can recall only one line in Yeats's poems in which violence is repudiated: in 'No Second Troy' where Maud Gonne's intentions include teaching 'to ignorant men most violent ways,' and even in that case it is the ignorance of her pupils that drags the violent ways down to commonplace.

[. . .]

I have implied that Yeats was not alone in Irish poetry in his ambivalence toward acts of violence. Conflict as such was dear to Yeats because it was the readiest form of his energy: he was more in need of conflict than of the peace that brings it to an end. He feared peace because he feared inertia. I do not mean that he was a propagandist for murder or that he condoned the Civil War; but he was afraid his poetry would stop if conflict stopped within himself; the grappling of opposites kept his art in force. This motive is still active in Irish poetry, but on the whole our poets have been turning their rhymes toward some form of transcendence.

Heaney is the most telling poet in this respect, and the success of *North* makes his case exemplary; it is clear that thousands of readers have found their feelings defined in that volume more than in any other. I shall maintain that Heaney's readers do not see themselves as lords of counter-positions, commanding a perspective in which all forms of conflict are held in poise. Rather, they find release in an area of feeling somehow beneath the field of violence and ideology; or imaginatively prior to such a moment. Heaney's poems in *North* point to such an area. The dominant analogy for his verses is archaeology, not history; his sense of time circumvents the immediacies of historical event by recourse to several different levels of experience, the accretion of cultures. He is, in *North*, a poet 'after Foucault', his knowledge archaeological rather than linear or sequential. . . .

. . . It strikes me that bogland, for Heaney, is the meeting-place between mineral and vegetable life, a state of nature which is soft, yielding, maternal, and full of secret lore. He has referred to 'images drawn from Anglo-Saxon kennings, Icelandic sagas, Viking excavations, and Danish and Irish bogs.' In 'Viking Dublin,' he says:

a worm of thought
I follow into the mud.

As a motto for the procedures of *North*, the lines would answer very well. Many of the poems in that volume follow those worms of thought into soft bogland. In the poem 'Belderg,' talking to the archaeologist:

So I talked of Mossbawn,
A bogland name. "But *moss*?"
He crossed my old home's music
With older strains of Norse.
I'd told how its foundation

Was mutable as sound
And how I could derive
A forked root from that ground
And make *bawn* an English fort,
A planter's walled-in mound,

Or else find sanctuary
And think of it as Irish,
Persistent if outworn.

Bawn can indeed mean a walled-in fort, if you take its meaning from the English or Scots planter; or it can mean a place for milking cows, if you leave its meaning in Ireland, especially the South. Heaney takes pleasure in these matters, as a poet should.

He also likes to think of his language as issuing from the accretion of centuries. In the poem 'Bone Dreams' he writes:

I push back through dictions,
Elizabethan canopies.
Norman devices,

> the erotic mayflowers
> of Provence
> and the ivied latins
> of churchmen
>
> to the scop's
> twang, the iron
> flash of consonants
> cleaving the line.

'Scop' means a poet, minstrel, or satirist in Old English, so Heaney is invoking the two strongest traditions in the forked tongue of English: the Anglo-Saxon and the Latin.

[. . .]

But Heaney likes to play off vowel against consonant, Latin pleasure against Anglo-Saxon reality, within the grand allowance which is Language itself, a concessive, permeable medium. So the topics or commonplaces on which his language relies are those in which nature and culture meet so harmoniously that we are not aware of a distinction between them.

[. . .]

The welcome extended to Heaney's *North* has been remarkably profuse. Part of the explanation is probably the consolation of hearing that there is a deeper, truer life going on beneath the bombings and torture. There are levels of action and responsiveness deeper than those occupied by Protestants and Catholics; there are archaic processes still alive despite times and technologies.

It is a comfort to receive such news, especially in poems such as Heaney's. The outrage of an obscene act such as the bombing of the La Mon Hotel is indeed the denial of humanity which it entails, but it is also its immediacy. What the act gives, without our asking, is immediacy, a quality which we are ready to accept when it comes as an attribute of chance and misfortune but which leaves us baffled when it comes with human motive. This outrage is not diminished by anything we can say of it. Heaney's poems are as helpless in this respect as any editorial after the event in a newspaper or the standard expressions of sympathy from politicians and bishops. But the archives presented as an archaeological site in Heaney's poems offer a perspective of depth upon local and terrible events. Precisely because he does not present history in linear terms, Heaney offers the reader not a teleology implicit in historical interpretation but a present moment still in touch with its depth. The procedure has the effect of releasing the reader – for the moment, God knows, and only for that – from the fatality which otherwise seems inscribed in the spirit of the age. There is little point in fancying ourselves free in space if we are imprisoned in time, but there are signs that poets and readers are turning away from time, having made such a mess of it, and seen such a mess made of it. [. . .]⁹ □

Criticism of Heaney's mythicising procedures was taken up again by Blake Morrison, in his book *Seamus Heaney* (1981), where he accuses Heaney in *North* of giving 'sectarian killing in Ulster a historical respectability which it is not usually given in day-to-day journalism'. Heaney, Morrison asserts, displays 'the tribal prejudices of an Irish Catholic'.

■ In 'Kinship', Heaney addresses one of the first foreign correspondents in Ireland, the Tacitus of Agricola and Germania: carefully choosing the word 'report' he asks:

> Report us fairly
> How we slaughter
> For the common good
>
> And shave the heads
> of the notorious,
> how the goddess swallows
> our love and terror.
>
> (*North*, p. 45)

I have spent many hours over these lines and come back to them many times. For that phrase 'slaughter for the common good' is reminiscent of, and in its own way as controversial as, Auden's phrase in 'Spain' about 'the necessary murder', a phrase that Auden changed after George Orwell had objected to it on the grounds that 'it could only be written by a person to whom murder is at most a word, . . . the kind of person who is always somewhere else when the trigger is pulled.' Heaney, acute as always, takes on board such an accusation when he writes later in *North*, 'We tremble near the flames but want no truck / With the actual firing'. But 'Kinship' itself embodies no such liberal conscience: like 'Punishment', it ends up speaking the language of the tribe, brutal though that language may be. And, if we cannot quite believe that Heaney really supposes slaughter such as the IRA carried out in Ireland and England in the 1970s to be 'for the common good', nor is there anything to suggest that the phrase is intended to be some kind of civilised irony – that would be to read into the poem a gap between the speaker and his subject which is simply not there. It is one of several points in *North* where one feels that Heaney is not writing his poems but having them written for him, his frieze composed almost in spite of him by the 'anonymities' of race and religion.[10] □

This view of Heaney's poems as expressions of sympathy with the terrorists drew a fiery rebuttal from Heaney's sympathetic and long-standing *Sunday Times* reviewer, John Carey. 'Such accusations', Carey retorted in his review of Morrison's book, 'seem blunderingly false to the scrupulous feeling of the poems. . . . Morrison's reading implies a deaf-ness to tone rare among native speakers of English.'[11]

The most sustained and detailed critique of Heaney's mythicising procedures in *North* was Edna Longley's essay '"Inner Émigré" or "Artful Voyeur"?', which first appeared in *The Art of Seamus Heaney*, edited by Tony Curtis (Poetry Wales, 1982). In this major text of Heaney criticism, Longley objects to Heaney's failure to 'distinguish between involuntary and voluntary martyrdom' in his handling of mythic archetypes. Regretting Heaney's exclusion of 'the intersectarian issue, warfare between tribes, by concentrating on the Catholic psyche as bound to immolation', she sees 'Kinship' as defining 'the battlefield in astonishingly introverted Catholic and Nationalist terms'. Consequently, Heaney's poetry, in Longley's view, is unable to offer 'a universal, Wilfred Owen-style image of human suffering'. She wonders if 'tribal pre-ordination, or ordination' has not 'any petrifying effect on poetic life'. The problem with *North*, according to Longley, is that Heaney has allowed his poetry to become the mouthpiece of 'a sophisticated version of Nationalist Ideology'. In another essay, 'Poetry and Politics in Northern Ireland', which was first published in *The Crane Bag* (1985), she advocates separation of art from politics:

■ Poetry and politics, like church and state, should be separated. And for the same reasons: mysteries distort the rational processes which ideally prevail in social relations; while ideologies confiscate the poets' special passport to *terra incognita*. Its literary streak, indeed, helps to make Irish Nationalism more a theology than an ideology. Conor Cruise O'Brien calls 'the area where literature and politics overlap' an 'unhealthy intersection'; because, 'suffused with romanticism', it breeds bad politics – Fascism and nationalism. But it also breeds bad literature, particularly, bad poetry, which in a vicious circle breed – or inbreeds – bad politics.[12] □

Poetry's separation from politics allows it to suggest new political possibilities. Longley's epigraph to 'Poetry and Politics in Northern Ireland' is a line from a statement by Derek Mahon:

■ The poets themselves have taken no part in political events, but they have contributed to that possible life, or to the possibility of the possible life; for the act of writing is itself political in the fullest sense. A good poem is a paradigm of good politics – of people talking to each other with honest subtlety, at a profound level. □

The excerpt from Longley's essay, '"Inner Émigré" or "Artful Voyeur"?: Seamus Heaney's *North*', reprinted below,[13] leads on from her statement that Heaney's myth-making, symbolic mode in Part I of *North* can 'represent as unreal an extreme' as the 'media jargon' of Part 2. The passage begins with a consideration of the relevance of the Bog People to the 'man-killing parishes' of Northern Ireland:

■ The prototype developed by 'The Tollund Man' is a scapegoat, privileged victim and ultimately Christ-surrogate, whose death and bizarre resurrection might redeem, or symbolise redemption for,

> The scattered, ambushed
> Flesh of labourers,
> Stockinged corpses
> Laid out in the farmyards . . .

Here Heaney alludes particularly to Catholic victims of sectarian murder in the 1920s. His comment to James Randall interprets the amount of family as well as religious feeling in the poem: 'The Tollund Man seemed to me like an ancestor almost, one of my old uncles, one of those moustached archaic faces you used to meet all over the Irish countryside.'[14] Thus related to 'the moustached/dead, the creel-fillers' elsewhere in *Wintering Out*, the Man becomes the logical conclusion, the terminal case, the *reductio* of ancestral dispossession and oppression. In 'Feeling into Words', having summarised Glob's account of 'ritual sacrifices to the Mother Goddess' for the sake of fertility, Heaney asserts: 'Taken in relation to the tradition of Irish political martyrdom for that cause whose icon is Cathleen Ni Houlihan, this is more than an archaic barbarous rite: it is an archetypal pattern. And the unforgettable photographs . . . blended in my mind with photographs of atrocities, past and present, in the long rites of Irish political and religious struggles.'[15] Heaney does not distinguish between involuntary and voluntary 'martyrdom', and the nature of his 'archetype' is such as to subsume the latter within the former.

[. . .]

Heaney's contracted or 'perfected' perception of the Bog People in *North* renders their emblematic function, as well as his poetry, less complex. If what was hypothetical in 'The Tollund Man' – the consecration of 'the cauldron bog' – has hardened into accepted doctrine, do these later images imply that suffering on behalf of Cathleen may not be in vain, that beauty can be reborn out of terror: 'The cured wound'? The females of the species also attain a 'leathery beauty'. For the girl in 'Punishment', the wind 'blows her nipples/to amber beads', and the tone of love-making compensates for any deficiencies:

> Little adulteress,
> before they punished you
>
> you were flaxen-haired,
> undernourished, and your
> tar-black face was beautiful.

As women cannot be 'bridegrooms', Heaney must find them a different place in the 'archetypal pattern'. The final moral twist of 'Punishment' has attracted a good deal of comment:

> I who have stood dumb
> when your betraying sisters,
> cauled in tar,
> wept by the railings,
>
> who would connive
> in civilized outrage
> yet understand the exact
> and tribal, intimate revenge.

This is all right if Heaney is merely being 'outrageously' honest about his own reactions, if the paradox 'connive . . . civilised' is designed to corner people who think they have risen above the primitive, if the poem exposes a representative Irish conflict between 'humane reason' and subconscious allegiances. But can the poet run with the hare ('I can feel the tug/of the halter') and hunt with the hounds?

[. . .]

Perhaps the problem is one of artistic, not political, fence-sitting. The conclusion states, rather than dramatises, what should be profound self-division, one of Heaney's most intense hoverings over a brink. In any case it remains unresolved, unless the poem does in a sense make a political point by endorsing the 'idiom', of something deeper than politics. (Although today's anthropology may only be yesterday's politics.)

He excludes the intersectarian issue, warfare between tribes, by concentrating on the Catholic psyche as bound to immolation, and within that immolation to savage tribal loyalties. This is what he means by 'slaughter / for the common good' ('Kinship'), and by 'granting the religious intensity of the violence its deplorable authenticity and complexity' – and, of course, no apologia for the 'male cult' of imperial power. 'Kinship' defines the battlefield in astonishingly introverted Catholic and Nationalist terms:

> Our mother ground
> is sour with the blood
> of her faithful,
>
> they lie gargling
> in her sacred heart
> as the legions stare from the ramparts.

If *North* doesn't cater for 'liberal lamentation', neither does it offer a universal, Wilfred Owen-style image of human suffering. It is a book of martyrs rather than of tragic protagonists. Only 'Strange Fruit' questions its own attitude, challenges inevitability:

> Murdered, forgotten, nameless, terrible
> Beheaded girl, outstaring axe
> And beatification, outstaring
> What had begun to feel like reverence.

The frank adjectives capsize what has previously been rather a decorative dawdle of a sonnet ('Pash of tallow, perishable treasure'; 'Diodorus Siculus confessed / His gradual ease among the likes of this'). They also capsize a good deal else in *North*. Heaney told John Haffenden: '['Strange Fruit'] had ended at first with a kind of reverence, and the voice that came in when I revised was a rebuke to the literary quality of that reverent emotion.'[16]

'Bog Queen' has the advantage of dealing directly with the goddess herself, so that questionable behaviour on the part of her acolytes may be ignored. The female figures in the poems, perhaps understandably, bear a family resemblance to one another: 'The pot of the skull, / The damp tuck of each curl'; 'My skull hibernated / in the wet nest of my hair'; 'They unswaddled the wet fern of her hair'; 'my brain darkening'; 'your brain's exposed / and darkened combs'. However 'Bog Queen', although over-amplified like 'The Grauballe Man', renews that well-worn genre the aisling by presenting Ireland as her landscape, weather, geography, and history, and by pushing her 'old hag' incarnation to an extreme:

My diadem grew carious,
gemstones dropped
in the peat floe
like the bearings of history.

Since this is the one Bog poem with true Irish antecedents, it can
begin with an apt analogue of dormant nationhood ('I lay waiting/
between turf-face and demesne wall'), and end with an equally plausible
'rising':

and I rose from the dark,
hacked bone, skull-ware,
frayed stitches, tufts,
small gleams on the bank.

These lines, and the poem's clearly shaped symbol, speak for themselves. But Heaney sometimes asks too much of his myth, as if all
statement has been shunted off to Part II, as if 'archetypes' remain
above or below argument. ('Punishment' suggests the contrary.) A
number of his comments on poetry nudge it towards the visual arts – a
surprising development from such a rhythmic prodigy: 'the verbal
icon'; 'a search for images and symbols'; 'The poetry I love is some
kind of image or visionary thing'; 'a painter can lift anything and
make an image of it'.[17] The notion of 'befitting emblems' also requires
examination. Their original context is section II of 'Meditations in
Time of Civil War', where Yeats defines the purpose of his art in terms
of 'founding' his Tower:

that after me
My bodily heirs may find,
To exalt a lonely mind,
Befitting emblems of adversity.

Yeats's 'emblems' are the many facets of the Tower and of his poetry as
a whole. Heaney seems to regard a symbol or myth as sufficiently
emblematic in itself: 'beauty' pleading with 'rage' within the icon of
'The Grauballe Man' – Man and poem synonymous – rather than
through any kind of dialectic. Nor does the myth, as the resemblances
between the poems suggest, undergo much evolution. Before the publication of *North*, John Wilson Foster said of the language poems in
Wintering Out: 'Heaney's conceit (landscape = body = sex = language)
and the way it sabotages emotion leads him into . . . difficulties'.[18] In
North the addition of = Ireland, of the aisling element, makes it still
harder to determine which level is primary, or whether they are all

just being ingeniously translated into each other. Presumably 'Come to the Bower' signifies the poet's imaginative intercourse with his country, but does the conceit do more than consummate itself?

> I reach past
> The river bed's washed
> Dream of gold to the bullion
> Of her Venus bone.

When England participates in the landscape-sex-Ireland poems, Heaney's edifice and his artifice wobble. In 'Bone Dreams' the poet's lady uneasily assumes foreign contours:

> I have begun to pace
> the Hadrian's Wall
> of her shoulder, dreaming
> of Maiden Castle.

'Ocean's Love to Ireland' overworks phallic symbolism: Ralegh 'drives inland'; 'his superb crest . . . runs its bent / In the rivers of Lee and Blackwater'; 'The Spanish prince has spilled his gold / And failed her'. Love poetry in political language risks even more than the reverse:

> And I am still imperially
> Male, leaving you with the pain,
> The rending process in the colony,
> The battering ram, the boom burst from within.
> The act sprouted an obstinate fifth column
> Whose stance is growing unilateral.

This poem, 'Act of Union', pursuing the parallel between sexual and political union, and between imperialism and maleness, casts the speaker in a role which fits uneasily. And the allegory could apply to begetting Loyalism as much as 'obstinate' Republicanism. In any case, the poem hardly persuades as a man's emotion towards his wife or child: 'parasitical / And ignorant little fists'.

Given Heaney's previous successful explorations of landscape, water, femaleness, what has gone wrong this time? His prose comments support the view that an obsession with stacking up parallels has replaced flexible 'soundings'. And in the case both of sex-and-landscape and of Bogland regions, Ireland is the straw that breaks the poems' backs. The Jutland connection does achieve certain archetypal dimensions but, as 'Punishment' indicates, the moral and political ground beyond the self-contained emblem is boggy indeed.

[. . .]

The sense in *North* that something is to be gained by going through the ritual, telling the beads, adopting a posture of supplication or worship, curiously aligns Heaney with the early rather than the later Yeats (the Catholic ethos of the Rhymers' Club). 'A Prayer for my Daughter', on the other hand, is not only a prayer but a contest in which 'custom' and 'ceremony' engage with their opposites.

The whole design of *North*, including its layout, proclaims a more punctilious patterning than that of Heaney's first three books: 'I had a notion of *North*, the opening of *North*: those poems came piecemeal now and again, and then I began to see a shape. They were written and rewritten a lot'.[19] In contrast with the fecund variety of *Wintering Out* there is system, homogenisation. Certain poems seem dictated by the scheme (rather than vice versa), commissioned to fill in the myth or complete the ritual. Conspicuous among these are three first-person quatrain sequences, all in six parts: 'Viking Dublin: Trial Pieces', 'Bone Dreams' and 'Kinship'. Neatly spanning the Vikings, England and Bogland, the sequences present the poet in a somewhat self-conscious physical and imaginative relation to each mythic territory: 'a worm of thought/I follow into the mud'; 'I push back/through dictions'; 'I step through origins'. Such announcements seem again a substitute for action, for genuine prospecting. 'Land' and 'Gifts of Rain' in *Wintering Out* began this kind of open quest, which owes a debt to the Ted Hughes of *Wodwo*. But the further back Heaney pushes, in default of a specific impulse, the more specialised or specialist he in fact becomes; so that the sequences exaggerate the book's anthropological, archaeological and philological tendency. The evolution since *Wintering Out* of the theme of language typifies other contractions. The place-name poems, if occasionally too calculated, stir mutual vibrations between landscape and language. But in 'Viking Dublin' Heaney's phonetic fantasy drives a huge wedge between word and thing: a longship's 'clinker-built hull' is 'spined and plosive/as Dublin'. 'Kinship', already off to a sign-posting start ('Kinned by hieroglyphic/peat') that has travelled far from 'We have no prairies' ('Bogland'), eventually goes into a swoon of synonyms:

Quagmire, swampland, morass:
the slime kingdoms,
domains of the cold-blooded,
of mud pads and dirtied eggs.

But *bog*
meaning soft,
the fall of windless rain . . .

'Bone Dreams', perhaps because of the poet's outsider position, relies more heavily on linguistic keys to unlock England: 'Elizabethan canopies, / Norman devices, / the erotic mayflowers / of Provence / and the ivied latins / of churchmen', 'the scop's / twang, the iron / flash of consonants / cleaving the line'. This comes uncomfortably close to the way Heaney talks about English in his lecture 'Englands of the Mind' (1976). In Geoffrey Hill's poetry: 'The native undergrowth, both vegetative and verbal, the barbaric scrollwork of fern and ivy, is set against the tympanum and chancel-arch, against the weighty elegance of imperial Latin.'[20] '[Hughes's] consonants . . . take the measure of his vowels like calipers, or stud the line like rivets.'[21] That the gap has narrowed between Heaney's creative and critical idioms, while widening between word and thing, underlines the extent to which the artist's own specialism also figures in these poems. Every poet worth his salt imprints his poetry with a subtext about poetry itself – as Heaney does, profoundly and skilfully, in 'The Forge' or 'Bogland'. A minority, because of the particular nature of their art, go public like Yeats as the poet-artist, taking on all comers. The protagonist's high profile in the *North* sequences, however, reveals him almost incestuously involved with the contents of his own imagination:

> My words lick around
> cobbled quays, go hunting
> lightly as pampooties
> over the skull-capped ground.
>
> ('Viking Dublin')

> I grew out of all this
> like a weeping willow
> inclined to
> the appetites of gravity.
>
> ('Kinship')

(Contrast: 'As a child, they could not keep me from wells' in 'Personal Helicon'.) Heaney's appetite for abstraction has certainly grown: 'ceremony', 'history', 'violence and epiphany', 'memory', 'dictions', 'the cooped secrets / of process and ritual'. Several commentators on *North* have headlined 'Hercules and Antaeus' as symbolising the different approaches of Parts II and I.

[. . .]

The poem certainly dramatises a conflict in Heaney (amply evidenced by *Preoccupations*) between an instinctive, 'feminine' artesian procedure ('the cradling dark, / the river-veins, the secret gullies / of his strength'), and an ordering, 'male' architectonic 'intelligence' ('a spur of light,/a blue prong graiping him/out of his element'). However, Hercules may be quite as responsible for the prescribed rituals of Part I as for the outbursts of Part II: telling yourself to 'Lie down/in the word-hoard' makes it less likely that you have done so. Stylistic examination suggests that Heaney has upset his strategic brinkman-ship, his former complex creative balance, by applying architectonic methods to artesian matters, by processing his rich organic resources into hard-edged blocks, by forgetting 'They'll never dig coal here.' [. . .]

Heaney's move South between *Wintering Out* and *North* must indeed have shifted the co-ordinates of his imagination: distanced some things, brought others closer. In an essay of 1975 Seamus Deane found Heaney (and Derek Mahon) apolitical in comparison with John Montague, whose *The Rough Field* (1972) had 'politicised the terrain' of his native Tyrone: 'it is in Montague, with his historical concentration, that this fidelity [to the local] assumes the shape of a political commit-ment'.[22] Interviewing Heaney after *North*, Deane encourages him to 'commit' himself: 'Do you think that if some political stance is not adopted by you and the Northern poets at large, this refusal might lead to a dangerous strengthening of earlier notions of the autonomy of poetry and corroborate the recent English notion of the happy limita-tions of a "well-made poem"?' Heaney replies:

> I think that the recent English language tradition does tend towards the 'well-made poem', that is towards the insulated and balanced statement. However, major poetry will always burst that corseted and decorous truthfulness. In so doing, it may be an unfair poetry; it will almost certainly be one-sided.[23]

('One side's as bad as the other, never worse.') This interchange logically, but oddly, ties in the espousal of a Nationalist attitude with divorce from 'English' modes. The combination marks a step across the border, away from 'vowelling embrace'. Similarly, whereas *Wintering Out* was written from the perspective of Belfast/South Derry, Heaney's hinterland interpreting the 'plague'-ridden city, *North* was written from the perspective of Wicklow/Dublin, and a broader Nationalism:

> I always thought of the political problem – maybe because I am not really a political thinker – as being an internal Northern Ireland division. I thought along sectarian lines. Now I think that the genuine political confrontation is between Ireland and Britain.[24]

The vision of 'The Other Side' is absent from *North*: 'the legions stare /
from the ramparts'. The 'Mossbawn' poems (though not the learned
debate about the place-name's origin in 'Belderg') prove the local
textures that Heaney's panoptic view omits. 'The Seed Cutters' also
shows how the English dimension of his technique lives on in a con-
creteness and empiricism reminiscent of nothing so much as Edward
Thomas's 'Haymaking' (written during the First World War): 'All of us
gone out of the reach of change –/Immortal in a picture of an old
grange'. *Preoccupations* salutes the varied influences that have fertilised
Heaney's imagination, and which render irrelevant the false distinction between 'well-made' and 'major' poetry, rather than good and
bad. (No *real* poem is 'well-made' in any limited sense; no major poem
ill-made.) Heaney here seems to join ranks with Montague and
Thomas Kinsella, who in different ways, and often too self-
consciously, have stressed the European and transatlantic alliances
which should be reflected in the outlook and technique of Irish poetry.

The Deane interview epitomises the intensive pressure on Heaney,
including his own sense of duty: to be more Irish, to be more political,
to 'try to touch the people', to do Yeats's job again instead of his own.
Printed in the first issue of the journal *Crane Bag*, it heralds successive,
obsessive articles on the relevance of his poetry to the Northern conflict.
Again, Deane sets the tone with an attack on Conor Cruise O'Brien:

> But surely this very clarity of O'Brien's position is just what is
> most objectionable. It serves to give a rational clarity to the
> Northern position which is untrue to the reality. In other words, is
> not his humanism here being used as an excuse to rid Ireland of
> the atavisms which gave it life even though the life itself may be in
> some ways brutal?[25]

Heaney demurs ('O'Brien's . . . real force and his proper ground is here
in the South'),[26] nor is he responsible for the conscription of his poetry
to bolster pre-set Nationalist conceptual frameworks, to endorse 'an
Irish set of Archetypes, which form part of that collectivity unearthed
by Jung, from which we cannot escape'.[27] But one of O'Brien's 'clarities'
is his distrust of the 'area where literature and politics overlap'. If they
simply take in one another's mythological laundry, how can the former
be an independent long-term agent of change? *North* does give the
impression of the urgent matter of Ireland bursting through the
confines of 'the well-made poem'. Heaney's most 'artful' book, it
stylises and distances what was immediate and painful in *Wintering
Out*. It hardens a highly original form of procedure ('pilot and stray')
into a less original form of content ('imperial power' *versus* 'territorial
piety'). By plucking out the heart of his mystery and serving it up as a

quasi-political mystique, Heaney temporarily succumbs to the goddess, to the destiny feared in Derek Mahon's 'The Last of the Fire Kings'[28] where the people desire their poet-king

> Not to release them
> From the ancient curse
> But to die their creature and be thankful. □

In Longley's view, Heaney had been taken over by a group of Southern intellectuals, chiefly Mark Patrick Hederman, Richard Kearney and Seamus Deane, who were associated with *The Crane Bag* (an influential journal of Irish arts and culture started in Dublin in 1977 by Mark Patrick Hederman and Richard Kearney) and Field Day (a theatrical company founded in 1980 in Derry by Brian Friel, Seamus Deane, David Hammond, Tom Paulin and Seamus Heaney, which developed an associated literary movement devoted to redefining contemporary Irish cultural identity), and who, in Longley's opinion, were determined 'to bolster pre-set Nationalist conceptual frameworks'.

Hederman robustly refuted the charge of bias and bigotry, reasserting the concept of 'the fifth province of the mind' which, he insisted, had been a guiding principle in both Field Day and *Crane Bag* thinking from their inception. The 'fifth province', he explained in his essay, 'Poetry and the Fifth Province', which appeared in *The Crane Bag* (1985), was a free space of the imagination, a kind of no-man's-land, a neutral ground, detached from all partisan and prejudiced connection, where the actualities of the other four provinces need not be so terribly insisted upon as they normally are in Ireland. He acknowledges the similarity between his concept of 'the fifth province' and Longley's 'terra incognita'. The two critics agree about the 'transcendent quality' of the 'fifth province', but differ about the way in which such a place can be reached and the historical effects that such an arrival can have. Hederman believes it can be reached only through our negotiations with the historical world, from which we can never entirely escape, and that our experience of the 'fifth province' crucially conditions our continued existence in the historical world.

For Hederman, therefore, there can be no separation of poetry and politics. Such a separation as Longley and O'Brien called for would, in Hederman's opinion, reduce poetry to mere 'aesthetic entertainment' and politics to 'rational pragmatism'.[29] Longley and O'Brien, he feared, were attempting 'to cordon poetry off into an anodyne, detached and insulated cocoon where it loses all its essential meaning and force':

■ There can, and indeed must be a connection between art and history which is neither the subjection of history to one's imagination, nor the subjection of one's imagination to history.[30] □

While acknowledging the possibility of dangerous liaisons developing between poetry and politics, he does not believe that these are justification for advocating an absolute separation of the two.

■ The point I am making is that both Longley and I would seem to agree about the existence of a 'fifth province' beyond any geographical or political dimension which forms a place of poetry, transcending any bigotted or partisan connections. What we would seem to disagree about is the way in which we reach such a place (although we would agree that only the 'defenceless spirit' can be received there) and the effect which such an arrival can have upon the 'history' of 'the people' after it has been accomplished. My view is that each one of us is prisoner to an 'assumptive' world which the religion, culture, education and psychology we have inherited weaves around us like a cocoon. The poet is required to journey back through this particular psychic hinterland towards the pure air of the fifth province. In other words the fifth province is always attached to the real provinces in which we live and move and have our being. It is not a detached and self-contained realm of its own. It is given existence by the very act of transcending the particular province to which we belong. Apart from this act of exodus through and from our 'assumptive' world, the fifth province is 'nothing'. However, I would interpret Derek Mahon's mushroom which 'develops from nothing' in a different way from Edna Longley. Although the fifth province is nothing in itself, the act of reaching this dimension has an effect upon the poet which allows him to be used as spokesperson for something new and unheard of. The space created by his arrival in the transcendent dimension of the fifth province is enough to allow the fresh air from this no-man's land or non-place to blow through the province he has just left. His breaking through creates a draught which blows the cobwebs from the ordinary and traditional.

Whereas I could agree with Edna Longley about the transcendent quality of the 'fifth province', I do not agree with her about the mode of access to it or the way in which it can influence our history once it has been reached. She would seem to regard it as a platonic realm irretrievably cut off from the real world in which we live. I would hold that our only means of access to it is through the assumptive world which is the make-up of our historical being and that it does have a decisive influence on the way we continue our historical existence once this point has been reached.

With regard to the mode of access, I would hold that there must be, in the North of Ireland, at least two psychic landscapes which have to be negotiated before either culture can have access to this transcendental realm. I also believe that the Irish language contains within its alluvial deposit of meaning a very pertinent truth in its word for a province (*coiced*) which means 'a fifth'. Although there would seem never to have been more than four geographical or political provinces in Ireland, this linguistic oddity suggests that the notion of a 'fifth province' was embedded in the language and that it has no reality other than the 'gift' of life it receives by the very act of transcending the other four provinces. This would mean that the place reached by any poet of any tradition would always be the same but that the way the place was reached would always be different. The reaching requires a great 'humility' in the poet, but this is not an identifiable virtue which can be cultivated in ethical terms, it is a metaphysical attitude which, as the word 'humus' implies, demands of each a journey which will lead to the very 'ground' (Humus) of being.

The assumptive world of the 'Protestant' and the assumptive world of the 'Catholic' are, for historical, psychological, social and educational reasons, very different. This could mean that the 'humility' of the poet in the one tradition could be almost unrecognizably different from that demanded of the poet in the other. The psychology of a politically 'dominant', socially 'secure' and religiously 'established' protestant will provide an entirely different assumptive world from that of an insecure, alienated and 'colonized' catholic. The task of both is to negotiate these psychic worlds until they can move beyond their restrictive dimensions. But the journeys they will have to undertake and the 'humility' which will be required of them will be entirely different.

[. . .]

The most important point is whether or not there is such a place as 'the fifth province'. Whether Seamus Heaney's poetry belongs to this place is another question. His first books showed both an interest in this Antaean region and an awareness of the option to dig elsewhere. The poem 'Door into the Dark' was, to my mind, the most explicit invitation to this 'ultramarine' territory. It described the 'outside' where 'old axles and iron hoops' lay 'rusting', while inside 'the anvil must be somewhere in the centre' of the 'dark', 'set there immovable: an altar'. Here it is possible for the poet to expend himself in shape and music, producing 'the unpredictable fantail of sparks' like Mahon's 'first-star-pierced dark'. Here was the challenge 'to beat real iron out, to work the bellows'.

Heaney is aware of the choice between this 'Antaean' forge and the more brilliant workshop of Hercules and, to my reading, he has not yet made the decision between the two, if, indeed such a decision is ever possible to make absolutely. However, I would not agree with Edna Longley, that the choice is between 'intelligence' and 'instinct', between the 'critical' and the 'creative', between 'philosophy' and 'poetry'. The choice, as I see it, is not between two faculties or parts within the poet himself, it is rather between two ways of being a poet. The poet is made up of all his faculties, both intellectual and instinctual. The poetry of the 'fifth province' is as much a 'thought' as it is an 'instinctive surety'. The difference is in the use of all these faculties. The Antaean use of intellect is one whereby this faculty is used, not in its authoritative and autonomous capacity, but as the receiver of something 'given'. The intellect recuperates for the realm of communicative discourse those instinctive gestures of poetic inspiration which, at the same time, reveal its source. The return to this source and its celebration must somehow become the substance of this poetry. Such poetry requires a 'conversion' towards the innermost region of interiority, where the possibility of transcendence within immanence is unfolded. Such poetry involves intellect, instinct and every fibre of the poet's being. If there is opposition here between two kinds of poet, two kinds of poetry, it is an opposition between two kinds of consciousness and, above all, of two kinds of 'willing'.

[. . .]

Now, whether Heaney actually achieved this kind of 'willing' in his collections *North* and *Field Work*, as I am inclined to say, or whether he is just an 'artful voyeur' who peeks into these realms and describes what he sees, is, as yet, an open question. Longley would claim that stylistic examination of his texts reveals the second outcome. I would claim that she pays too much attention to what Heaney says about his work and gives almost as much credence to his 'preoccupations' as to the language of the poetry itself. I would hold that the poet who speaks about his work is every bit as fallible as the critic who views it from the outside.

However, I do think that Heaney has been subjected to two kinds of pressure which make it difficult for him to occupy himself with those inward qualities of the imagination: detachment, patience, silence, a 'cold dream/of a place out of time' which Longley so elegantly enunciates. These two pressures are stardom and criticism. The popularity and success of his poetry make it difficult for him not to try to please and the endless stream of advice to him about where his true genius lies makes it difficult to 'get back into harness . . . to let go, unclench, forget, and fill the element with signatures on your own frequency.' The two last books read to me like someone on a 'station island' simply flying around like the bird-man Sweeney, this time cursed by his brush with the poetic rather than the priestly establishment, allowing the rush of voices to pass through him. And yet, all the way through, there is that still small voice which is waiting for the moment and the space to make itself heard.[31] □

In the same essay, Hederman goes on to accuse Longley of showing little understanding of the psychic make-up of a poet like Heaney – an Irish Catholic inhabiting 'the assumptive world of the "colonized" person'. Longley's 'superior attitude', Hederman says, prevents her from responding to Heaney's 'vulnerability', such as finds expression in 'The Ministry of Fear'.[32] Hederman's further complaint against Longley is that by selective quotation she has actually misrepresented what he has said:

■ In my own case, I find that the various quotations which are culled from my articles, when removed from the context in which they were originally written and when placed in the tapestry which Longley has woven, give the impression that I am saying something quite alien and removed from what I had intended. When I look to Heaney, for instance, 'to lead us through that psychic hinterland which we shall have to chart before we can emerge from the Northern crisis', I do not mean by this that I want to use his poetry 'to bolster a sophisticated version of Nationalist ideology'. On the contrary, I mean that Heaney is one of the few people who might be able to lead us out of the 'assumptive world' of 'Nationalist ideology'; that such a task cannot be achieved by either ignoring or wishing away this pervasive psychic condition; that the dispelling of its narcotic aura can only be achieved by a dedicated and subtle dialogue between poetry and thinking. Such a dialogue is neither the creation of poetry by thinkers, nor is it the creation of politics by poets. It is the recognition by both that we are living in destitute times when all the things that we have to say to one another, all the structures we have learned to create for one another and all the 'truth' which we believe to be fundamental to the reasonable progress of our common history are inadequate to the task of catering for the future.[33] □

In her 'Reply' to Hederman's article (in the same issue of *The Crane Bag*), Longley says she 'admires' the concept of 'a fifth province' but not the Field Day version, and offers her own preferred metaphor for the 'fifth province', one which de-centres the national component: 'a shifting cloud, now soaking moisture from the Atlantic, now from the Irish Sea, now from the Channels. Or, as a working model, what about Patrick Kavanagh's neglected cultural vision which bypasses the nation to connect the "parish" with the universe?'[34]

The same issue of *The Crane Bag* contained yet another contribution to the debate over Heaney's 'mythological impulse'. This is Maurice Riordan's essay 'Eros and History: On Contemporary Irish Poetry'. Riordan argues that Heaney's mythological tendency derives from the aesthetic of the Irish literary revival, which was concerned with evoking 'the spirit of Ireland as a sustaining power, usually in the form of a goddess who is bride of the poet's imagination' and who must be reclaimed from the colonial clutches by her warrior sons. Heaney's poetry, Riordan claims, conforms to this traditional nationalist discourse:

■ its summons is to be the sacred ground beyond history. It is nostalgic and melancholic, sporadically ecstatic, in its hunt for lost origins, for the lost site of bliss, where the self would feel its wholeness and potency. It is, in a word, Rousseauistic, a nationalistic mutation of romanticism.[35] □

In opposition to this 'backward look', Riordan proposes a modern Irish poetry 'prepared to embrace the varied adventure of its becoming the gay responsibility of making, rather than remaking, history'.[36]

Richard Kearney, in his book, *Transitions: Narratives in Modern Irish Culture*, ranges before him a variety of 'revivalist' readings of Heaney, including Longley's and Timothy Kearney's, but it is Riordan's that he is particularly keen to challenge in proposing his own anti-revivalist re-evaluation of Heaney:

■ I will argue that a modernist or post-modernist reading of Heaney's work exposes an irony and ambiguity in his approach to mythology; and that this approach, far from being a Rousseauistic nationalism or romanticism, does succeed in *making* rather than simply *remaking* history – the two options being, in the final analysis, inseparable.[37] □

Kearney's specific analysis of Heaney's poetry is reprinted on pages 55–64. It emphasises Heaney's ambivalent attitude to home, the tension between nostalgic desire and the corrosive modern sense of alienation and absence. Underlying Kearney's critique is a recognition not only of the value, but the inescapability of mythic representation. Myth, Kearney says, is a means of communal integration, providing a community with a communal set of images whereby it can know itself and represent itself. In this sense, myth has an ideological function. But Kearney also recognises that myth can imprison a people in outmoded images of the past. Thus, myth must be continually subject to a process of rational critique so that its negative, alienating potential can be identified. Having demythologised the ideologies of false consciousness, there follows the challenge of creatively reinterpreting the past to release new possibilities of meaning. Myths are authentic or inauthentic depending on the interests they serve. These interests can be either emancipatory or oppressive: 'The myths of Irish Republicanism can be used to enhance a community or to incarcerate that community in tribal bigotry'.[38] Myth can only move towards its proper universalist potential when its Utopian forward look reinterprets its ideological backward look in such a way as to produce new historical understanding. An authentic myth, says Kearney, thus always knows itself to be an imaginative construct, and is always subject to critique.

The trouble with Heaney's mythicising, according to Edna Longley and George Watson, is precisely its exclusivity, its failure to speak for a radically pluralist culture. Longley praises 'The Other Side' (in *Wintering Out*) – 'The point of the poem is Heaney's imaginative entry into the mind and idiom of the other side, into the "other", beyond psychic hinterlands, across psychic frontiers' – but regrets that in his next book (*North*), he retreats 'within one tribe, one nation', within 'psychic hinterlands' that 'can be imaginative dead ends'.[39] Similarly, Watson wishes Heaney had made more effort to straddle and speak to both traditions. Watson regrets 'how few poems from this enormously sympathetic imagination deal with the "other side"',[40] and laments 'how even this most compassionate and sensitive imagination can fall victim – even temporarily – to the temptation . . . of myth-making'.[41] Watson objects to Heaney's 'fatalistic historicism' and to his 'atavistic vision', which he sees as symptomatic of the 'Catholic imaginative obsession with mythological history and racial landscapes'.[42] This obsession stems, in Watson's view, from the feeling among Catholic writers (his examples are Heaney and John Montague) that they have history and tradition on their side, in contrast to the Protestant imagination (exemplified by Derek Mahon and Tom Paulin) which, Watson suggests, 'feels excluded from history and tends to regard its own culture with a contempt and bitterness which betokens a kind of inferiority complex, a lack of cultural self confidence'.[43] He concludes his commentary on Heaney with an anxious warning against allowing the 'power of the poems' to obfuscate the dangerous moral and political ideas from which it derives. The responsible critic, says Watson, 'must register alarm the more urgently because of the very power of the poems which mediate Heaney's atavistic vision'.

Seamus Deane, in an interview with Heaney in the first issue of *The Crane Bag* (1977) (quoted in Longley's essay '"Inner Émigré" or "Artful Voyeur"?'), and in his essay 'The Timorous and the Bold' in *Celtic Revivals* (1985), suggests that atavistic rootedness is in fact a source of poetic power. Where for O'Brien, Carson, Watson and Longley the use of myth is simply a recycling of old ideas and images that inhibits the free imagining of alternative possibilities and promotes dangerous politics such as fascism and militant republicanism, Seamus Deane, along with Hederman, sees myth as representing the primitive, atavistic dimension of public consciousness that any real understanding of the situation in the North must take account of. Deane's essay offers not only some provocative ideas about the relation between poetry and violence ('the roots of poetry and of violence grow in the same soil'), but also some interesting observations on the development of Heaney's poetic after *North* ('In *Field*

Work, all trace of a consoling or explanatory myth has gone'), and a compelling demonstration of how 'the boldness of writing' itself transforms the relationship between poetry and politics ('we are witnessing a revision of our heritage which is changing our conception of what writing can be').

■ When myth enters the poetry, in *Wintering Out* (1972), the process of politicization begins. The violence in Northern Ireland reached its first climax in 1972, the year of Bloody Sunday and of assassinations, of the proroguing of Stormont and the collapse of a constitutional arrangement which had survived for fifty years. Heaney, drawing on the work of the Danish archaeologist P. V. Glob, began to explore the repercussions of the violence on himself, and on others, by transmuting all into a marriage myth of ground and victim, old sacrifice and fresh murder. Although it is true that the Viking myths do not correspond to Irish experience without some fairly forceful straining, the potency of the analogy between the two was at first thrilling. The soil, preserving and yielding up its brides and bridegrooms, was almost literally converted into an altar before which the poet stood in reverence or in sad voyeurism as the violence took on an almost liturgical rhythm. The earlier alliance with the oppressed and archaic survivors with their traditional skills now became an alliance with the executed, the unfortunates who had died because of their distinction in beauty or in sin. The act of digging is now more ominous in its import than it had been in 1966. For these bodies are not resurrected to atone, in some bland fashion, for those recently buried. They are brought up again so that the poet might face death and violence, the sense of ritual peace and order investing them being all the choicer for the background of murderous hate and arbitrary killing against which it was being invoked. In 'The Digging Skeleton (after Baudelaire)' we read:

> Some traitor breath
>
> Revives our clay, sends us aproad
> And by the sweat of our stripped brows
> We earn our deaths; our one repose
> When the bleeding instep finds its spade.

Even in this frame of myth, which has its consoling aspects, the violence becomes unbearable. The poet begins to doubt his own reverence, his apparent sanctification of the unspeakable:

> Murdered, forgotten, nameless, terrible
> Beheaded girl, outstaring axe

And beatification, outstaring
What had begun to feel like reverence.
                    ('Strange Fruit', *North*)

The sheer atrocity of the old ritual deaths or of the modern political killings is so wounding to contemplate that Heaney begins to show uneasiness in providing it with a mythological surround. To speak of the 'man-killing parishes' as though they were and always would be part of the home territory is to concede to violence a radical priority and an ultimate triumph. It is too much. Yet how is the violence, so deeply understood and felt, to be condemned as an aberration? Can an aberration be so intimately welcomed?

I who have stood dumb
when your betraying sisters,
cauled in tar,
wept by the railings,

who would connive
in civilized outrage
yet understand the exact
and tribal, intimate revenge.
                    ('Punishment', *North*)

Heaney is asking himself the hard question here – to which is his loyalty given: the outrage or the revenge? The answer would seem to be that imaginatively, he is with the revenge, morally, with the outrage. It is a grievous tension for him since his instinctive understanding of the roots of violence is incompatible with any profound repudiation of it (especially difficult when 'the men of violence' had become a propaganda phrase) and equally incompatible with the shallow, politically expedient denunciations of it from quarters not reluctant to use it themselves. The atavisms of Heaney's own community are at this stage in conflict with any rational or enlightened humanism which would attempt to deny their force. Heaney's dilemma is registered in the perception that the roots of poetry and of violence grow in the same soil; humanism, of the sort mentioned here, has no roots at all. The poems 'Antaeus' and 'Hercules and Antaeus', which open and close respectively the first part of *North*, exemplify the dilemma. Antaeus hugs the ground for strength. Hercules can defeat him only by raising him clear of his mothering soil.

the challenger's intelligence

is a spur of light,
a blue prong graiping him
out of his element
into a dream of loss

and origins . . .

This is surely the nub of the matter – 'a dream of loss / and origins'. Origin is known only through loss. Identity and experience are inevitably founded upon it. Yet Heaney's loss of his Antaeus-strength and his Herculean postscript to it (in Part II of *North*) is only a brief experiment or phase, leading to the poem 'Exposure' which closes the volume. In 'Exposure', the sense of loss, of having missed

The once-in-a-lifetime portent,
The comet's pulsing rose . . .

is created by the falseness of the identities which have been enforced by politics. This is a moment in Heaney's work in which he defines for himself a moral stance, 'weighing / My responsible *tristia*', only to lose it in defining his imaginative stance, 'An inner emigre, grown long-haired / And thoughtful', and then estimating the loss which such definitions bring. To define a position is to recognize an identity; to be defined by it is to recognize loss. To relate the two is to recognize the inescapable nature of guilt and its intimacy with the act of writing which is both an act of definition and also the commemoration of a loss. The alertness to writing as definition – the Hercules element – and the grief involved in the loss that comes from being 'weaned' from one's origins into writing – the Antaeus element – dominate Heaney's next book, *Field Work*. But it is worth repeating that, by the close of *North*, writing has itself become a form of guilt and a form of expiation from it.

In *Field Work*, all trace of a consoling or explanatory myth has gone. The victims of violence are no longer distanced; their mythological beauty has gone, the contemplative distance has vanished. Now they are friends, relations, acquaintances. The violence itself is pervasive, a disease spread, a sound detonating under water, and it stimulates responses of an extraordinary highly-charged nervousness in which an image flashes brightly, a split-second of tenderness, no longer the slowly pursued figure of the earlier books:

In that neuter original loneliness
From Brancloseon to Dunseverick

I think of small-eyed survivor flowers,
The pined-for, unmolested orchid.
                    ('Triptych, After a Killing')

The recent dead make visitations, like the murdered cousin in 'The Strand at Lough Beg' or as in 'The Badgers', where the central question, in a very strange poem, is:

How perilous is it to choose
not to love the life we're shown?

At least a partial answer is given in the poem in memory of Robert Lowell, 'Elegy':

The way we are living,
timorous or bold,
will have been our life.

Choosing one's life is a matter of choosing the bold course, that of not being overwhelmed, not driven under by the weight of grief, the glare of atrocious events. Among the bold are the recently dead artists Robert Lowell and Sean O'Riada; but the victims of the recent violence, Colum McCartney, Sean Armstrong, the unnamed victim of 'Casualty', are among the timorous, not the choosers but the chosen. Among the artists, Francis Ledwidge is one of these, a poet Heaney can sympathize with to the extent that he can embrace and surpass what held Ledwidge captive:

In you, our dead enigma, all the strains
Criss-cross in useless equilibrium . . .

Perhaps the poet was playing aspects of his own choice off against one another. Leaving Belfast and the security of a job in the University there, he became a freelance writer living in the County Wicklow countryside, at Glanmore. In so far as he was leaving the scene of violence, he was 'timorous'; in so far as he risked so much for his poetry, for the chance of becoming 'pure verb' ('Oysters'), he was 'bold'. The boldness of writing confronted now the timorousness of being there, gun, not pen, in hand. The flute-like voice of Ledwidge had been overcome by the drum of war, the Orange drum. But this, we may safely infer, will not happen to Heaney:

I hear again the sure confusing drum

You followed from Boyne water to the Balkans
But miss the twilit note your flute should sound.
You were not keyed or pitched like these true-blue ones
Though all of you consort now underground.

In 'Song' we have a delicately woven variation on this theme. Instead of the timorous and the brave, we have the mud-flowers and the immortelles, dialect and perfect pitch, main road and byroad, and between them all, with a nod to Fionn McCool,

And that moment when the bird sings very close
To the music of what happens.

This is the moment he came to Glanmore to find. It is the moment of the *Field Work* sequence itself, four poems on the vowel 'O', envisaged as a vaccination mark, a sunflower, finally a birthmark stained the umber colour of the flower, 'stained to perfection' – a lovely trope for the ripening of the love relationship here. It is the remembered moment of 'September Song' in which

We toe the line
between the tree in leaf and the bare tree.

Most of all, though, it is the moment of the Glanmore sonnets, ten poems, each of which records a liberation of feeling after stress or, more exactly, of feeling which has absorbed stress and is the more feeling. The sequence is in a way his apology for poetry. In poetry, experience is intensified because repeated. The distance of words from actuality is compensated for by the revival of the actual in the words. This paradoxical relationship between loss and revival has been visible in all of Heaney's poetry from the outset, but in these sonnets it receives a more acute rendering than ever before. The purgation of the ominous and its replacement by a brilliance is a recurrent gesture here. Thunderlight, a black rat, a gale-warning, resolve themselves into lightning, a human face, a haven. As in 'Exposure', but even more openly, the risk of an enforced identity is examined. But the enforcement here is that desired by the poet himself, the making of himself into a poet, at whatever cost, even the cost of the consequences this might have both for himself and his family. The fear of that is portrayed in the Dantesque punishments of 'An Afterwards'. But in the sonnets there is nothing apologetic, in the sense of contrite, in the apology for poetry. This is a true *apologia*. It transmits the emotion of wisdom. What had always been known is now maieutically drawn out by these potent images until it conjoins with what has always been felt. The chemistry of the timorous and the bold, the familiar and the wild, is observable in Sonnet VI, in which the story of the man who raced his bike across the frozen Moyola River in 1947 produces that wonderful final image of the final lines in which the polarities of the enclosed and the opened, the domesticated and the weirdly strange, are crossed, one over the other:

> In a cold where things might crystallize or founder
> His story quickened us, a wild white goose
> Heard after dark above the drifted house.

In such lines the sense of omen and the sense of beauty become one. In *Field Work* violence is not tamed, crisis is not domesticated, yet they are both subject to an energy greater, more radical even, than themselves. By reiterating, at a higher pitch, that which he knows, his familiar world, Heaney braves that which he dreads, the world of violent familiars. They – his Viking dead, his dead cousin and friends, their killers – and he live in the same house, hear the same white goose pass overhead as their imaginations are stimulated by a story, a legend, a sense of mystery.

It is not altogether surprising, then, to find Heaney accompanying Dante and Vergil into the Inferno where Ugolino feeds monstrously on the skull of Archbishop Roger. The thought of having to repeat the tale of the atrocity makes Ugolino's heart sick. But it is precisely that repetition which measures the scale of the atrocity for us, showing how the unspeakable can be spoken. Dante's lines:

> *Tu vuo' ch'io rinovelli*
> *disperato dolor che 'I cor mi preme*
> *gia pur pensando, pria ch'io ne favelli*
> > *(Inferno,* Canto XXXIII, II. 4–6)

have behind them Aeneas's grief at having to retell the tragic history of the fall of Troy:

> *Infandum, regina, iubes renovare dolorem,*
> *Troianas ut opes et lamentabile regnum*
> *eruerint Danai, quaeque ipse iniserrima vidi*
> *et quorum pars magna fui . . .*
> > *(Aeneid,* It, II. 3–6)

The weight of a translation is important here because it demonstrates the solid ground-hugging aspect of Heaney's language and concerns, and reminds us once again, as in Kinsella, of the importance of the Gaelic tradition and its peculiar weight of reference in many poems. 'The Strand at Lough Beg' is enriched in the same way by the reference to the Middle Irish work *Buile Suibhne*, a story of a poet caught in the midst of atrocity and madness in these specific areas:

> Along that road, a high, bare pilgrim's track
> Where Sweeney fled before the bloodied heads,
> Goat-beards and dogs' eyes in a demon pack
> Blazing out of the ground, snapping and squealing.

Atrocity and poetry, in the Irish or in the Italian setting, are being manoeuvred here by Heaney, as he saw Lowell manoeuvre them into a relationship which could be sustained without breaking the poet down into timorousness, the state in which the two things limply coil. Since *Field Work*, Heaney has begun to consider his literary heritage more carefully, to interrogate it in relation to his Northern and violent experience, to elicit from it a style of survival as poet. In this endeavour he will in effect be attempting to reinvent rather than merely renovate his heritage. In his work and in that of Kinsella, Montague and Mahon, we are witnessing a revision of our heritage which is changing our conception of what writing can be because it is facing up to what writing, to remain authentic, must always face – the confrontation with the ineffable, the unspeakable thing for which 'violence' is our helplessly inadequate word.[44] □

Heaney himself is much absorbed by this question of the proper relation between poetry and politics. He returns to it again and again in both his prose and his poetry. At least in an early phase of his poetic career, he saw himself as a spokesman of his people:

■ Poetry is born out of the watermarks and colourings of the self. But that self in some ways takes its spiritual pulse from the inward spiritual structure of the community to which it belongs; and the community to which I belong is Catholic and nationalist . . . I think that poetry and politics are, in different ways, an articulation, an ordering, a giving form to inchoate pieties, prejudices, world-views, or whatever. And I think that my own poetry is a kind of slow obstinate papish burn, emanating from the ground I was brought up on.[45] □

Where Watson, O'Brien and Longley would have Heaney renounce his atavisms, Heaney acknowledges the importance they have for his poetry, and is concerned to understand them. In 'Belfast' he confesses to being

■ fatigued by a continuous adjudication between agony and injustice, swung at one moment by the long tail of race and resentment, at another by the more acceptable feelings of pity and terror.[46] □

And a little further on in the same essay he remarks:

At one minute you are drawn towards the old vortex of racial and religious instinct, at another time you seek the mean of humane love and reason.[47] □

Describing his response to the outbreak of the Troubles in 1969, he says:

■ From that moment the problems of poetry moved from being simply a matter of achieving the satisfactory verbal icon to being a search for images and symbols adequate to our predicament . . . I felt it imperative to discover a field of force in which, without abandoning fidelity to the processes and experience of poetry . . . it would be possible to encompass the perspectives of a humane reason and at the same time to grant the religious intensity of the violence its deplorable authenticity and intensity.[48] □

He acknowledges both an aesthetic ('satisfactory verbal icon') and an ethical ('our predicament') imperative (though to whom the 'our' refers is unclear: Northern Irish Catholics? The entire Ulster people? The modern world?). Using the parallel between contemporary Ulster and the Iron Age bogs, he explores his own ambivalent feelings about his native place. 'Punishment' articulates the awful tension in him between the rational and the instinctive, between 'civilized outrage' and 'understanding' of the tribal lust for 'revenge'. His mythicising approach to the contemporary situation may thus be seen as Heaney's way of asserting the primacy of imagination, an effort to avoid becoming merely a mouthpiece for dogma and opinion.

However, as Deane notes, by the time we reach the end of *North*, the bodies exhumed from the bog have lost their imaginative appeal. Heaney himself has pre-empted the critics of his mythic, archaeological and symbolic methods. He is his own hardest critic. He recognises the possibility that fascination with the goddess and the artistry of the myth may only distract from the real horror of atrocity and lead to a sterile escapism. In 'Strange Fruit' he finally wrenches the language away from elaborating a romantic dream and, instead, emphasises the stark reality of 'Murdered, forgotten, nameless, terrible / Beheaded girl outstaring /

What had begun to feel like reverence'. The poem ends with a ringing indictment of his archaeological and aestheticising approach. He caricatures himself as 'Hamlet the Dane, /skull-handler, parablist, /smeller of rot/in the state, infused/with its poisons, /pinioned by ghosts/and affection, /murders and /pieties'. 'Exposure', the last poem in *North*, is an anguished confession of the poet's sense of isolation, exile and failure. He feels exposed to every wind that blows. Though he has distanced himself from events in his homeland by moving to County Wicklow, he has not been able to shed guilt and the sense of social responsibility.

Repeatedly, he confronts the question: to what extent should he concede to the pressures of his own time and people, and to what extent should he follow the demands of his own imagination? The question is at the heart of his second volume of essays, *The Government of the Tongue*. John Carey's review of the essays, 'A Plea for Poetry in our time', in the *Sunday Times* (12 June, 1988), is as elegant as it is succinct:

■ Heaney's whole poetic output could be seen as a hymn to doubt, a tribute to the wise, inconclusive, circling that is as needful to the mind's survival as the circulation of blood to the body's.

The title of his new collection of essays is fittingly ambiguous, encoding doubt. *The Government of the Tongue* could mean the subordination of the poet's voice to ethical or political dictates. Or it could mean the opposite – the tongue's autonomy, surmounting logic and morality, obedient only to the inner rightness of its own song. Which it ought to mean, the reader of this book will certainly not know by the end. Nor does Heaney. But in journeying towards not knowing, he provides a professional overview of the possibilities for poetry in our time, as well as of the misgivings that have shaped his own work in recent years.

The prime question Heaney engages is whether poetry has a right to exist at all. Is not its very being an affront, a betrayal of the suffering that surrounds it and is ignored by it? He cites, for the prosecution, the discomfort critics feel in the presence of Wilfred Owen's poetry. Its *lived* horrors expose the critics' aesthetic cavils as piffling, and reassert the superiority of suffering to song, of life to art. Yet as an antidote to that view Heaney carries in his mind another image – a bottle of cognac, the gift of friends and well-wishers, which Chekhov took with him to the Sakhalin penal colony, and drank on his first night there, surrounded by the clinking of convicts' chains. The cognac's amber luxury, savoured in cruelty's thin lair, symbolises for Heaney the poet's gift, justified and unabashed by the evils that beleaguer it.[50] □

In *The Government of the Tongue* Heaney is intent on articulating a concept of poetry that accommodates both a social and an aesthetic demand. He draws on the Biblical story of the woman taken in adultery whom the crowd drags before Jesus demanding that she should be stoned. At the time Jesus was writing in the sand with his finger. He interrupted his writing only to say to the crowd: 'He that is without sin among you, let him first cast a stone at her'. Heaney connects Jesus' writing with that of the poet:

■ The drawing of those characters is like poetry, a break with the usual life but not an absconding from it. Poetry, like the writing, is arbitrary and marks time in every possible sense of that phrase. It does not say to the accusing crowd or to the helpless accused, 'Now a solution will take place'; it does not propose to be instrumental or effective. Instead, in the rift between what is going to happen and whatever we would wish to happen, poetry holds attention for a space, functions not as distraction but as pure concentration, a focus where our power to concentrate is concentrated back on ourselves.[51] □

What Jesus wrote wasn't important. What was important was the space he created in which the crowd could examine themselves and then, having done so, quietly disperse. Ultimately, Heaney aspires to a poetry that is, paradoxical though it may seem, both socially responsible and creatively free, a double imperative suggested by the double meaning in the the title of his essay 'The Redress of Poetry':

■ Poetry cannot afford to lose its fundamentally self-delighting inventiveness, its joy in being a process of language as well as a representation of things in the world . . . . Which is to say that its power as a mode of redress in the first sense – an agent for proclaiming and correcting injustices – is being appealed to constantly. But in discharging this function, poets are in danger of slighting another imperative, namely, to redress poetry as poetry, to set it up as its own category, an eminence established and a pressure exercised by distinctly linguistic means.[51] □

CHAPTER FOUR

Gender, Colonialism, Nationalism

FROM EARLY on Heaney has tended to see the landscape as female. It is a feared and fecund mother; also, an insatiable lover. He remembers bathing naked in a moss-hole: 'treading the thick-liver mud, unsettling a smoky muck off the bottom and coming out smeared and weedy and darkened . . .' This incident is recalled as a 'betrothal' and an 'initiation',[1] the language suggesting both religious and sexual intensities. Language as well as land is gendered: 'I think of the personal and Irish pieties as vowels, and the literary awarenesses nourished on English as consonants'. He hopes, he says, that his poems will be 'vocables adequate to my whole experience'.[2] Poems emerge from the dark, female depths of imagination and are worked upon by the masculine intelligence:

■ I have always listened for poems, they come sometimes like bodies come out of a bog, almost complete, seeming to have been laid down a long time ago, surfacing with a touch of mystery. They certainly involve craft and determination, but chance and instinct have a role to play in the thing too. I think the process is a kind of somnambulistic encounter between masculine will and intelligence and feminine clusters of image and emotion.[3] □

This opposition between architectonic masculinity and female feeling for mystery and divination underlies much of Heaney's writing, and may be seen in the two-part divisions of *Wintering Out* and *North*. It is the opposition between the arena of public affairs and the intimate, secret stations of culture and consciousness. He uses it to describe the tension between English influence and Irish experience: 'The feminine element for me involves the matter of Ireland and the masculine strain is drawn from involvement with English literature'.[4] It underlies two different responses to landscape, one that is 'lived, illiterate and unconscious', and one that is 'learned, literate and conscious'.[5] His poetry can be seen as an attempt to reconcile these oppositions, as the paradigmatic 'Lovers on

Aran' suggests: 'Did sea define the land or land the sea?/Each drew new meaning from the waves' collision./Sea broke on land to full identity'. This is an emblem of poetry as an act of love. In its embrace the intractable raw materials of experience are brought into relationship with each other in a way that promotes 'new meaning' and 'full identity'.

David Lloyd refers to the 'inanity' of Heaney's opposition between oral, feminine, unconscious image and emotion on one hand, and, on the other hand, cultured, masculine, conscious will and intelligence. Such 'rigid, dualistic schematisation', Lloyd argues, is only the more rigid for its pretension to be unsystematic and natural, and acutely registers 'the form of integration which is projected' (see page 46). Other critics emphasise the strategic and aesthetic function of Heaney's archetypes, cults and rituals, seeing them as stylistic arrangements of experience that help him, as Yeats was helped by his 'system', to speak more fully out of his own nature.

Seamus Deane argues that Heaney's is a ritualising imagination rather than a political one: 'his central trope is marriage, male power and female tenderness conjoined in ceremony'. But, according to Deane, such has been the impact of the Troubles that the trope of marriage has been broken and, from *Field Work* onwards, the poet has had to develop other forms of 'reconciliation'.

■ His guilt is that of the victim, not of the victimizer. In this he is characteristic of his Northern Irish Catholic community. His attitude to paternity and authority is apologetic – for having undermined them. His attitude to maternity and love is one of pining and also of apology – for not being of them. Maternity is of the earth, paternity belongs to those who build on it or cultivate it. There is a politics here, but it is embedded in an imagination given to ritual. That which in political or sectarian terms could be called nationalist or Catholic, belongs to maternity, the earth itself; that which is unionist or Protestant, belongs to paternity, the earth cultivated. What Heaney seeks is another kind of earth or soil susceptible to another kind of cultivation, the ooze or midden which will be creative and sexual (thereby belonging to 'art') and not barren and erotic (thereby belonging to 'society' or 'politics'). Caught in these tensions, his Ireland becomes a tragic terrain, torn between two forces which his art, in a healing spirit, will reconcile. Thus his central trope is marriage, male power and female tenderness conjoined in ceremony, a ritual appeasement of their opposition. One source of appeasement is already in his hands from an early age – the link between his own, definitively Irish experience and the experience of English poetry. There was a reconciliation to be further extended by Kavanagh and Montague in their domestication of the local Irish scene in the English poetic environment. But what was possible, at one level, in poetry, was not possible at another, in politics. Part of the meaning of Heaney's career has been in the pursuit of the movement from one level to another, always postulating the Wordsworthian idea of poetry as a healing, a faith in qualities of relationship which endure beyond the inclinations towards separation. Yet such has been the impact of the Troubles in the North, that Heaney's central trope of marriage has been broken, and in *Field Work* (1979) a new territory has been opened in pursuit of a reconciliation so far denied, although so nearly achieved.[6] □

The 'new territory' that Deane goes on to map out is that of poetry itself, for in Heaney's work, Deane believes, 'we are witnessing a revision of our heritage which is changing our conception of what writing can be'.[7]

The strain which Heaney's trope of marriage comes under is the subject of Jonathan Allison's study of Heaney's marriage imagery, 'Acts of Union: Seamus Heaney's Tropes of Sex and Marriage':

■ Even after the outbreak of the troubles in 1968, Heaney continues to use the metaphor of marriage, but it ceases to represent resolution and harmony. Instead, it represents unstable, anxious, and even forced union, and is associated with constriction and even destruction. Indeed, some of Heaney's earliest metaphors of marriage present the possible harmony of marriage as troubled by the bridegroom's fear of imprisonment and subjugation by female power. These fears reach a climax in *Wintering Out* (1971) and in the image of the devouring earth goddess in 'The Tollund Man,' who grotesquely demands that her lovers be dead. In that poem, the necrophilic female goddess has intercourse with the corpse of the young male, the 'Bridegroom to the goddess,' whose death and symbolic castration coincides with her genital pleasure and impregnation: 'She tightened her torc on him / And opened her fen.'

Reproduction and marriage or cohabitation are generally considered necessary for the coherence of perpetuity of the social order, and Heaney's presentation of marriage as fearful suggests his perception of a pathology not only in the individual liaisons described, but in the social order itself. This pathology is registered in images like the 'infected sutures' of 'No Man's Land' (*WO* 40), and in other tropes of tragic sexuality and unequal union. Heaney's metaphors of sex and marriage in these years are emblems of personal and cultural crisis, they are 'semaphores of hurt' (*WO* 74).

In the first poem of Seamus Heaney's poetic sequence 'Clearances' in *The Haw Lantern* (1987), the Catholic speaker's great-grandmother, who appears to have been a Protestant, crosses tribal boundaries by marrying a Catholic: 'A cobble thrown a hundred years ago / Keeps coming at me, the first stone/Aimed at a great-grandmother's turncoat brow.' This exogamous bride is viewed by her fellow Protestants – who cast stones at her – as a traitor to her people: 'He whips on through the town to cries of "Lundy!"' 'Lundy' was a Protestant convert to the Jacobite side during the siege of Derry, 1689; for loyalists his name is the badge of traitor. The poem shows that marriage in Ulster, as elsewhere, can be seen as a betrayal of the traditions of family and tribe – not merely a ritual bonding, but also a transgression that invokes the anger and hatred of one's community. The emblematic significance of marriage as a resolution of opposites is thus undermined by the presentation of the union as transgressive because exogamous.[8] □

'The Tollund Man', Allison argues, expresses the association in Heaney's imagination 'between marriage as initiation and symbolic death':

■ The bog where they exhumed the Tollund man is the location of marriage, engendering, and genital satisfaction, but also a place of execution and necrophilia where the bridegroom becomes the passive object of the goddess's desire. The poem depicts the bogland as female and sexually hungry: 'Those dark juices working him/to a saint's kept body.' But the erotic aspect of the goddess is, of course, tied to her generative needs: the Tollund man is both lover and husband who fertilizes the land, impregnating the goddess with the seed for the future season's crop.

[. . .]

In the Nordic fertility sacrifice, which Heaney views as continuous with Celtic decapitation rituals and which he uses as a metaphor for Irish republican martyrdom, we may read an image of castration in the act of copulation, as the young male corpse becomes absorbed in the vagina of the goddess. To the degree that the goddess is a mother goddess, as Heaney claims in his prose account, so the sacrifice may also be viewed as a symbol of the man's incestuous copulation with his mother.

Nowhere in Heaney's poetry, however, is Irish republican violence criticized in such horrific terms, where the bog corpse or political martyr is seen as a sacrificial, oedipal, castrated object of the grotesque goddess's erotic love and reproductive needs. Of course, the speaker of 'The Tollund Man' does not adopt the moralistic tone towards bog sacrifice and political violence that this account implies. One strength of the poem is its capacity to convey the seductive power of the bog goddess, as well as of the exhumed bridegroom, while also suggesting the terrible barbarity of the ritual. The poem's power lies in its ability to

show us why the speaker finally feels 'lost, unhappy, and at home,' uncertain as to whether he is a wedding guest, a voyeur, or a mourner.[9] □

Many of the marriage poems written during the 1970s, Allison shows,
'foreground the pain rather than the pleasure of marriage', and he cites
the 'ambivalence' about marriage in 'Wedding Day', the 'discomforting
strangeness' of marriage in 'Honeymoon Flight', the mixture of sadness
and celebration in 'Mother of the Groom', the woman's experience of
marriage as 'both constricting and endangering' in 'Shore Woman'.
Allison goes on to note that 'Aisling' presents both sexual desire and
nationalist fervour as 'potentially tragic and self-destructive', and that in
'The Betrothal of Cavehill' the notion of 'betrothal' is ironically undermined by the potential violence beneath the surface of the poem.

Allison concludes with a close analysis of 'Act of Union', in which, as
in 'Traditions' and 'Ocean's Love to Ireland', the colonisation of Ireland
is presented as a rape. He highlights some problems with Heaney's
allegorical approach:

■ The poem pictures the triangular relationship between Britain,
Ireland, and Loyalist Ulster in terms of an unhappy family. The
brutish child's birth is likely to be violent: his fists 'Beat at your
borders and I know they're cocked / At me across the water.' The Ulster
fetus beats at his mother's womb from inside, and threatens England
across the waters of the Irish Sea. The problem with this metaphor,
however, is that it tries to convince us that the 'wardrum' of Ulster
loyalism is unborn, although Heaney was writing at a time when such
loyalism was actually in full force. Presumably what the British
speaker fears is the birth of an *independent* Ulster, and only on those
terms does the metaphor make sense. But it is not clear how, if the
child is unborn, the father knows him to be an 'obstinate fifth
column.' The terms of the metaphor of the Ulster child are, therefore,
not entirely clear and the analogy of Ireland with the mother also
remains obscure, since the 'heaving province' is presumably her pregnant womb, yet in terms of the topographical metaphor Ulster should
be her head. This kind of complication shows the limitations of the
poem's central trope and points to one possible reason why Heaney
has steered clear of such national allegories after *North*, but 'Act of
Union' demonstrates very dramatically how for Heaney the metaphor
of sexual relations had become expressive of political crisis.[10] □

Central to Allison's thesis is the relationship between Heaney's representation of marriage as 'unstable union' and the social and political context
in which the poet was writing:

■ It is quite appropriate that marriage, an important symbol of the coherence and perpetuity of the social order, should be presented as inherently unstable, threatened, and even threatening, at a time when ideological conflict and political violence were fragmenting the social and symbolic order in Northern Ireland.[11] □

Heaney's poetry has recently been coming under increasing scrutiny from feminist critics. Of particular interest to them is the way he seems unquestioningly to have taken over the traditional view of Ireland as a woman – Cathleen Ni Houlihan, the Shan Van Vocht (the poor old woman) or Mother Ireland. David Cairns and Shaun Richards, in *Writing Ireland: Colonialism, Nationalism and Culture*, are concerned with this image of the nation as female victim: 'The achievement of such a stance is problematic in the extreme, and not least because of the extent it relies on the reappropriation of essentially Arnoldian categories'.[12] Their reference is to Matthew Arnold's essay 'On the Study of Celtic Literature' in which Arnold characterised the Celtic psyche in terms of a passive, ineffectual femininity as opposed to Saxon, practical, masculine strength. While literary revivalists played on this image of Irish imagination and eloquence, it was also used, as Cairns and Richards show, to justify the colonial subjection of the Irish.

In her useful study of the intersection between gender and nationalism in '"Thinking of Her . . . as . . . Ireland": Yeats, Pearse, and Heaney', Elizabeth Cullingford is at pains to emphasise that this idealisation of Irish womanhood, far from conferring any real power upon women in Irish society, has in fact trapped them within a reductive stereotype of purity and passivity. And far from acting as a liberating and empowering myth of national identity, the feminisation of Irish society has served English colonial interests.

■ The allegorical identification of Ireland with a woman, variously personified as the Shan Van Vocht, Cathleen Ni Houlihan, or Mother Eire, is so common as to be rhetorically invisible. Yet it is neither natural nor archetypal. Historically, the personification of Ireland as a woman has served two distinct ideological purposes: as applied by Irish men it has helped to confine Irish women in a straitjacket of purity and passivity; and as applied by English cultural imperialists it has imprisoned the whole Irish race in a debilitating stereotype.

The representation of the land as female is a function of the patriarchal opposition between male Culture and female Nature, which defines women as the passive and silent embodiments of matter. Politically, the land is seen as an object to be possessed, or repossessed: to gender it as female, therefore, is to confirm and reproduce the social arrangements which construct women as material possessions, not as speaking subjects. A striking contemporary example of thinking by sexual analogy is to be found in Seamus Heaney's account of his betrothal to the bog:

> To this day, green, wet corners, flooded wastes, soft rushy bottoms, any place with the invitation of watery ground and tundra vegetation . . . possess an immediate and deeply peaceful attraction. It is as if I am betrothed to them, and I believe my betrothal happened one summer evening, thirty years ago, when another boy and myself stripped to the white country skin and bathed in a moss-hole, treading the liver-thick mud, unsettling a smoky muck off the bottom and coming out smeared and weedy and darkened. We dressed again and went home in our wet clothes, smelling of the ground and the standing pool, somehow initiated.[13]

This image parallels Yeats's metaphor of a love-affair with a proud woman as falling into a 'fecund ditch' ('A Dialogue of Self and Soul'). Although both Yeats and Heaney intend to convey a sense of awe at woman's boundless fertility, their depictions of her as damp and smelly demonstrate how easily a focus on the female as body can slide into disgust and contempt.

Even when the 'feminine principle' is worshipped as a goddess rather than identified with 'liver-thick mud' and 'smoky muck', her cult does not ensure a high status for human females. Although the power, energy, and freedom of Celtic mythological heroines may correlate with the relatively favourable legal status of pre-Conquest women, nineteenth-century devotion to the Mother of God coincided with the most violent misogyny. Mary's role as the embodiment of maternity reinforces a biologistic insistence on woman's function as reproducer and nurturer, while adoration of her paradoxical virginity masks a hatred of the unclean female body and a denial of female desire. Mariolatry in Ireland must be understood as the deliberate identification of a conquered people with a cult which was anathema to their Protestant oppressors, yet its effects on Irishwomen have been repressive.

When the myth of the goddess is used as a political instrument, the consequences are too often credited to the so-called 'feminine principle', rather than to the male imagination which has created and manipulated it. Images of women that originated as the projections of male anxieties and aggression are used as evidence of the need to control and subordinate the whole female sex. Seamus Heaney draws an analogy between the preserved bodies of human sacrifices found in the peat-bogs of Denmark and the corpses on the streets of Belfast: both, he suggests, are victims of the goddess:

You have a society in [the] Iron Age where there was ritual blood-letting and killing to a goddess of the territory of the ground. You have a society where girls' heads were shaved for adultery, you have a religion centering on the territory, on a goddess of the ground and of the land and associated with sacrifice. Now in many ways the fury of Irish Republicanism is associated with a religion like this, with a female goddess who has appeared in various guises. She appears as Cathleen Ni Houlihan in Yeats's play; she appears as Mother Ireland, she appears you know playing her harp. I think that the kind of republican ethos is a feminine religion in a way.[14]

Heaney's ambivalence, his mixture of fear and fascination, is generated as much by his feelings about women as by his feelings about the IRA. He vacillates between the positions of detached anthropological observer and dismayed devotee of the Goddess. Although he describes the psychological economy underlying the conflict between 'feminine' Catholic and 'masculine' Protestant as 'bankrupt', he seems unable to understand how the habit of thinking in immutable gender polarities helps to sustain the political problem he deplores: to call the Republican ethos a 'feminine' religion is to imply that femininity and barbarism are inseparable. In his poem 'The Tollund Man', he depicts the Goddess of the ground as demanding

new bridegrooms each winter to bed with her in her sacred place, in the bog, to ensure the renewal and fertility of the territory in the spring. Taken in relation to the tradition of Irish political martyr-dom for that cause whose icon is Cathleen Ni Houlihan, this is more than an ancient barbarous rite: it is an archetypal pattern.[15]

[. . .]

While the poet Heaney is possessed by and even reproduces the atavistic myth which he deplores, the critic Conor Cruise O'Brien is firmly opposed to all deployment of mythology for political ends, describing the intersection between literature and politics as 'unhealthy'. He lays the blame for the confusion between symbol and reality in Northern Ireland firmly at the door of W.B. Yeats, author of *Cathleen Ni Houlihan*:

Nor does one have to go to the top, to the leaders of great states, to find people who are seeking in history for an immortality promised in literature. You find this, for example, in a particularly pure and deadly form in a guerrilla movement like the IRA. . . . One permanent feature of such a movement is the conception of

> history as a series of blood sacrifices enacted in every generation.
> . . . Now this is most essentially a literary invention. The great
> propagandist of this notion, as far as Ireland is concerned, was the
> poet Yeats.

O'Brien attacks what he sees as the contamination of literary discourse
by political statements, as if it were possible to write verse that has no
ideological reference. His position is endorsed by Edna Longley, who
feels that in Northern Ireland 'Poetry and politics, like church and
state, should be separated'. It is, however, possible to critique the
political implications of specific myths without rejecting the notion of
political poetry altogether.[16] □

In her essay, '"Bog Queens": The Representation of Women in the Poetry
of John Montague and Seamus Heaney' (in *Gender in Irish Writing*, edited
by Toni O'Brien Johnson and David Cairns, 1991), Patricia Coughlan
raises the question of how a gendered poetry with a 'partial perspective'
can fulfil 'poetry's implicit claim to universality of utterance and to
Utopian insight'.[17] Heaney's constructions of the feminine, she shows,
derive from images of 'the sovereignty goddess from early Irish literature
and myth as well as *magna mater* figures from other European contexts',
from a neo-Jungian 'feminine principle', and from images of 'woman-
as-land-and-national-spirit' popularised by nationalist political
rhetoric.[18] This mythic (male) appropriation of femininity is achieved,
she argues, by an 'elision of history'. History is no longer an open-ended
process of transformation but a predetermined cycle of events in which
women figure as 'immemorial archetypes'.[19] Their actuality as human
individuals is subordinated to the demands of the stereotypical ideal.
Heaney's women, Coughlan argues, are domesticated, compliant and
denied 'a fully self-conscious ego'. His ploughmen, thatchers, diviners
and diggers are all figures of the artist, but his women are never role
models. Indeed, his self-definition requires that he distance himself from
their secure and familiar world of home: 'What ostensibly offers itself as
a celebration may rather be read, then, as a form of limiting definition, in
which certain traditional qualities of the feminine are required to persist
for a fit wife, mother or Muse to come into being'.[20]

■ Turning to the representation of gender roles in Heaney's work, we
find that he tends towards two opposing and possibly complementary
representations of gender interaction. One constructs an unequivocally
dominant masculine figure, who explores, describes, brings to
pleasure and compassionates a passive feminine one. The other proposes
a woman who dooms, destroys, puzzles and encompasses the man,
but also assists him to his self-discovery: the mother stereotype, but

merged intriguingly with the spouse. Members of the first group, representing masculine domination, are 'Undine' and 'Rite of Spring', in which the man's victory is achieved in agricultural terms; 'Punishment' and 'Bog Queens', which combine an erotic disrobing narrative (as in Renaissance and other love poetry) and a tone of compassionate tenderness, with a very equivocal result; and the political group including 'Ocean's Love to Ireland', 'Act of Union' and 'The Betrothal of Cavehill', which usually rehearse narratives of rape and sexual violation. The second group contains 'The Tollund Man', 'The Grauballe Man' and the intense and intriguing 'Kinship', which merges mother and spouse as well as active and passive and, I shall argue, functions primarily as a masculine-identity myth, despite its political ending and the political criticism it has chiefly attracted.

In Heaney's first two collections, the most prominent form of attention to gender roles is what may be termed vocational: an allocation of special domains to the masculine and feminine, of a triumphantly traditional kind. Masculine actors find the greater space: in *Death of a Naturalist*, the very first poem 'Digging' foreshadows later, explicitly sexual, bog poems, with its all too relevant succession of phallic surrogates – pen, 'snug as a gun', spade – and its sensuously rich material which waits passively to be 'dug' ('He . . . buried the bright edge deep', in the 'squelch and slap / Of soggy peat'). The active prowess of the speaker's male ancestors is stressed, and he is concerned to present his own displacement to intellectual performance as not interrupting his place in that succession. Parallel to this insistence on inheritance, however, these early poems also rehearse the construction of an individuated masculine self: in the title poem 'Death of a Naturalist', the croaking bullfrogs – 'croaked on sods' – may be perceived as an invasion of maleness into the child's pre-pubertal feminized world, governed by 'Miss Walls' the teacher, whereas two poems later in 'An Advancement of Learning' the boy successfully faces down the slimy, 'nimbling' rat in a test of courage which confirms his own masculinity.

With increasing definiteness in the successive collections, the memory of an essentially unchanging rural world is rehearsed, with its traditional crafts and trades; and as a central part of that dispensation, male and female subject positions are also construed as immemorially fixed. Once natural threats such as those represented by the rat, or by the eel-nits in 'Vision', (*Door into the Dark* 45) have been overcome, the speakers of the poems identify admiringly with active natural creatures such as the bull in 'Outlaw', and the trout which is rendered in strikingly phallic terms – 'Gun-barrel', 'torpedo', 'ramrodding' ('Trout', *Death of a Naturalist*). The trout's ballistic activity is contrasted with the neighbouring 'Cow in Calf' (38), where bulk, slowness and recurrence of the same are stressed: 'Her cud and her milk, her heats and her calves / keeping coming and going'.

There are human versions of such continuities: 'The Wife's Tale' with its rare female speaker is typical in celebrating, without obvious intentional irony, the separate spheres of farm and home labour: 'I'd come and he had shown me / So I belonged no further to the work'. But Heaney's imagination is already dwelling more intensely on metaphors of *nature* as feminine than on the human version. Other strongly conventionalized female figures do also appear, especially mother figures signifying domesticity, intermittently from the earliest poems. But the centre of imaginative intensity is undoubtedly his curious and compelling construct of the land-cum-spouse-cum-death-bringer, with its active and passive aspects.

The hags and goddesses, classical and Celtic, of Montague's poems are replaced in Heaney's by this figure. Its more politicized version, as it appears tentatively in *Wintering Out* and assertively in *North*, represents a merging of the north European fertility goddess, whom Heaney found described in P. V. Glob's study of Iron Age bog burials, with the rather vaguely realized notion of the land of Ireland as seeker of sacrifices, from nationalist political tradition. In his bog poems Heaney sexualizes the religious conceptions of Celtic and north European prehistory. Gender in Celtic and other early mythologies was a metaphysical concept, one of several dyadic means of cosmic organization (male : female lining up with black : white, left : right, north : south, and so forth); a proper service to male and female divinities of earth and air was connected with successful cultivation. This is, of course, markedly different from the predominantly *sexual* interpretation of gender in our culture, which sees it as inextricably bound up with individual personal identity and affective fulfilment, an understanding deriving from Christian theology, the European tradition of courtly love, and the insights of psychoanalysis, among other sources. Heaney's archaizing projection of specifically sexual feeling on to agricultural practices ('Rite of Spring', 'Undine') (*Door into the Dark*) and human sacrifices to a fertility goddess (the bog poems) seems to be a bid to reach past urban and intellectual social forms and their accompanying thought-world, which are implicitly judged as wanting, to a notional state of physical naturalness and 'anonymities' whether folk or prehistoric. An obvious casualty of this attempt, were it to succeed, would be the impulse to individual self-determination and reflexivity. This is an impulse noticeably present in the self-construction of poets, but it is its assumed absence as a defining figure in the lives of Irish rural people and Iron Age Danes which seems to be being celebrated. Thus a disjunction appears between the speaking subjects of these writings and their unspoken objects. In particular the female figures in this conjured world are the epitome of a general silence, at the opposite pole from the describing, celebrating, expressing poet. Whether active or passive, these figures are spoken for, and this division is a highly problematic one.

[. . .]

'Punishment', the poem describing Glob's 'Windeby girl' – the drowned body of a young woman with a halter round her neck – has attracted much commentary, chiefly about the analogy it makes with tarring and feathering in Northern Ireland. The speaker of it does to a certain degree interrogate his own position, discerning it as that of 'the artful voyeur', but the words' overt application here is to his sense of his political ambiguity: he would 'connive / in civilized outrage', but understands the 'tribal, intimate revenge' being exacted (*North*).

The publicly expressible 'civilized outrage' belongs to a language which the persona of all these poems feels is denied him and his ethnic group; he constructs Northern Irish Catholics as, like Celts to the ancient Romans, a race mysterious, barbarous, inarticulate, lacking in civility. But, one might argue, the result of this expressed sense of marginalization by the speaker is to make the girl seem doubly displaced: the *object* of equivocal compassion by a *subject* himself forced to be covert, himself the *object* in turn of others' dominant and therefore oppressive civility. Thus the fascinated details of the description which composes the girl as passive and observed object have the effect, whatever the intention, of outweighing the initial assertion of a shared subjectivity ('I can feel the tug / of the halter at the nape / of her neck . . . '). The compassion is equivocal, not just because of the half-sympathy with the punishers, but because of the speaker's excitement (can we not identify it as specifically sexual?) at the scopic spectacle of the girl's utter disempowerment ('It blows her nipples / to amber beads . . . '). Hence the usual sense of the word 'voyeur' must suggest itself strongly.

Turning to the active feminine, Heaney's engagement with a female destructive principle is particularly intense, as an examination of his Ireland-spouse poems 'The Tollund Man' (*Wintering Out*) and 'Kinship' (*North*) shows. In the 'Tollund Man', the sacrificed corpse is described as 'bridegroom to the goddess', who is credited with a murky amalgam of lethal and sexual acts:

> She tightened her torc on him
> And opened her fen,
> Those dark juices working
> Him to a saint's kept body . . .
> > (*Wintering Out*)

This, like 'Punishment', aestheticizes the horror of a murdered corpse and presents it as a natural phenomenon 'The mild pods of his eye-lids, / His pointed skin cap'). But here it is also made an effect of erotic absorption and incorporation by a female energy conceived as both inert and devouring. If one turns the motif this way round, for the moment understanding it primarily as a way of thinking about woman rather than about Irish political murder, it reveals an intense alienation from the female. Eros-Thanatos pairings generally do seem to rely on a perception of woman as channel for masculine fear and desire, and this is no exception. When one readmits into one's mind the poem's parallel between Stone Age sacrifices to the fertility goddess and Irish political murders in the 1970s, one's increased awareness of the erotic-aesthetic frisson in the first section makes the analogy seem all the more shaky and difficult to assent to. Can this sexual thrill really have anything other than mischief to bring to our thought about the actual perpetration of torture and murder?

'Kinship', at the dead centre of the collection *North*, also represents a centre of Heaney's project. Developing a hint at the end of the earlier 'Bogland' ('The wet centre is bottomless' *Door into the Dark*) it presents Ireland's bogland as above all an encompasser – ruminant, storer, embalmer, 'insatiable bride', swallower, mideen, floe. At the end of the passage is a disrobing moment: the ground 'will strip / its dark side' as if undressing. As the poem's hero pulls out, then replaces, a turf-spade in the bog, 'the soft lips of the growth / muttered and split', leaving the spade-shaft 'wettish / as I sank it upright . . .' (*North*). Following this moment of phallic discovery (evidently granted with some reluctance by the bog) and reinsertion, recalling Heaney's many earlier digging and ploughing passages, there is an explicit merging of birth and death – 'a bag of waters / and a melting grave' – in this per-sonified ground, a 'centre' which, unlike Yeats's, 'holds' (*North*). The poet identifies himself as having grown out of this bog 'like a weeping willow / inclined to / the appetites of gravity'. In a turn to the overtly political at the end of this poem, he addresses Tacitus, Roman describer of Celtic Europe, wryly acknowledging the practice of 'slaughter for the common good' (which presumably represents both the ritual human sacrifices described in the Germania and Northern Ireland's deaths):

> Our mother ground is sour with the blood of her faithful,
> report us fairly,

> How the goddess swallows
> our love and terror.
>
> (*North*)

First, taking this passage politically, one might argue that the evident irony in the expression 'slaughter for the common good' does not solve the more general problem of a projection of the mythic and ritual onto history and the resulting blockage of rational understanding and possible action. The poet compulsively predicates his claim to intuitive identification with his landscape on personifying it as feminine and equating it with death ('The goddess swallows / our love and terror'). As others have suggested, this further entangles the gloomy facts of Irish political history with the heady rhetoric of nationalist ideology instead of interrogating them. My second point concerns the poem's real priorities. It privatizes and sexualizes the political. Its early sections show much greater intensity than the later (which has probably contributed unnoticed to critics' questioning of the ending): the charged personal ode to the bog as mother and partner – giver and receiver of the spade-phallus – is no more than tenuously related to the political references at the end, which risk seeming merely dutiful. I think the real focus is on the speaker's private myth of identity formation, on wresting a self from the 'feminine' unbounded indeterminacy of the bog. This poem attempts a synthesis of the stereotypes of femininity: the bog-goddess is imagined as both mother and spouse, and as destroyer and provider, but it is still persistently (and in both senses) the *ground* on which the speaker's self and his very identity is predicated. The feminine is thus once again an Other but not really envisaged as an alternative subject or self: a relation of complementarity, certainly, but not of equality, and one which enshrines difference in the oppressive sense of that word.

Following the privatized and sexualized bog-Ireland poems, there is also a series of poems in *North* which mount a specifically political gender-historical narrative of English conquest and colonization in Ireland. This series includes 'Ocean's Love to Ireland' and 'Act of Union'. Both these poems employ the conceit representing political conquest by acts of sexual possession, and 'Act of Union' makes the male/English violator its speaker; and/or: it is a love poem to a pregnant spouse. There is a crucial ambiguity about the sexual act in both poems: rape (indicated by a reference to Elizabethan massacres) or seduction by a male force whose energy is attractively irresistible? The language of 'Act of Union' strongly recalls that of the exploring lover in 'Bone Dreams':

> . . . I caress
> The heaving province where our past has grown.
> I am the tall kingdom over your shoulder
> That you would neither cajole nor ignore.
> Conquest is a lie . . .
>
> (*North*)

133

Her mutuality is said by the male speaker (England) to have sup-
planted violation of an unwilling woman (Ireland). How ironically is
that speech to be read? Does not the tone strongly recall the gender
triumphalism of 'Rite of Spring', which, after all, enthusiastically
celebrated the farmer's sexualized thawing of the pump? The speaker
in 'Act of Union' regrets the pain of his partner's imminent childbirth
('the rending process in the colony, / The battering ram') but also reads
it as the promise of a forthcoming Oedipal struggle: 'His parasitical and
ignorant little fists already . . . cocked / At me across the water'. One
can credit Heaney with a vivid rendering of the complications, the
tangled intimacy, of Anglo-Irish political relations. But one might also
feel that to rehearse the narrative of these relations in these terms is to
re-mystify rather than to attempt an understanding of the phenomena.
What is especially questionable is the apparently unconscious equivo-
cation in Heaney's deployment of gender. The application of force in the
agricultural handling of nature, imagined as male sexual domination, is
felt as deeply right. But the occurrence of the same structure in political
relations is (presumably, in the work of a poet of Catholic nationalist
origins) to be taken as reprehensible and grievous. Further, in the
structure of *North* the death-bringing goddess's claiming helpless
victims (female force) in the bog poems is matched with the rape-
narratives in the pendent colonization series (male force). The
symmetry of this deepens the sense of inevitability generated by the
whole project of the mythicization of history. The social, economic and
constitutional conditions of modern Ireland are elided in this reductive narrative which merges the chthonic personifications of the Iron
Age with a presentation of gender roles as immemorial.

[. . .]

It may seem that I am ignoring one of the prominent developments of
Heaney's later work, namely his 'marriage poems', particularly in *Field
Work*, and indeed the sprinkling of earlier personal love poems. I
believe, however, that these poems are mostly also recuperable to this
broadly dualistic active-passive pattern I have outlined. Poem VI in
the sequence *Station Island*, for example ('Freckle-face, fox-head, pod of
the broom'), is motivated by an autobiographical 'plot', but centres on
the constitutively masculine gestures of watching and actively desir-
ing an uncommunicative and mysterious female figure, who is
associated with bags of grain, like the sheela-na-gig in *Station Island*:

    Her hands holding herself
    are like hands in an old barn
    holding a bag open

and what one might term a genial voyeurism is typical of the love poems in general: 'The Skunk' is a classic example (*Field Work*). 'Polder' (*Field Work*), one of the 'marriage poems', is a kind of psychologized reprise of 'Kinship', shorn of political extrapolation. It retains the land-woman metaphoric equation: in the combined metaphor of possession and origination re-employed from 'Kinship', the woman is the territory where the man, 'old willow', has his 'creel of roots', and 'I have reclaimed my polder,/all its salty grass and mud-slick banks'. One might read the sequence *Field Work* itself, and its stress on the erotic excitement of retracing physical marks and stains on the spouse's limbs, as working to fetishize woman's body in much the same way as Montague's *The Great Cloak* does.

So must we not conclude that the poetry of Montague and Heaney as a whole is insistently and damagingly gendered? Its masculine personae, whether in the narrative of personal identity, or that of nationality, must, it seems, possess or be possessed by a counter-force personified as feminine: an encounter of the genders as of aliens – dog eat dog, possess or be swallowed up – is forever occurring, even within and beneath politics. On this evidence, it remains very difficult for men, when they imagine self-formation as a struggle, to escape conceiving that struggle, however metaphorically or virtually, as *against* the feminine. The integral self counted as so precious to the capacity for expression of these poets is won against a necessarily subordinated ground of merely potential, never actual feminine selves. In Lacanian terms, they seem to be stuck in the self/not-self dualism of the mirror stage, failing to arrive at an acknowledgement of the existence of an autonomous subjectivity in others: a structure common to sexism and racism. Just as 'every document of civilization is a document of barbarism', in Benjamin's phrase, so one is tempted to conclude that every feat of self-discovery by these masculine poets entails the defeat of a feminine ego. Or as Irigaray puts it:

the/a woman fulfils a twofold function – as the mute outside that sustains all systematicity; as a maternal and still silent ground that nourishes all foundations.[21] □

Catherine Byron, in her book, *Out of Step: Pursuing Seamus Heaney to Purgatory* (1992), a mixture of autobiography, literary criticism, travel writing and self- and social analysis, also laments Heaney's failure to critique the repressive male discourse that defines both women and nation in terms of inferiority and subordination to colonial male power. Herself a poet of Ulster background, she tells how for many years Heaney's poetry had afforded her essential nourishment. The Heaney of the early work 'seemed to be something rare amongst contemporary poets – a man who spoke out of the feminine in himself'. However, 'Station Island', she says, is a particularly disappointing poem for her. Despite the poet's religious heterodoxy, the poem, she finds, 'assumes a patriarchal men-only version of the world with just the same easy unconsciousness of difference as the island's priests do'.[22] So intrigued is she by Heaney's poem that she makes the pilgrimage to Station Island in Lough Derg herself. Barefoot, fasting and deprived of sleep, she follows Heaney's ghost and listens for the unvoiced feminine in his silences and omissions. Questions are raised about Irish spirituality, the nationalist tradition, the current Troubles, about her own Catholic upbringing, about Heaney's poetry and 'the male orthodoxy of Ireland'. She sees the pilgrimage to 'the stone island set in the midst of the waters' as 'an entering of the female realm that is intimate, in darkness, with the cycle of growth and death'. But Heaney eventually emerges from this mythic realm of 'powerlessness and supplication' braced by James Joyce's sternly masculine advice to turn his back on 'That subject people stuff' and strike out on his own on 'a distinctively masculine "quest"'.[23] Byron feels that Heaney has left her behind along with all that is feminine in his craft and in his life, in his people and his landscape. Though Joyce has the last word in the poem, it should not perhaps be identified too closely with Heaney's. It is one of many voices that Heaney uses to present his drama of the self. If a precursor is to be invoked, why not Dante, whose *Purgatorio* is the obvious conceptual and formal model for Heaney's poem, and who, for both Heaney and Byron, represents a powerful synthesising imagination? Though Byron regrets that Heaney seems to have resolved on a (masculine) poetry of 'the tangent' rather than a (feminine) poetry of 'circles and circuits', his post-'Station Island' work still finds him 'walking round and round a space / Utterly empty, utterly a source ('Clearances 8', *The Haw Lantern*). The passage excerpted below contains her commentary on Section VI of the poem, which presents the pilgrim-poet's encounter with the first important female presence included in the poem.

■ He [the pilgrim-poet] sets foot in the other direction, against the 'stream of pilgrims answering the bell': he is 'sunstruck', out in the unroofed outdoors. He doesn't even stay for a bite and a sup.

He walks into childhood's playing at houses, but also through centuries, through civilisations, through faiths. The flock of today's faithful is hurdled away inside the basilica. The ancient beds lie open to the sun, unpeopled. But out here, on the cleared circles, the *genius* of the place materialises for him, and she is unmistakably female – girl-child, fairy, play-wife from 'mothers and fathers'. 'Freckle-face, fox-head, pod of the broom', she arrives as mysteriously as the aisling of Ireland's eighteenth century dream-vision poetry, but without the haunting distress that hovers even over O Rathaille's loveliest 'Gile na gile' – 'Brightness of brightness I beheld on the way . . .' Heaney's 'she' brings affirmation, not distress: the rooted assurance of a land that is not in subjection, and the promise of fertility, of harvest. The 'tramped neolithic floor' of her 'house' is like a timeless threshing circle, ready for the gold of the grain that will be spilled on it. The musk of an unashamed sexuality is in the air: Innocence in the time before Experience, bodies before the Fall.

Inside the built basilica there is only Mary, the virgin mother, and Eve, mother of all our woe, to choose from. Outside, there is the possibility of a sexual love innocent of that polarity and all its works. This open air, this hallowed and ancient place, is a setting now for sacraments that are pagan and integral: here grain and wine will be both the 'outward signs of an inward grace', and still unmistakably themselves; here even children playing at houses are rehearsing a sacred and secret rite. No wonder Heaney's pilgrim self 'shut[s his] ears to the bell', and walks away into paganism and the timeless, mythic shelter of a tree. The actual and fine-leaved solitary sycamore that has stood by the largest of the beds for over three hundred years offers, now, 'the bottle-green, still/shade of an oak': a Roman oak, with perhaps a strain of the oaks that the druids revered, and of the oakwood that gave Derry – *doire* – its name. It may even have a slip of Eden in its heartwood.

In this poem Heaney is at the halfway point in his sequence, and at the threshold of adulthood in its autobiographical sub-plot. It is rite of passage time. The poem opens its heart to intimacy and to the female, moving from the foxy Eden of the freckle-faced girlchild to the possibility of making 'grown-up' love. As the pilgrim remembers his own passage to Experience, two long-dead poets act as his invisible spiritual fosterers: Horace to urge him to delight in the intelligence of the body's sensuality, and another Italian, Dante, to give a mystical blessing to the delight he finds.

They are *invisible* fosterers in the sense that neither is named within the text. Each speaks an underword – italicised to indicate its fragmentary, translated nature – that is seamlessly integrated into Heaney's sonnet-stanzas. He could, by being more showy about them, have had two such charismatic poets act as creaking hinge points into vast philosophical hinterlands, both pagan and Christian; but this is a poem of hiddenness, not of big gestures: 'Eyes shut. Leaf ears. *Don't tell. Don't tell.*' Any hinges are oiled into silence in the text. In the sparse 'Notes' at the back of the collection, their words are unobtrusively but precisely attributed; follow the trail, and there, in the original context of each quoted section, are some of the most radiant of the silent women in (or, in this case, not in!) Heaney's whole sequence.

The effect is subtle and extraordinary. The light it shines on this pivotal poem is, in the widest sense of the word, religious.

'Shades of the Sabine farm / On the beds of Saint Patrick's Purgatory.' Italy. Warm weather. Conviviality. Imperial Rome's dropout rural philosopher urges an easy sensuality that is a far cry from Irish Catholicism in a cold climate. What brings Horace to the narrow north? What can he offer Heaney except distress at such narrowness, and an unbearable contrast?

His very language sharpens the anomaly: Latin, the *lingua franca* shared, at different periods, by both the Imperial and the Holy Roman empires. For the bright schoolboy in Catholic Ireland, that long history would have been telescoped in a single day's hearing of the 'dead' tongue, the soft c's of the Mass's pronunciation and the hard c's of the schoolroom's making a fine, scholastic distinction. But Quintus Horatius Flaccus! What a dangerous thing even classroom learning can be – and what unsuitable role-models it can introduce to Catholic adolescents in the name of classical scholarship!

And was Horace also a presiding spirit at a later turning-point in Heaney's life? Both poets, having come from humble origins and achieved early literary acclaim, left the big city (Rome, Belfast) for rural seclusion, and devotion to their art. And they made the move – with the generous help of patrons – at a very similar age, their early thirties. The 'Glanmore Sonnets' are Heaney's celebratory 'odes' on that mid-life rural 'singing school' as much as they are his Ovidian 'Tristia' of (in his case chosen) exile. And the distinctive steep and wooded glens around Glanmore are an Irish approximation to the hill country beyond Tivoli where the house called Horace's can still be seen, its layout redeemed from vines and underbrush.

For a still moment the carefree but serious Epicureanism of Horace's ode (the twenty-third of his third book) smiles on the stones of Station Island. Wine is the companion of philosophy, the loosener of anxiety and secrecy, the disabler of pomp and war. And when – best of all – Bacchus is accompanied by Venus, then living lanterns will light up the hours of darkness, 'Till Phoebus returning routs the morning star.'

This, then, is the full context of the one line that Heaney carries over – 'trans-lates' – direct from the Latin. The reference is so swift and light of touch that only Heaney's clue would alert the reader to its discreet company. The goddess of love and her attendant Graces are its hidden women whose radiance leaves an afterglow even in this fragment of an ode. It is as though Horace's poem is a glass hologram: even a shard of it holds this image of Venus rejoicing.

And Heaney's poem unquestionably has woman in mind, even in this case when it leaves her out. A 'somnolent hymn to Mary' cuts across Horace's words in praise of sensuality – the Church's version of woman, exemplum of virginity and restraint. Despite 'leaf ears', and wine, and poetry, the twentieth century pilgrimage and its pieties are never quite out of the pilgrim's earshot. The resultant discord revives painful memories of 'long virgin/Fasts and thirsts' in a Catholic adolescence dominated by the intertwined guilts of ignorance and the confessional. The accoutrements of the land's fertility – 'bags of grain/ And the sloped shafts of forks and hoes' – mock the boy's exclusion from such natural rhythms.

The abstinence and the guilt seem to last for years. Then, through a key hole, through a window, a particular girl shines out both in her own perceived beauty and as an emblem of love's transforming kindness:

> . . . that night I saw her honey-skinned
> Shoulder-blades and the wheatlands of her back
> Through the wide keyhole of her keyhole dress . . .

She is wheat and honey, she is the boy's 'America, [his] new-found-land'. But the door is not yet opened, the window not shinned through; the girl has not revealed her face or her self. She keeps her back to the poem, and this reluctance of women to show their face within Heaney's text continues in the much fuller quotation from his second unseen fosterer – Dante.

Or Heaney takes the lovely simile from near the end of the second canto of the *Inferno* and almost fills the sestet of his own concluding sonnet with his translation of it:

> As little flowers that were all bowed and shut
> By the night chills rise on their stems and open
> As soon as they have felt the touch of sunlight,
> So I revived in my own wilting powers
> And my heart flushed, like somebody set free.

The lines are beautiful as they stand. But again a trail is quietly arrowed by the notes' precise attribution.

It is dusk on Good Friday. Dante's first day in Hell. His fear of 'the road and the pity' that lie before him have disabled him utterly. Virgil has already rescued him from the wild beasts of worldly sin. Now it is his own infirmity of purpose, his own too-much thinking, that stop him in his tracks. But it is also now that he learns for the first time of the loving care of three women: Our Lady, Lucia and Beatrice are all watching over him from the court of heaven as he begins his arduous pilgrimage. And Beatrice, whom he loved on earth as Beatrice dei Portinari, is the very one who has sent Virgil to his side.

These 'tre donne gentile' enact with human grace and delicacy an allegorical model of divine grace: for the fearful Florentine it is grace abounding. It is this overflowing of love that revives him and frees him to continue both pilgrimage and poem. In Beatrice's words:

amor mi mosse, che mi fa parlare.
It is love that moves me, that makes me speak.

The figures of the allegory – Mary the vessel of divine grace, Lucia its illumination, and Beatrice its wisdom – exist above and beyond the words that Heaney has translated, yet their presence in the canto from which he draws the simile leaves after-images that persist in its transplanted life, even more clearly than in the borrowing from Horace. Is it because, however remote the lost world of that great medieval architecture of faith, Dante's love of divine philosophy is rooted, like Heaney's own vision of love, in a very particular flesh-and-blood woman? In the *Commedia* human love becomes an expression of divine grace, and the individual beloved a bodying forth of Sophia, the wisdom of God.

What is Heaney doing here? It's possible that, far from objectifying and marginalising the female through his back-view-only icon of her presence, he may subtly be invoking Dante's help to express the elusive feminine within the psyche of us all, men as well as women. Both these male pilgrim-poets, Dante and Heaney, will have to learn about waiting, about not forcing either themselves, or others. 'This is the [feminine] way of non-interference and acceptance which has been praised by poets throughout the centuries,' writes Sukie Colegrave in *The Spirit of the Valley*, her investigation into the integration of the masculine and feminine within each of us. 'Trust is central to the feminine consciousness . . . It is the capacity to surrender the individual ego to a meaning and direction which may not, at first, be intelligible.' Of the other side of the psyche, the masculine consciousness, she writes:

It gives us the certainty that we stand utterly alone in this world, unsupported by institutions . . . It brings the extraordinary and often alarming knowledge that we can look to no one and no thing other than ourselves for directions and answers.

She could have been writing about the demands that this very pilgrimage makes on its bewildered participants.

But why is it all quite so hidden in Heaney's poem? Am I too eager to discover such possibilities in his references simply because I am finding the Mass of my own pilgrimage so difficult, and Heaney's walking out of 'all that' so enviable? Surely he must have found some-thing better out there in the open air of the deserted 'beds' than I have, held in the paternalistic embrace of the basilica! I hesitate, rethink that last Dantean lifting, its juxtaposition with the image of the girl's half-uncovered back. If he is indeed, by quoting Dante here, raising the possibility of a spiritual merging or consummation beyond the literal and physical, how is this to be achieved on any level within the remaining half of the sequence? For he is now moving into the most heavily masculine part of it, into other men's stories far more than his own. Just at the crucial point in his sub-plot of growing-up, just when an image of the feminine flickers almost into actuality on the island, he leaves the girl's image hanging, and it is faceless as well as voiceless.

There comes the uneasy feeling that Dante's image of the flowers rising up on their stems could suggest, in Heaney's rather different context, just a voyeur's arousal, and not a philosophical confirmation at all. Nor can I, at this moment, recall that there is any foreground narrative in the rest of the sequence that continues the story begun here into a face-to-face consummation. Will I find other, less literal, feminine presences to continue the 'argument' as I walk my new bare-foot way through the difficult poems that I know are coming? Will it move on to a different plane altogether, and offer an indirect way for-ward from these radiant but disturbing images of the sixth poem?[24] □

CHAPTER FIVE

Powers of Earth and Visions of Air

CRITICAL OPINION is agreed that one of the most notable develop-ments of Heaney's career occurs in *Field Work*, though it is signalled earlier. It is accompanied by a long period of self-interrogation and inner struggle, and it is not until *Seeing Things* that it is confidently achieved. Heaney explains the shift in his poetics in an interview with James Randall in 1979:

■ I wrote a fairly constricted freeish kind of verse in *Wintering Out* and North in general, and then in the new book *Field Work*, I very deliber-ately set out to lengthen the line again because the narrow line was becoming a habit. The shortness of line constricts, in a sense, the breadth of your movement. Of course, a formal decision is never strictly formal. I mean it's to do with some impulsive things, some instinctive sense of the pitch you want to make. And with *North* and *Wintering Out* I was burrowing inwards, and those thin small quatrain poems, they're kind of drills or augers for turning in and they are narrow and long and deep. Well, after those poems I wanted to turn out, to go out, and I wanted to pitch the voice out; it was at once formal but also emotional, a return to an opener voice and to a more – I don't want to say public – but a more social voice. And the rhythmic contract of a meter and iambic pentameter and long line implies audience.[1] □

This shift from 'burrowing inwards' to turning outwards is indicated in one of Heaney's favourite tropes, the allegorical victory of the 'sky-born' Hercules over native, earth-grubbing Antaeus. Clair Wills discusses the poem 'Hercules and Antaeus' as a struggle between the two principles of 'rationality' and 'mythic atavism', and offers this important reminder:

■ In an interview with Seamus Deane, Heaney describes the poem as evincing a 'nostalgia' for Antaeus' sense of place, a sense which he

connects with a primitive, tribal, and hence bigoted view of the situation in Northern Ireland, while assenting to the rationalism of
Hercules. (Importantly Heaney qualifies the poem in the phrase, 'but I
think that is wrong now'.)[2] □

The poetry after *North* is usually discussed in terms of Heaney's struggle
to move from the Antaean darkness into the Herculean light, to find a
balance between the claims of attachment and an ideal of personal and
artistic freedom. 'I was mired in attachment', the poet complains in 'The
First Flight', one of the poems in the 'Sweeney Redivivus' section of
Station Island. 'Mired' effectively recalls the early interest in puddling
through muck, probing the rich alluvia of decay, excavating the dark
recesses of the past. His attachment of course was not only to the landscape of his native place but also to family, tribe, community. Heaney
may have found that his ideal culture, his 'first kingdom', was irretrievable ('the wet centre is bottomless'; 'the ground . . ./ Is flayed or
calloused . . ./ Our island is full of comfortless noises'), but he discovers a
new kingdom of the imagination. 'I no longer wanted a door into the
dark', he said, 'I wanted a door into the light'. 'Oysters', the first poem in
Field Work, sets the pattern of what follows: the poet longs to 'repose/ in
the clear light . . . Leaning in from sea'. Writing about Sylvia Plath in *The
Government of the Tongue*, Heaney concentrates on the moment in 'Mussel
Hunter at Rock Harbour' when Plath's poetry 'soars from the crustacean
to the cerulean'.[3] 'Oysters' is expressive of the longing for the same
amplitude and freedom of mind. It is also representative, however, in the
acknowledgement it gives to the resistant drag of a troubling political
and historical consciousness. Heaney may have made good his escape
from the massacre in the North to a kind of Wordsworthian pastoral
romanticism when he and his family moved from Belfast to Glanmore in
July 1972, but his thought is still burdened by history and politics. As if
to compensate for desertion, he displays an unusually explicit degree of
tribal solidarity in some poems in *Field Work*. In 'The Toome Road', for
example, he speaks as a resentful native staking his claim to home
ground against the armed incursion of the colonial invader, while in
'Badgers' he identifies with the 'bogey of fern country', representative of
a dark, atavistic force associated with terrorism.

Other poems, such as 'Casualty' and 'The Singer's House' celebrate the
kind of poetic 'release' Heaney writes about in *The Government of the Tongue*:

■ The achievement of the poem is an experience of release . . . The
tongue, governed for so long in the social sphere by considerations of
tact and fidelity, by nice obeisances to one's origin within the minority
or the majority. This tongue is suddenly ungoverned. It gains access to
a condition that is unconstrained.[4] □

If he is simply 'dumb' witness to atrocity in 'Punishment', unable to speak out against the violence, in 'Casualty' he proclaims the necessary freedom of the creative imagination, 'As you find a rhythm / Working you, slow mile by mile, / Into your proper haunt, / Somewhere, well out, beyond . . .' It is the advice James Joyce gives him on Station Island: 'fill the element / with signatures of your own frequency, / echo soundings, searches, probes, allurements . . .'. It is also the advice that poet and critic, Andrew Waterman, would give him: 'Casualty', in Waterman's view, is a landmark poem in Heaney's career for it was there the poet reached full awareness of his 'proper haunt' beyond any socially ordained constraint.[5]

Field Work may be seen to affirm the possibility of transcendence despite death and loss. Ensconcing himself as pastoral field worker in the gatehouse of Glanmore Castle, Heaney finds a respite from the political violence of the North. In contrast to the earlier imagery of 'exposure' and 'no sanctuary', the Glanmore sonnets offer a series of images of farmhouse, hedge-school, Wordsworth's Rydal Mount, tree-house, harbour and classical rural sanctuary. Rededicating himself to the 'versus' of poetry, to nature, to personal feeling and experience, to the familiar, the ordinary and the known, he wants to be quickened into 'verb, pure verb', to raise a voice that 'might continue, hold, dispel, appease'. Seeking a renewed lyricism (note the number of poems alluding to song or singing) attuned to the natural world, he thinks of his poems as everlasting flowers: in the words of a poem called 'Song', they are 'the immortelles of perfect pitch'. The bucolic world of Glanmore, just like the childhood world of Mossbawn, is pervaded by death and horror, the Glanmore imagery often recalling earlier references to the horror at the heart of nature and everyday life. In the fifth sonnet, for example, the description of the elderberries as 'caviar of shot / A buoyant spawn, a light bruised out of purple' reprises the frightening spawn in 'Death of a Naturalist', the bullet references in 'Trout', 'Dawn Shoot' and 'After a Killing', the fatal purple bruise in 'Mid-Term Break', and brings to mind the image of that other 'dark/elderberry place' that was the site of the Grauballe Man's terrible wounding. In the ninth poem, the black rat swaying on the briar 'like infected fruit' recalls both 'Blackberry Picking' and 'Strange Fruit'. Surveying the 'blood on a pitch-fork, blood on chaff and hay, / Rats speaked in the sweat and dust of threshing', the poet asks 'What is my apology for poetry?', echoing the similar query in 'A Northern Hoard'. But *Field Work* also includes images of clearing storms, a disappearing rat, the passing of night, a new vision of a wife's face, the quickening power of nature, 'story' and love. All this suggests the poetic invigoration that comes from a rediscovered domestic muse. The poems of wifely celebration such as 'The Otter' and 'The Skunk' confirm the poet's re-siting of himself within the personal and the familial.

Mark Patrick Hederman, writing in 1979, without benefit of the knowledge of the direction Heaney's poetry was to take subsequently, insists that it is the Antaean force in Heaney's poetry that produces his 'most powerful and original poetry'.[6] Heaney's strength, Hederman argues, is his 'gift of expressing in words the secrets of the earth', his Heideggerean ability to penetrate behind and beneath 'the everyday world and the normal kind of saying'[7] to pre-literate, pre-conscious levels of consciousness and culture. When he leaves the world of Antaeus to re-enter the world of Hercules, the poetry, in Hederman's view, loses force, a failure that is spelt out in the poet's inability to provide 'A Drink of Water' in the poem of that title.

■ Hercules and Antaeus represent two different kinds of poet: the first composes his own poetry; the second is composed by his own poetry. The first is the self-assertive poet, the political poet, who has a definite vision of things, who chooses his style and his words, who decides what kind of poet he is going to be. The second kind of poet is he whom Martin Heidegger calls the 'more daring' . . . because he works from the heart and . . . articulates a song 'whose sound does not cling to something that is eventually attained', but which has already shattered itself even in the sounding . . . [8] □

Hederman's preference for a poetry of the dark has been overtaken by the developments in Heaney's poetic since Hederman was writing in 1979. In the poetry after *Field Work* the characteristic imagery changes spectacularly, from the archaeological and excavatory to the aerial and ornithological, from earth to air, darkness to light, expressive of the poet's desire for transcendence – 'When goldfinch or kingfisher rent the veil of the usual'. Heaney's desire for release from history, politics, the self, expresses itself in various ways. It is represented not only in the opposition between native, earth-grubbing Antaeus and the superior intelligence of the 'sky-born' Hercules, but also in his use of the Sweeney myth (notably in *Sweeney Astray* and *Station Island*). *Sweeney Astray* speaks of the longing for a depoliticised poetry that draws instead from nature: 'I prefer the elusive / rhapsody of blackbirds / to the garrulous blather / of men and women'. The bird-man, Sweeney, is a figure of the divided poet who relishes his freedom yet is unable to slip personal and social attachment. Sweeney lives a life of lonely exile far from home and society, but whilst he laments his loss he cherishes his solitude. He represents the poet as 'trespasser, pursuing tabooed secrets of the Irish historical landscape, penetrating the hidden self: 'As if a trespasser / unbolted a forgotten gate / and ripped the growth / tangling the bars – / just beyond the hedge / he has opened a dark morse / along the bank' ('The King of the Ditchbacks') – an image of the poet's leaving the civilised world of history and language and entering the pre-verbal, illiterate realms of whisper. Escaping the modern world, Sweeney/Heaney stays clear of all processions, refusing conformity to religious or political orthodoxy, excursing into unknown, darkly pagan zones. The figure of Sweeney allows the poet to view the world from new, detached perspectives, to overcome the 'appetites of gravity' and consider things from a Kavanaghesque point of view of 'weightlessness'. At the same time, Sweeney never entirely loses contact with the earth. Contact with the natural world gives renewed vitality to his senses and imaginative life. 'The First Flight' (in *Station Island*) enacts both the fear of flying and the exhilaration of an unbearable lightness of being. The poet, in fact, as 'Station Island' and his essay 'Envies and Identifications: Dante and the Modern Poet' (1985) suggest, aspires to a Dantean aesthetic that would reconcile the claims of both the earthly and the spiritual, the political and the transcendent, allowing him to combine the roles of 'sky-born' Hercules and 'earth-hugging' Antaeus.

Ciaran Carson's review of *Sweeney Astray*, 'Sweeneys Ancient and Modern' in *The Honest Ulsterman* (1984) discusses the use Heaney made of the medieval Irish story of King Sweeney in terms of both theme and language. Carson, himself a poet whose first language was Irish, judiciously weighs Heaney's translation against both the original text, *Buile Suibhne*, and other translations:

■ 'The ruined maid complains in Irish', writes Seamus Heaney in 'Ocean's Love to Ireland' (from *North*), a poem which refers – among other things – to the linguistic colonization of the island. Despite the inexorable erosion of the language over the past few centuries, the ruined maid still complains in Irish: its position as the language of revolution is, for better or worse, enshrined in Sinn Fein's cultural policy; poetry and prose is being written in Irish, largely ignored by students of Irish literature. And if Irish is still alive, however vestigially, the position of English can never be wholly authoritative, as Stephen Dedalus recognises in *A Portrait of the Artist*:

The language in which we are speaking is his before it is mine. How different are the words home, *Christ, ale, master* on his lips and mine! I cannot speak or write these words without unrest of spirit.

Heaney uses that quotation as preface to his poem 'The Wool Trade', from *Wintering Out*, and the book as a whole is informed by its concerns: take, for example, 'Toome' and 'Broagh', which are playful extensions of the Irish tradition of *dinnshenchas*, or lore of place-names; or 'The Backward Look':

A stagger in air
as if a language
failed . . .

The language in question is, presumably, Irish, whose ghost is sub-
liminally present throughout the book; this is one way of trying to
ease the unrest of the linguistic dilemma which is, to a greater or lesser
extent, the heritage of every Irish writer. Joyce invented a language;
Beckett wrote in French; others translated, or received their inspiration
from translation. We can see how Thomas Kinsella's version of the
Tain, for example, with its violent narrative, its deep and prophetic
utterances, mirrors Kinsella's own work; it is an historical and linguistic
imperative. Translation is one way of trying to come to terms with the
already created conscience of the Irish language.

So, Seamus Heaney's version of *Buile Suibhne*. Briefly, this is the
story of Sweeney, king of Dal Araidhe, who offends the distinguished
cleric Ronan Finn, firstly by throwing his psalter into a lake (it is
miraculously recovered, unblemished, by an otter), then by killing
one of the holy man's acolytes and – worse, perhaps – by throwing his
spear at Ronan and denting the sacred bell he wears around his neck.
Ronan curses Sweeney on both occasions, prophesying that he will
take the form of a bird and eventually die, by the spear. Sweeney goes
to fight at the Battle of Moira, and the first part of the malediction is
fulfilled. The bulk of the text is taken up by his subsequent peregrina-
tions and hardships, until he is eventually mortally wounded by a
spear and reconciled, somewhat unconvincingly, to Christianity.

The story's linguistic embodiment is complex: like many early
Irish compositions, it consists of alternate prose and verse, the latter
constituting by far the greater part of the work. It might be said that
the prose delineates the outward events of the story; the verse recounts
an inward, psychological journey; and certainly, much of the effect of
the original is gained by this creative interplay. Heaney sees Sweeney
as 'a figure of the artist, displaced, guilty, assuaging himself of his
utterance' (p. viii); he is also the product of the tension between
paganism and Christianity, between the natural world and linguistic
order. The dialogue is embodied in a significant quibble in the Irish
text on the word *eolas*, which Dineen's Irish Dictionary defines
variously as 'knowledge of direction, way, guidance, bearings; knowledge, learning, skill; a habit, particularly of frequenting a place; a
recipe, a prescription or formula; an incantation'; for his part' O'Keefe
sometimes renders the word as 'home'. All these readings are possible: home is where the heart is; it is a state of mind, an incantation.
The text is, at times, a catalogue of place-names recited with loving
care, all the more so because Sweeney is homeless: it is a significant

extension of the *dinnshenchas* tradition, which existed to give historical legitimacy to territorial claims. A place was not simply a place; it was a story, a history, a creative act, an ordering of time. The ambiguity is seen at its most concise in the lines

> *cian om eolus-sa*
> *crioch gusa ranag-sa*

Unfortunately I cannot give Heaney's version of these lines, since they occur in one of four consecutive stanzas in Section 45 which he omits without acknowledgement. O'Keefe renders them as 'far from my home / is the country I have reached', but the matter is more complex. *Cian* means far, both in time and space. For *crioch*, we can take some definitions from a column-long entry in Dineen: 'furrow, boundary; limit, end; region, territory; a definite end or object; business; *ceithre criocha deidheanna an duine*, the 'four last things' (death, judgement, heaven, hell)' . These meanings are all possible; with the added ambiguity of *eolas*, they combine to give a dense, riddling effect appropriate to Sweeney's state of mind. I do not know if we can call this usage metaphorical; it is, rather, exploitative, the words themselves generating lines of implicit enquiry; or to put it another way, the technique emerges from the 'deep structure' of the language. We see the ploy at its most effective in the sixty-five quatrains of Section 40, where the key word *beann* and its oblique forms *binn* and *benn*, together with the adjectival homophone, meaning, 'sweet, melodious', occurs no less than forty-three times. Here is Dineen again: 'a point, a peak; a crest, a spire; a wing, a branch; a prong; a horn.' Again, all these meanings, and others, are played on; their inherent ambiguity represents Sweeney's schizophrenia, his obsession with mountain-tops, antlers, the tops of trees, spears. His original transgression was caused by a spear; so, he will die by the spear. The manic expansion and diminution of his life is summed up in the lines

> *a mbeinn ar gach beinnine*
> *beinnini ar gach mbenn*

A complete translation is impossible. O'Keefe renders this as 'If I were on every little point / There would be a pointlet on every point', which sounds pretty silly in English. Heaney glosses it as 'I would roost among / Her mazy antlers'. What the Irish implies, by its play on the subjunctive of the verb 'to be' (*da mbeinn*), is that the physical world of antlers, mountain-peaks, spears, has become microscopically internalized in a kind of *Third Policeman* logic. The literal world of the noun has become verb. Sweeney himself is not unaware of the play; a few verses later he calls himself *fer benn*, man of the points or peaks, and, by implication, man of being. His is the chronicle of a death foretold; he is living out the knowledge of a prophecy. The intricate circularity of purpose is mirrored in the convention of the Irish verse forms, that they must begin and end on the same word; the effect, at times, is like taking one step forward and two steps back.

With all this in mind, it is no accident that Flann O'Brien used *Buile Suibhne* as an integral part of *At Swim-Two-Birds*, another book about the responsibility of authorship (Sweeney is the author of his own woes, as well as being largely the author of the verse). Or that Heaney himself, in the first poem in the Sweeney section of *Station Island*, should recall his own fascination with writing:

> Take hold of the shaft of the pen.
> Subscribe to the first step taken
> from a justified line
> into the margin.

('The First Gloss')

The succinctness of those lines is at least partially informed by the poetic method of *Buile Suibhne*, whose basic unit is the 'thin small quatrain . . . kind of drills or augers for turning in and they are long and narrow and deep'. Eleven different types of quatrain are in fact used in the original, each with its complex set of rules of metre, assonance (or rhyme) and alliteration. Clearly, to attempt an English equivalent is out of the question; even a 'literal' translation, with its difficulties of the text's many ambiguities, is a daunting task – and indeed, O'Keefe's English text rarely gives an adequate idea of the hypnotic density of the original:

> O briar, little arched one,
> thou grantest no fair terms,
> thou ceasest not to tear me,
> till thou hast thy fill of blood.
>
> O yew tree, little yew tree,
> in churchyards thou art conspicuous;
> O ivy, little ivy,
> thou art familiar in the dusky wood.
>
> O holly, little sheltering one,
> thou door against wind;
> O ash tree, thou baleful one,
> hand-weapon of a warrior.

O birch, smooth and blessed,
thou melodious proud one,
delightful each entwining branch
in the top of thy crown.

The aspen a-trembling;
by turns I hear
its leaves a-racing –
meseems 'tis the foray!

In his introduction, Heaney claims that he has 'now and again
invested the poems with a more subjective tone than they possess in
Irish'; this is not entirely true of his rendition of these lines. Granted,
the original has a litanic, manic formality; but here, nature is not
observed, it is addressed; in their personification, the trees become
cyphers for Sweeney's state of mind; nature is internalized. Heaney's
descriptive method alters the relationship to that of observer and
observed, an attitude that is at once more romantic and less dramatic;
it is, perhaps, more meditative:

Briars curl in sideways,
arch a stickle back,
draw blood and curl up innocent
to sneak the next attack.

The yew tree in each churchyard
wraps night in its dark hood.
Ivy is a shadowy
genius of the wood.

Holly rears its windbreak,
a door in winter's face;
life-blood on a spear-shaft
darkens the grain of ash.

Birch tree, smooth and blessed,
delicious to the breeze,
high twigs plait and crown it
the queen of trees.

The aspen pales
and whispers, hesitates:
a thousand frightened scuts
race in its leaves.

In the original, that last verse reads:

Crithach ara criothugudh
atchluinim ma seach
a duille for riothugudh dar leam as i an chreach

where *crithach* (aspen, or, literally, 'shivery' or 'shaky') is a near homophone of *creach* (raid or foray). Heaney's verse necessarily loses that dramatic ambiguity; but its own aural ambiguity, though different in emphasis, is appropriate.

[. . .]

If Sweeney's voice is sometimes that of Heaney, we cannot quibble too much. Until *Sweeney Astray, Buile Suibhne* has lain nearly moribund in the shelves of libraries. No organisation charged with promoting the Irish language has undertaken to make it more easily available. Its resurrection in a new voice can only be commended.[9] □

Seamus Deane, in his review of Heaney's *New Selected Poems*, 'Powers of Earth and Visions of Air', in the *Times Literary Supplement* (16 March 1990), emphasises the dialectical quality of Heaney's mature work. Deane speaks of the coexistence of a 'devotion to the ground' and a 'Herculean effort to lift off from the old Antaeus-like hugging of the holy and violent ground into the realm of air and fire, the zone of vision, not merely the dry air of rational enlightenment'. Heaney, Deane suggests, 'wants the powers of earth to give him sufficient lift-off to carry him into the regions of the air'. As Deane's gloss on the terms 'Antaean' and 'Herculean' suggests, they are indeed flexible and capacious concepts. Excerpts from the review are reproduced below.

■ Since his first book, *Death of a Naturalist* (1966), Seamus Heaney has been much concerned with deaths of various kinds. His life as a writer has almost exactly coincided with the most recent period of crisis in Northern Ireland, and the degeneration of that rancid statelet over the past twenty years has provided enough violent killings to deepen a preoccupation that was already there in the early work. In Heaney's poetry, as in the political world that subsists with it, there is a need to possess or to repossess a territory that is always there in its specific actuality and yet evades all attempts to seize and hold it in one stabilizing grasp.

It has often been observed that Heaney's work – especially the first four volumes, including *Door into the Dark* (1969), *Wintering Out* (1972) and *North* (1975) – has a remarkably large vocabulary for earth, especially earth in a state of deliquescence, earth mixed with water.

Mud, slime, mould, silt, and *slicks* are words that note the ambiguity of the ground itself; they appear in those man-made workings that Heaney endlessly explores, in trenches, drains, pits, wells and furrows. These in turn belong to particular kinds of territory – fens, bogs, loanings, keshes – and all of these are finally embedded in political and religious division of the land: baronies, parishes, counties, and parklands. Even the local place-names are seduced into their alluvial origins. To name a place is to pronounce the kind of ground it occupies; to fail to pronounce the name properly is to fail to possess it truly, to be foreign. This devotion to the ground and its names, the constant ascent from original slime to the nominations of geography and history, provides Heaney's poetry with a highly complex sonar architecture in which vowels and consonants dispute between themselves for an equilibrium that will allow to each its separate function and yet acknowledge for both their interdependence. The vowel, especially the vowel *O*, is originary: but it cannot speak the emptiness it represents without the consonantal surround. Looms and honeycombs, seeds splitting into root systems, interconnected deltas of archaeological remains, develop their ramifications around these gaping open ground vowels, the eyes, sores, valves and wounds that are the characteristic marks of the creature who is the ultimate victim of and possessor of the ground – the buried corpse.

In *Wintering Out* and in *North*, more than in any previous volume, Heaney found a way to make the ground speak in a human voice. The act of ventriloquism by which he made the Viking dead speak for the contemporary victims of violence in Ireland was a brilliant stroke – it enabled to a higher degree than before the tone of reverence and piety that had been and has continued to be the most notable aspect of Heaney's mode of address to his subject. The violence of the actions that had produced these sacrificial victims was only partly muted. By deflecting into these archaeological remains, he could brood on it without risking that pornographic observation of atrocity which is so frequently found in the reportage of political crises. More importantly, though, it brought him back to the inexhaustible trope of origin (since the violence is, in a sense, originary, prehistoric) and death as manifested in the earth itself. The territory now assumes yet another vocabulary – of souterrain, flint, and hoard – the words of archaeology that support and reproduce the words of farming and cultivation. A digging is now both a cultivation of the ground and an exploration of it. The ground is never firm; like the bog, with its moss and peat and its aqueous nervous system, it absorbs and preserves the dead it receives, making them like itself but allowing them to retain their own identity, an embrace of vowel and consonant. For Heaney, this is a linguistic as well as a historical and political drama, an actual place in time, geography intersecting history, in and through which he can gaze at the nub, node, or centre his poetry craves.

[. . .]

Heaney's ultimate home is not Station Island, or the island of Ireland, but, as he titles it in *The Haw Lantern*, 'The Disappearing Island.' In this poem the imagined situation is that of a band of wandering Irish monks, voyaging in the western seas and making camp on an island that disappears as they light their fire. (The old tales mention such islands that turned out to be whales, sea monsters.) The final stanza restores to us memories of Heaney's earlier explorations of that boundary between the actual and the visionary. 'Water and ground in their extremity' (from 'The Peninsula,' in *Door into the Dark*) is one version of it; another is registered in the recurrent images of eye, needle, notch, the infinitesimally small opening through which the actual flows, as through an isthmus, into the visionary. For that to happen, the fidelity must be there; but it must be given to a vision and in such a manner that it is the actual that becomes the product rather than the precondition of the vision.

> The land sustaining us seemed to hold firm
> Only when we embraced it *in extremis*.
> All I believe that happened there was vision.

Perhaps it is this probing, exact and exacting measurement of the fictive distance between actualities and their representation that so attracts audiences and readers to Heaney's work. He gives the double impression that nothing gets lost in the translation of the world into poetry, and that it is only through the poetry that the world to which it refers comes fully into existence. He so narrows the discrepancy between world and word, so winningly lends a tongue to emptiness, that the effect is genial. His is an earth that speaks directly and in recognition to the body. It is without even the vestige of alienation. At the root of every word there is a tentacular handshake between the speaker and the thing spoken of. In 'A Postcard from Iceland' (in *The Haw Lantern*), we learn that the word 'lukewarm,' describing the temperature of the water from a spring, derives from the old Icelandic word *luk*, meaning 'hand.' Heaney characteristically shares this knowledge with his reader by making it more intimate, by making hand into 'palm' and by telling us we knew it already. Of course we did; but never this way

> And you would want to know (but you know already)
> How usual that waft and pressure felt
> When the innerpalm of water found my palm.

Here the reader is acknowledged as a lover in a world that is 'usual' and yet, as in love, extraordinarily perceived.

Heaney's *New Selected Poems, 1966 –1987* does not include this poem, but then there are very few indeed from the last three volumes that I would have had the heart to exclude. The work gets more and more Herculean, but the Antaean root does not snap. In *The Place of Writing*, the inaugural Richard Ellmann Lecture in Modern Literature delivered at Emory University, Heaney broods on the question of place and writing, with Yeats finally taking here a priority never assigned him in Heaney's own poetry. Heaney's reading of Yeats is also a reading of himself, particularly what he calls Yeats's 'desire for foundedness' and the accompanying 'fear of unfoundedness which might lurk beneath it.' Heaney is exploring his own recent preoccupation with an origin that is empty, because writing reveals its absence, and yet is actual because writing envisions its presence. Yeats's tower is transposed into the poems; for Heaney these themselves become buildings, stanzas return to their origin by becoming rooms, and the verbal architecture of the poem locates itself in a space that is also a place. The actuality of place queries the insubstantiality of space; but space is what place becomes in vision. This affirmation and denial are an operatic affair in Yeats. The music is Wagnerian, the libretto Nietzschean. Heaney loves the Gotterdammerung atmosphere, but his admiration is more pronounced than his affection. He prefers what his contemporaries, such as Kinsella, Montague, Mahon, and Muldoon, do when they refuse the limited destiny of place and go in search of 'the problematic place of the writer.' In Ireland, where the place has been invested with such political energy, this is a difficult problem. In one sense, it is the struggle to become a writer rather than an Irish writer. You can't be one without the other; yet to be too self-consciously Irish might rob one of the freedom to be a writer, an author. These poets have to authorize their Irishness by giving primacy to authority; only then will the place of Ireland become real. Otherwise it is merely a stereotype, a place that is given, not found.[10] □

The poetry in and after *Field Work*, the critics agree, is marked by the sense of drama and struggle to move from the Antaean darkness into the Herculean light. Guilt and self-doubt persist alongside a sense of great imaginative power and freedom. The prolonged self-interrogation that is carried through 'Punishment', 'Strange Fruit', 'Viking Dublin' and 'Exposure' reaches a climax in the purgatorial rites of 'Station Island' and *The Haw Lantern*. In a powerfully written essay, 'The Witnessing Eye and the Speaking Tongue', Terence Brown, Professor of English at Trinity College Dublin and a critic who has followed Heaney's development with a discriminating and sympathetic attentiveness, refers to *The Haw*

Lantern as a volume 'absorbed by occasions of judgement, attentive to the moment of verdict, as if the poet yearns for some release from the stresses of public trial'.[11] Brown identifies the emergence of a poetry that takes account of 'a true witnessing, a bearing witness to the intractable aspects of experience' and at the same time 'possesses the lyric faith'. This happens, Brown argues, in the 'Clearances' poems and in 'The Mud Vision':

■ The truly witnessing eye opens without apologetic self-regard or self-accusation. The poet is ready to accept the public's gaze. For he once again possesses the lyric faith. Not the ardent freedom of youthful exuberance discovering the lyric potential of the given and familiar, but something hard-won which takes the duty of the witnessing eye for granted, which does not avert its face from 'the beggar at the gate'. And in such writing guilt is transcended in an art which, wholly responsible to its own form and the language of its expression, can rest easy in a kind of chastened delight, knowing its own untrammelled possibility.[12] □

Brown, like Deane, emphasises the strenuous effort of crossing the frontier of writing, achieving clearance from the scrutiny of the public world and finding release into the airy playgrounds of the imagination. These crossings from darkness into light constitute a rite of passage, variously figured by Heaney as the voyage of the Anglo-Saxon 'ship of death', the Dantean journey through Inferno, Purgatorio to Paradiso, Aeneas's crossing into the underworld, Kavanagh's discovery of the 'placeless heaven'. In his essay, Brown expertly shows how Heaney, with the kind of somnambulist poetic assurance he celebrates in 'The Harvest Bow', now seeks to transform loss and absence by absorbing them into a luminous, supra-historical realm of the imaginary.

Heaney's next collection, *Seeing Things* (1991), both confirms the validity and explores the nature of the visionary impulse. Echoing the sentiment of 'The First Flight', Heaney refers to his previous poetry as being 'sluggish in the doldrums of what happens'. He wants to cast off 'heaviness' and embrace an unbearable lightness of being: 'Me waiting till I was nearly fifty / To credit marvels . . . / so long for the air to brighten, / Time to be dazzled and the heart to lighten' ('Fosterling'). Impelled by a longing for the visionary, he wants to open a door into the light rather than the dark. The book is bathed in dazzling light, the estranging, irradiating blaze of the imagination. The 'cascade of light' for which he had longed in 'North' has at last arrived. Yet, installed at the heart of Heaney's visionary seeing (and encoded in the double meaning of his title, *Seeing Things*) is the continual awareness that vision may be delusion. John Bayley's analysis of Heaney's poetry in terms of

Blanchot's aperçu that 'la négation est liée au langage' (see pages 26–9) would still seem to hold true, as indeed would Patrick Crotty's recognition that Heaney brings 'caution and distrust to his own visions . . . because they are founded on contradictory apprehensions of the nature of poetic language' (see pages 75–6).

With Heaney's new visionary seeing come new experiments in language and style. Seeking to devise a form that will complement and enact the fluid and the phantomatic, Heaney, in Part II of the book, experiments with a series of forty-eight twelve-liners, each of the poems arranged in four unrhymed tercets in freely handled iambic pentameter – a kind of free version of Dante's intricately patterned *terza rima* with which Heaney had earlier experimented in 'Station Island'. The sequence is composed out of diverse materials – chance observations, versions of old stories, personal memories, dreams, snippets of quotations, aesthetic questionings – that he aims to turn into poems having a kind of emblematic suggestiveness and brilliance: 'And strike this scene in gold too, in relief / So that a greedy eye cannot exhaust it' ('Squarings' xv). The astonishing thing about the sequence is the imaginative freedom it exhibits. The poems are what Heaney calls 'squarings', a term he remembers from playing marbles as a child: 'Those anglings, aimings, feints and squints / You were allowed before you'd shoot . . . / Test-outs and pull-backs, re-envisagings' ('Squarings' iii). Heaney is demonstrating a renewed interest in the incomplete, the suggestive and the experimental that we find in earlier work such as 'Viking Dublin: Trial Pieces', with its 'buoyant/migrant line', evocative of jaw-bone, a bill in flight, a basket of eels, a longship, a worm cast. The 'Squarings' poems are like the suggestive outline of the trial-piece: 'a cage / or trellis to conjure in'. They may, in fact, be seen to enact a view of poetry expressed in *The Government of the Tongue*:

■ Poetry is more a threshold than a path, one constantly approached and constantly departed from, at which reader and writer undergo in their different ways the experience of being at the same time summoned and released.[13] □

The continual cycle of approach and departure, summoning and releasing, 'free passage and return' ('Squarings' xxviii) is also enacted thematically in, for example, Heaney's re-envisagings and reappraisals of his childhood world, and in his return to Glanmore (in the 'Glanmore Revisited' sequence).

In an interview with Blake Morrison, Heaney explained his intentions in the 'Squarings' section, emphasising a dual concern with freedom as well as constraint:

■ The 12-line form felt arbitrary but it seemed to get me places swiftly. So I went with it, a sort of music of the arbitrary that's unpredictable, and can still up and catch a glimpse of a subject out of the blue. There's a phrase I use, 'make impulse one with wilfulness': the wilfulness is in the 12 lines, the impulse in the freedom and shimmer and on-the-wingness. Until recently I had no titles or numbers for these poems, as if they were afloat all at once and moving separately, like mosaics.[14] □

Fluidity and flying on one hand, rootedness and attachment on the other: these are the two poles of Heaney's work. The need to maintain a strenuous dialectical tension between them has long been recognised by the poet as well as his critics. The early 'Gravities' (in *Death of a Naturalist*) speaks of keeping the lines taut between 'riding high' and being rooted: 'High-riding kites appear to range quite freely / Though tied by strings, strict and invisible'. Flying a kite with his sons in 'A Kite for Michael and Christopher' (in *Station Island*), he makes them take the string to feel 'the strumming, rooted, long-tailed pull of grief'. 'Old Smoothing Iron' (*Station Island*) reiterates a poetic ideal as he admiringly watches his mother iron: 'to pull your weight and feel / exact and equal to it. / Feel dragged upon. And buoyant'. The challenge is echoed in *Seeing Things*, as the poet watches clouds moving across a flooded quarry. Contemplating this collocation of the 'diaphanous' and the 'massive', he asks: 'Were you equal to or were you opposite / To build-ups so promiscuous and weightless?' ('Squarings' x). Heaney's poetry is an attempt at reconciling opposites. It is constructed out of a series of contrasting images. Previous work featured a dialogue between Antaeus and Hercules, or the man in the wellingtons and the travelled intelligence ('Making Strange'); in *Seeing Things* we have the airless attic and the wide skylight ('The Skylight'); the light, whispering cast and the ratcheting gather of the fishing line: 'One sound is saying, "You are not worth tuppence, / But neither is anybody. Watch It! Be severe." / The other says, "Go with it! Give and swerve. / You are everything you feel beside the river"' ('Casting and Gathering'). In this parable of the poetic life there is, on one side, the voice of cautious reason, self-deprecating, doubtful about the validity of its powers; on the other, the adventurous self-expressing confidence in the enabling rhythms that carry one out of oneself. The half-rhyme of 'severe' and 'swerve' reflects the inextricable connection between the two voices, but also the transformations that can be worked through the play of language. In earlier poems the tension threatened to split the poetry apart into, for example, the symbolic, mythic outreach of Part I of *North*, and the direct, documentary engagement with the actual situation that we find in Part II. But, in 'Casting and Gathering', Heaney rejoices in the challenge of dualism: 'I love hushed air. I trust contrariness'.

Henry Hart, in his essay, 'What is Heaney Seeing in *Seeing Things*?', in the *Colby Quarterly* special Heaney issue (March 1994), concentrates on the 'theme of harmonized contraries – of limits crossed, of the natural and the supernatural wedded, of the confused infused with the sublime'.

■ When we call a poem 'visionary' we usually mean that it contains things that are conspicuously fantastic to the ordinary observer. Blake's poems are fervently 'visionary'; William Carlos Williams' are not. When Blake looked at the sun he saw angels crying 'Holy, Holy, Holy is the Lord God Almighty.' When Williams looked at the sun he probably saw 'a round disk of fire somewhat like a Guinea' (617). Because of Pound and the Imagist movement, most twentieth-century poets fear abstractions and feel compelled to focus closely on objects. But they also know that language mediates both things and ideas, transforming both into an artificial medium that is simultaneously abstract and concrete. In the word the world is both idea and object. Realizing that the visionary and the real are symbiotic rather than exclusive, Marianne Moore called for 'imaginary gardens with real toads in them' ('Poetry'). In his most recent collection of poems, *Seeing Things*, Seamus Heaney calls for a similar synthesis of the imaginary and real, and repeatedly explores the dynamic relations between them.

As critics tirelessly point out, Heaney's career has moved from a deeply visceral engagement with the earth and the historical bodies buried in it to a preoccupation with more transcendental matters. In the early poems from *Death of a Naturalist* to *North*, his feet are solidly planted in the bogs and potato drills of rural Ireland. In *Station Island* and *The Haw Lantern* he is more willing to make pilgrimage to other worlds inhabited by spirits and ghosts. If the visionary smacks of escapism for the younger Heaney – a culpable flight from past and present Irish troubles – for the older man it becomes a justifiable maneuver. Much of Heaney's recent poetry and criticism is a kind of apology for the sort of vision and voyage that transcends the 'complexities of mire or blood' (as Yeats phrased it in 'Byzantium') of Ireland's sectarian strife. Patrick Kavanagh is one of his guides in this levitation. In 'The Placeless Heaven,' an essay printed in *The Government of the Tongue*, Heaney empathizes with Kavanagh's move from an early poetry that 'is supplied with a strong physical presence and is full of the recognitions which existed between the poet and his place' to the later poetry in which 'the world is more pervious to his vision than he is pervious to the world. When he writes about places now, they are luminous spaces within his mind' (4, 5). He also empathizes with Philip Larkin, the subject of an adjacent essay and of the first poem in *Seeing Things*, whose 'unsettled quarrel [was] conducted all through the mature poetry between vision and experience'.

For Heaney the appeal of metaphysical visions and voyages is countered by a similar devotion to the quotidian.

[. . .]

What distinguishes *Seeing Things* from books by predecessors, and from Heaney's previous books, is both stylistic and thematic. Heaney harmonizes the heavy, earthbound 'plop and slap' sound effects of his first books and the more subliminal, philosophical style of *Station Island* and *The Haw Lantern*, creating what might be called a 'middle style.' While his long poetic sequence (48 sections of 4 tercets) called 'Squarings' in some ways recalls the way he strung together 'spots of time' in *Stations* (his sequence of prose poems), it is also a radical departure. As in many modernist sequences, the events and objects dwelled upon are arranged with apparent randomness. There is no ostensible plot or logical argument, only a flow of often disconnected associations.

M. L. Rosenthal's and Sally Gall's *The Modern Poetic Sequence*, which Heaney reviewed for *The New York Times Book Review* in 1983, no doubt encouraged him in the form the authors argue is '*the* modern poetic form within which all the tendencies of more than a century of experiment define themselves and find their aesthetic purpose' (vii). Heaney in his review takes note of the developments championed by Poe and Pound that led to:

> a changing wind of sensibility that finally blows away chronological and rational ordering from long poems. It tilts them away from discourse and narrative and renders them amenable to the terms of praise recurrent in these pages – 'centers of intensity,' 'units of affect,' 'progression of tonalities' . . . They see Whitman's defiant readiness to contradict himself as characteristic of the modern sequence, where the relationship of the poems 'is like that within a planetary system: a process of tensions and countertensions, self-contained yet not rigid.' ('Common Bed' 3, 31)

Heaney's sequence, as well as the poems collected in the first part of *Seeing Things*, repudiate traditional narrative order to map the tensions and countertensions at work in poetic memory. In theme and form he is working in a well-trodden Romantic and modernist arena, but his voice and his particular angle of vision are distinctly his own.

[. . .]

Throughout *Seeing Things* Heaney dwells on what is seen as much as why it is seen the way it is. His poems continually draw attention to gates, thresholds, borders, limits, lines, doors, ceilings, roofs, circles, and squares. The situation he obsessively delineates is one where the mind comes up against a confining boundary, is checked by it, but then is stimulated to transcend it. In the end all of his forms of resistance and containment are resisted. To his dialectical mind, limits provoke sublimation and sublimity – journeys or visions below or beyond the threshold (as the etymology of *sublime* – *sub-limen* and *sublimis* – paradoxically indicates).

The last poem in *Seeing Things* is entitled 'Crossings,' but most of the poems before it describe crossings as well – from boringly mundane reality to scenes made sublime by altered perception or poetic tropes. The repressive limits, as in Heaney's other books, can be political, religious, psychological, literary, or an allegorical combination of these. They evince pain, ennui, or some other kind of blockage that challenges the mind to overcome them. Kant described a situation similar to the one that reappears in Heaney's poetry when, in *The Critique of Judgement*, he pointed out that sublime experiences begin when overwhelming natural phenomena check the mind's ability to conceive of them, but then 'raise the forces of the soul above the height of vulgar commonplace, and discover within us a power of resistance of quite another kind, which gives us courage to be able to measure ourselves against the seeming omnipotence of nature'. For Kant the meditating or envisioning mind, when suitably challenged, reduced all seemingly omnipotent natural phenomena to concepts and declared its own omnipotence. For Kant the reason was transcendent, divine. It was the seat of sublimity.

While inheriting Kant's ideas about the sublime from Romantic tradition and its current expositors (Bloom, Weiskel, Eagleton, Hertz, and others), Heaney puts his own spin on the old aesthetic concept. It's tempting to use Robert Lowell's term from 'Sunday Morning,' 'the monotonous sublime,' to describe Heaney's particular brand of sublimity. But the sublime isn't monotonous for Heaney so much as motivated by monotony, by the 'vulgar commonplace' referred to by Kant or the 'ennui' that launched Baudelaire's exotic voyages. For Lowell the sublime was born out of oedipal power struggles and erupted in pathological enthusiasm, mania, and violence. For Heaney it comes from a quieter struggle and leads to a mellower transformation. He and his staring woman in 'Field of Vision' attain the sublime or the 'distinctly strange' after first being blocked by the 'well-braced gate' and the monotony of 'The same small calves . . . / The same acre of ragwort, the same mountain.' In the end, they triumph over commonplace checks to vision simply by pitting their meditative powers against them.

Throughout *Seeing Things* Heaney illustrates his dialectical concept of limits and sublimities, repressive occlusion and visionary release, with homely examples. Frequently he goes to boyhood sports to embody this subtle process. In 'Markings,' for instance, he recounts how he and his friends delimited a football pitch: 'And then we picked the teams / And crossed the line our called names drew between us.' Already delimited by Catholic and Protestant identities, the boys 'cross' them by playing with and against each other. The game itself, Heaney suggests, is a kind of acknowledgement of boundaries and rules that seeks to transcend them. Like all good athletes, Heaney's football players are 'playing in their heads,' so assured are they that their bodies will follow what their minds dictate. Heaney asserts: 'Some limit had been passed, / There was fleetness, furtherance, untiredness / In time that was extra, unforeseen and free.' In their humble way, the athletes have attained a timeless, transcendental release from the rules that restrict them. They have become another example of Heaney's down-to-earth visionaries. 'Blessed be down-to-earth! Blessed by highs,' he says in 'Man and Boy.' He knows 'our spirits must be lightly checked' by earthly constraints for those spirits to yearn for unearthly releases.

'Damn braces: Bless relaxes,' Blake exclaimed in 'The Marriage of Heaven and Hell,' even while admitting, 'Without Contraries is no progression. Attraction and Repulsion, Reason and Energy, Love and Hate, are necessary to Human existence' (152, 149). Heaney's poems are testaments to the necessity of these oppositions. In 'Casting and Gathering' he says 'I trust contrariness' and exemplifies the idea with two fishermen on opposite banks of a river. One is severe and repressive; the other is laid-back and expressive. Heaney's point at the end, however, is that they are interchangeable: 'I see that when one man casts, the other gathers / And then *vice versa*, without changing sides.' In 'Fosterling' he finds this 'contrariness' illustrated in a picture of Dutch windmills. He speaks of 'The immanent hydraulics of a land' – of the Netherlands, Ireland, but also the 'lowlands of the mind' – in which pressure must be exerted downward for the water to move upward. The science of hydraulics is his metaphor for the dynamics of the visionary imagination. Repression, for Heaney as for Freud, leads to sublimation. An awareness of the heaviness or sinfulness of existence – he refers to the 'picture's heavy greenness' and the 'Heaviness of being' – sooner or later compels the mind to seek refuge in visions that transcend that heaviness. In 'Fosterling' Heaney concedes that a propensity for the extraordinary was long in coming: 'Me waiting until I was nearly fifty / To credit marvels . . . / So long for air to brighten, / Time to be dazzled and the heart to lighten.' He also concedes implicitly that the lightening – one of his favorite words in *Seeing Things* – would never have come if he hadn't felt weighed down by the political, religious and poetic 'doldrums of what happens.' He might as well say that Ireland, with its various oppressions and repressions, hurt him into poetic vision.

[. . .]

Although some critics felt Heaney was not working at the top of his form in *Seeing Things*, the poems have a strong, cumulative effect. Like many modernist poems, and like the modernist sequence in general, they forgo conventional patterns of narrative and logic for a more musical, free-flowing discourse. The conversational clarity of many of the poems may disappoint those readers bent on pyrotechnic rhetoric. The style, however, fits the theme of harmonized contraries – of limits crossed, of the natural and supernatural wedded, of the confined infused with the sublime. Like his fictional predecessor Stephen Dedalus, Heaney flies over the nets of Irish religion, politics, literature, and self but primarily 'to encounter for the millionth time the reality of experience' (*A Portrait* 228). He accedes to visionary flight but mainly to see the things of this world more truly and strangely. *Seeing Things* adds another chapter to the career of one of the most consistently skilful and engaging poets in the postmodern era.[15] □

Balance – the central theme of Deane's, Brown's and Hart's essays – is a theme taken up again by Nicholas Jenkins in his review of Heaney's latest volume in the *Times Literary Supplement* (5 July 1996). Indeed, the theme is highlighted by Heaney himself in the title of his volume, *The Spirit Level*. Jenkins entitles his review 'Walking on Air' – a phrase from one of the poems in the volume, and also, as Jenkins notes, from Heaney's Nobel lecture, where Heaney spoke of 'permitting myself the luxury of walking on air' in spite of a 'temperamental disposition towards an art that was earnest and devoted to things as they are'. Jenkins sees *The Spirit Level* marking a definite development in Heaney's work: it demonstrates, he believes, a greater subtlety and fluidity than ever before, the refinement of a '"give and take" poetry which is continually crossing and re-crossing boundaries'.

■ The Caesar of the *Gallic Wars* might have put it *this* way: like Ireland, Seamus Heaney's poetry is divided into two parts. And Caesar would have had a point; fractures and self-oppositions are elemental features of Heaney's work. So, as all his previous collections have been, his dazzling new book, *The Spirit Level*, is an intricately doubled entity, a thing that strives to be both buoyant and sombre, cryptic and forthright, as it weaves back and forth across the line between myth and memory, lightness and heaviness, a 'nowhere' and (Heaney's own word-play) the 'here' and 'now'. The two-mindedness is perfectly captured in the book's title — the hierarchy of reference abolished, the words shimmer almost undecidably between meaning a thing and meaning a psychological plane.

If *Seeing Things* (1991), his last volume, adumbrated a poetics of charmed stillnesses, of 'Omnipresence, equilibrium, brim', *The Spirit Level* seeks out a more slippery and transitional state of being where, even in moments of balance, there are shivers of movement, where, on a loaded-down weighbridge, for instance, 'every-thing trembled, flowed with give and take'. This is, in short, not just a new book but a book with newness in it, as all Heaney's collections have been. It marks a sustained effort, not exactly to unite the two parts of himself and his cultural inheritance but rather to make the line between them more permeable than before.

The advance is, paradoxically, into a special kind of retrospection. In a benign lyrical language that is one of this collection's most appealing notes, Heaney declares elegiacally that ' My last things will be first things slipping from me'. In looking forwards, he also finds himself gazing back, revisiting his old subjects and writings, re-inscribing them into an historical setting, re-contextualising them like the travellers who at 'cruising altitude' fly over the 'same house/ They'd left an hour before'. ('Transportation', at both the carnal and spiritual levels, is one of the book's main themes; and its pages are therefore crowded with vehicles. Among other things, Heaney looks increasingly like one of the great travel writers – writers, that is, who relish the physical sensations of travel. From the early 'Night Drive' to the relatively recent 'From the Frontier of Writing', has anyone else, even Proust, even Kerouac, written as sensually about the modern experience of being in a car?)

[. . .]

The Spirit Level's main sequence, 'Mycenae Lookout', placed at its solid centre, is far less sanguine, far more bloody. Its mood lies closer to the dynamics of the cessation of hostilities enunciated in *North* (1975): 'exhaustions nominated peace'. Ostensibly, 'Mycenae Lookout' is Heaney's investigation of the 'peace' wrought after the fall of Troy. The Irish parallels, though, jut out like bones in the grass. The speaker is a familiar Heaneyan observer, at times a voyeur, a tongue-tied prophesier, so indecisive that finally, almost self-parodically, he even moves 'beyond bad faith', caught as he is between his awareness of the adulterous love-shouts of Clytemnestra below him and his guilty imagining of the far-off 'yell of troops/Hurled by King Agamemnon from the ships':

> I balanced between destiny and dread
> And saw it coming, clouds bloodshot with the red
> Of victory fires, the raw wound of that dawn
> Igniting and erupting, bearing down
> Like lava on a fleeing population . . .

Heaney's apprehension of peace is extraordinarily savage; it is something that has 'come upon us', a fresh configuration in the endless rounds of massacre. Water seems to exist in order to be polluted by blood. Agamemnon, the victor, comes home from Troy to death at the hands of his wife and her lover in his own bathtub, and in a spectacularly beautiful but horrific invasion of the future, the watchman recounts how he saw a man who 'Jumped a fresh earth-wall and another ran / Amorously, it seemed, to strike him down'. It is a premonition of eternal civil and fratricidal conflict, simultaneous love and hate, not just at Troy, or Mycenae, or Athens (in the place where 'what was to be / Greek met Greek'), but further away in distance and time (at the founding of Rome where Romulus kills his boundary-crossing brother Remus), and then, of course, further away still.

There is an impressive muscularity to this 'heavy', panoramic side of *The Spirit Level*. But the imaginative heart of the book is located further over towards its 'lighter', more fractured and exploratory side – the part that occupies itself with a delicate and innovative groping after half-sensed, airy realities, mysterious states of mind, and the things of the spirit. The music of this masterful book, then, is as much gentle woodwind and strings as pounding percussion. It is a poetry of micro-worlds and micro-events, of slight, almost missable sounds ('small plinkings from a dulcimer' or a singing voice 'like hoisted water / Ravelling off a bucket at the well head'), fragrances (the whiff of mint, or of 'a sick beast's water'), minute visual stirrings (the tiny bubble trapped in the spirit level, a thread passing through a needle-eye, the wind shaking a poplar), and people often with the aid of some artefact serving as an extension of themselves who reach tenderly into otherwise inaccessible regions (a girl using a stick to hook down high-branched blackberries, children drawing their finger-tips across braille lettering, an adult listening over the furred silence of a telephone line to a clock that ticks faraway in his parents' hall).

The poet who once wanted to quicken himself into the intransitive, self-authenticating power of 'verb, pure verb', now searches for milder states of transitiveness. Indeed, simply to run through some of the variations that Heaney plays on the 'trans-' prefix in *The Spirit Level* is to see how essential this fluid, relational, 'give and take' activity has become for him. It is also to realize how many different kinds of boundary are crossed in the book, and how many eerie George Herbert-like in-between moments of balance, rocking, counterweighting and reversal occur there. Besides the meditations on transience (his own and others'), there are transitions, transparency, transports, translations, and transformations. What was once 'the music of what happens' is now 'the music that transpires'. It probably isn't stretching things too far to see the prefix's shadow cast in both the hard material

facts of the trains and the frail memory trances which abound in *The Spirit Level*.

The most far-reaching 'transition' is from earth to air. Helen Vendler, a scholar of Herbert and Heaney and the book's dedicatee, once aptly described it as a move towards a 'poetics of "a listening"'. The early Heaney understood himself to be an Antaean writer, a chthonic artist, 'mould-hugger', a cherisher of rootedness and ooze, a poet with an overwhelmingly aural and tactile imagination obsessed with the 'guttural muse' and the 'furrowed brain', of 'Words entering almost the sense of touch'. This total earthiness was so pervasive in his writing that his people were seen, as if caught in an imaginative force-field, bent over towards the ground in a 'Processional stooping through the turf', sometimes, of course, as sacrificial victims, being dragged down into the womb of the 'dark mother'. The pulls of gravity and of local piety were almost identical: indeed, in the word 'Mass' they became imaginatively superimposed.

Heaney strove for *solidarity* with his world, his myths and landscape. To have lost that vital contact with the soil, to have been lifted off the ground and into the element of air, as Hercules, in an early poem, heaved up Antaeus until his feet kicked on nothingness, seemed to mean creative death, and an afterlife merely as consolatory 'pap for the dispossessed'. The grounded downward trajectory, the early etymological digging and boring, culminated in *North*. But a counter-movement in Heaney's work did not get under way until around the time of *Sweeney Astray* (1984) – a man transformed into a bird – and the dazed, ascetic visions of *Station Island* (1984). It has been going on ever since.

In 'Seeing Things', for example, after all that 'Heaviness of being. And poetry/Sluggish in the doldrums of what happens', Heaney wanted 'the heart to lighten', and he courted a sense of release, partly through an investigation of moments of take-off: a 'fabulous high-catcher suspended momentarily in mid-air', children sliding on ice, the 'phantasmal flow-back' of the road (driving suddenly looked like a form of earthbound gliding), and ships drifting through the sky. At points in *The Spirit Level*, everything seems to be going upwards or seeking to relate itself, if only verbally, to the ether. On a swing for instance, the Heaney siblings 'all learned one by one to go sky high,/Backward and forward in the open shed'. A sofa, its 'castors on tip-toe', has 'achieved/Flotation'. The 'solid letters of the world' grow 'airy' in a story where the Virgin's house 'rose and flew'. Credos are 'light-headed', time is a question of 'light years' and tunes, too, in this phase of Heaney's imaginative history, are always on the point of 'turning into "airs"'.

The Spirit Level, buttressed by Heaney's comments in recent prose, shows how all-consuming this drive to a liberating, upward evolution can become. (Remember now the portents hidden in his sympathetic description of Chekhov's deliberate turning-away, his time-out with a bottle of spirits, in *Station Island*: 'first he drank cognac by the ocean, / With his back to all he travelled north to face'.) Even so, in 1988, well into his 'airy' phase, Heaney could still express genial doubts about how far away a poet could actually get from his native ground and still flourish. That year he remarked that Paul Muldoon had gone so far from any kind of tribal solidarity that he had 'practically achieved the poetic equivalent of walking on air' and made it sound slightly spurious, a smoke-and-mirrors miracle, as much a trick as a gift.

[. . .]

This 'walking on air' phrase has become, then, an organizing preoccupation for Heaney. In his Nobel lecture, for instance, delivered in December, he avowed that 'for once in my life, I am permitting myself the luxury of walking on air'. But 'walking on air' means something more than simply the conventional sense (of being exultant or delighted), though of course it includes that. For Heaney, it also conveys an effort of determination and defiance, as much remaking as relaxing. In the Nobel lecture, he explained this new aspiration as a reaction against his 'temperamental disposition towards an art that was earnest and devoted to things as they are'.

[. . .]

It would be hard to think of another writer whose faith in the power of writing and whose hard-earned sense of the status of the poet were greater. In *The Redress of Poetry*, his recently published Oxford lectures, Heaney spoke startlingly of poetry's 'angelic potential' and of 'its function as an agent of possible transformation, of evolution towards that more radiant and generous life which the imagination desires'.

Grandiosely Yeatsian in his prose, in verse Heaney's sense of the poet's centrality takes on a kind of practical and exemplary viability. There, his mobility within himself, his weaving between his two halves, forms a possible model for a way towards the future that can emphasize the process without prescribing the goal. *The Spirit Level*, then, is spotted with moments of the release and freedom, when the worlds of the tribal and the individual, the natural and the cultural, seem to blur or to reverse their usual planes: 'The rafters aching in our shoulder-blades, / The give and take of branches in our arms'. Throughout, Heaney memorably inducts himself into a world of 'open darkness' – strange gaps, openings, irresolutions and transitions, moments when old barriers might be falling and the blending of what had previously seemed distinct entities might actually be taking place. A reader's first reaction might be intense literary fascination. But this vision of imaginative crossing and re-crossing also serves as a subtle political paradigm. If the two sides, the two parts, of Heaney's writing are never completely joined, they are now more open to each other than ever before, and can no longer be clearly divided – even in Caesar's imperial eye.[16] □

I end this chapter with John Wilson Foster's stimulating piece, which also acts as a kind of summarising conclusion to the Guide as a whole, since Foster conducts his discussion of the 'decisive shift in Heaney's thinking about poetry' in terms that are recognisably those that I have used to structure this study of Heaney's poetry: place, identity, language, politics, gender, nationalism and colonialism. Having noted Heaney's early celebration of his native place, of the fishermen, ploughmen, thatchers, diviners and blacksmiths, of 'lives in their element' as Heaney puts it in 'Away From it All', Foster goes on to indicate how education and poetry placed a distance between the poet and his world, so that from the beginning he always had some sense of being 'out of his element'.

In terms of the Antaeus and Hercules paradigm, the poet is hoisted out of his 'first world', like the lobster forked out of its tank in 'Away From it All', the 'hampered one, out of water'. The poet can neither return to his native habitat nor 'participate / actively in history'. 'Out of his native element', Foster says, 'Heaney early made "exile" his writer's chosen ground, making poignant poetry out of "a dream of loss / and origins"'.[17] This in-between poetic stance, with the poet 'parleying in midstream', declaring that 'Two buckets were easier carried than one / I grew up in between', accords with Richard Kearney's view of what he calls the 'transitional crisis' of modern Irish culture: 'Heaney', Kearney observes, 'defines his poetry as journeywork, a migrant preoccupation with threshold and transit, passage and pilgrimage, with the crossing over of frontiers and divisions'.[18] But what Foster emphasises, along with Kearney, Deane, Welch and others, is the groundedness of Heaney's poetry as a prerequisite for flight. The poetry of vision gives life and expression to what is doomed and would otherwise be lost forever. A feminised nature and a feminised Ireland are carried over, translated into, possessed by, a poetry that has acquired a new freedom, virility, and governing power – 'a kind of repossession of the female by her mate and not the rhetorical colonisation of a Jonson, Hopkins or Yeats'. The process of masculine redress Foster traces to the parable poems in *The Haw Lantern* and the search for the father in *Seeing Things*. This sexual redress is also a political redress: 'The search for a justifying (and justified) masculinity is the search for power which, in political form, Irish Catholics were deprived of for centuries'. Poetry is a form of self-determination that can redeem the past. Foster believes this new kind of poetry, even in *Seeing Things*, 'is still more a thematic than a formal accomplishment'. So busy is his brilliantly conceptualising mind that he misses the actual power, the performative mastery of the poems in the 'Clearances' sequence in *The Haw Lantern* or of poems such as 'The Pitchfork', 'The Skylight', 'Wheels within Wheels', 'Man and Boy' or the title poem in *Seeing Things*. The substance of his analysis may also seem to hark back to the traditional view of Irish cultural achievement, which sees art's symbolic resolutions as a kind of compensation for political and material failure.

■ Even though it has been fitfully anticipated from the start, there has been one decisive shift in Heaney's thinking about poetry, a shift registered in his second book of criticism and to a lesser extent in his poetry from *Station Island* onwards. [. . .] To telegraph the shift: poetry's proper element is no longer seen as earth (or sea) but as air. Poetry is no longer a door into the dark but a door into the light; it must climb to its proper light, no longer descend to its proper dark.

It is possible that Heaney is responding to a new weather in Ireland created by the revisionist historians who have rendered his earlier gender-based nationalist mythography suspect. Or perhaps he has grown uncomfortable with the warmly reassuring presence he now is for the Common Reader who, alienated by much modern poetry and by the ideological stridency and theoretical introversions of criticism, has, judging by the enormous sales of Heaney's books, found in him a haven ('the hammered shod of a bay'). In any case, when 'Sweeney' describes his previous earthbound life as his 'old clandestine/pre-Copernican night' ('Alerted' in 'Sweeney Redivivus'), it is Heaney describing his own sensuous miring in the Ulster countryside. The Hughesian raid into darkness, the troubling secrecies underfoot, rich opacities of sound, rootedness: these that brought Heaney his fame have been subjected to a Copernican revolution, a shift from earth's centrality. If the requisitions of society have always been one potential captivity for the poet, then those of origin and background have by now become another, from which his poetry must also lift itself clear.

Still, chiefly through his adoption since *Sweeney Astray* and *Station Island* of the tree as a major site and symbol, Heaney has attempted to seam smoothly his two poetics. One gains the air only through the agency of the rooted. From the tree 'Sweeney' can launch himself into the air more than a stone's throw beyond those who would have him return to their battles. Heaney in 'Sweeney Redivivus' imagines the banished king as a poet (like himself) who wrote of conflict, was taken to task for doing it in the way he did, turned his back on auxiliary art, then (in 'The First Flight') 'upped the ante' in the poetry stakes:

I was mired in attachment
until they began to pronounce me
a feeder off battlefields

so I mastered new rungs of the air
to survey out of reach
their bonfires on hills their hosting

and fasting, the levies from Scotland
as always, and the people of art
diverting their rhythmical chants

to fend off the onslaught of winds
I would welcome and climb
at the top of my bent.

In this eloquent wish-fulfilment, the reference to hillside bonfires establishes an Ulster dimension of meaning.

The plant of honour in that beautifully swaggering poem 'In the Chestnut Tree', has cropped up in Heaney's work before. In his 1977 lecture at the Ulster Museum, 'The Sense of Place', reprinted in *Preoccupations*, he recalled 'the green chestnut tree that flourished at the entrance to the Gaelic Athletic Association grounds', which 'was more abundantly green from being the eminence where the tricolour was flown illicitly at Easter or on sports days'. It was, if you like, a symbol of that constitutional nationalism (cutting a republican dash on ritual occasions) I have remarked on. In its implied femaleness it also stood over against the male totem of the Protestant red, white and blue (man-made) flagpost at Hillhead.

Tree = Nature = native Ireland = femininity. The familiar equation is familiarly extended when the tree in 'In the Chestnut Tree', gorgeously female, is earthed and breathes like poetry. In 'The Placeless Heaven: Another Look at Kavanagh', an essay collected in *The Government of the Tongue*, Heaney writes of a family chestnut tree planted the year he was born and with which he connected his own life (and, I surmise, on hindsight his poetry). The tree was cut down and forgotten about.

Then, all of a sudden, a couple of years ago, I began to think of the space where the tree had been or would have been. In my mind's eye I saw it as a kind of luminous emptiness, a warp and waver of light, and once again, in a way that I find hard to define, I began to identify with that space . . . Except that this time in was not so much a matter of attaching oneself to a living symbol, of being rooted in the native ground; it was more a matter of preparing to be unrooted, to be spirited away into some transparent, yet indigenous afterlife.

That is the occasion and most succinct explanation of Heaney's one revolution in thought, and *The Haw Lantern* (1987) was the immediate result in verse, though it is continuous with some of the poetry in Part Three of *Station Island*. The implication is that in Heaney's future verse, Sweeney's chestnut tree is doomed in its reality and therefore in its gorgeousness: it is to be immaterialized and purified; and so must the poetry, too, be translated into a new spirituality, a different tonality, a 'neuter allegiance' to use Sweeney's words in 'The Cleric', the adjective carefully displacing the word 'neutral'.

At the heart of *The Haw Lantern* is a suite of eight sonnets in memory of the poet's mother who died in 1984.

[. . .]

The suite of sonnets is called 'Clearances'. The title suggests all manner of changes: endings – the cutting down of trees, emptyings, sweepings clean; and also middles – clarifications and respites. And beginnings too – necessary preparations for actions, buildings, fresh starts. It even suggests transcendence: more than unhamperings or leaps over hurdles, clearances can mean those absences caused by death but turned by love into their luminous opposite; clearances are translations, not extinctions.

[. . .]

Heaney has always championed the ungoverned tongue, a 'feminine' and permeable resistance to the 'masculine' demands of society. In *Preoccupations* the ungoverned or unhampered tongue is the Wordsworthian organ of origins, roots, background speaking the authority of primal conditions. Recently, however, Heaney has sought to describe and educe a more confident form of ungoverning for poetry. Now it *is* a problem should poetry evade challenges to it; such ungoverning, it seems, is an oblique acceptance of the primacy of society. Heaney seeks self-government for poetry in the sense of sovereignty, not self-constraint, and in which the 'masculine' traits of government are appropriated by a verse that nevertheless retains or creates as a result the field of the original Wordsworthian force and without being – as far as I can make out – the 'mere' rhetorical mastery of Jonson, Hopkins or Yeats. He seeks a third poetry that is not the poetry of conscience and responsibility, even if the latter can achieve equilibrium between poetry and society, art and life.

The Government of the Tongue is dominated, like *Preoccupations*, by the double nature of poetry, and many of the previous polarities are rehearsed – art versus life; song versus suffering; poetry versus politics; rhetoric versus reality; beauty versus truth; relish versus penitence; artistic self-respect versus submission to the times. But on the artistic side of the equation, the uprooted is now privileged. So too are absence, placelessness, the unsaid, impersonality, weightlessness, vision, even dream – all most un-Heaney-like. Kavanagh is re-evaluated and found to have moved from a substantial, local and self-expressive poetry to a weightless, placeless self-mastery. This is not a reading that convinces me, but it aligns with Heaney's current 'stance towards life'. Indicting his earlier reading of the verse Kavanagh wrote after 'Epic', Heaney writes: 'To go back to our original parable [of the chestnut tree], I still assumed Kavanagh to be writing about the tree which was actually in the ground when he had in fact passed on to write about the tree which he held in mind'. Kavanagh 'had cleared a space' to be filled from an inner source that could irrigate the world beyond the self.

The world beyond the self, which Sylvia Plath is judged not quite to have reached, is most authentically imagined in terms of air and light, of the vacancy left by events passed, objects removed, people departed . . .

Solidities of natural object, rural implement and folk artefact, once the texts of Heaney's poems, are now asserted to be pretexts for their insubstantial consequences.

[. . .]

Heaney professes now to value glimmerings, traces, spoors, sensings: the after-lives rather than the lives of things. He had already implied this in an earlier poem, 'The Harvest Bow', in *Field Work*.

[. . .]

Heaney's third poetry, a poetry of light, air, glimmer, manoeuvre, is still more a thematic than a formal accomplishment, and this is evidenced not just by *The Haw Lantern* but also by its successor, *Seeing Things* (1991). This is the case partly because Heaney must faithfully record the palpable in order to register its traces. The title *Seeing Things* is a pun: seeing things is also, in the popular phrase, *not* seeing things, but instead imagining them. The palpable creates a field of force: the imagined, a field of vision; the first is the burden, the second the task, of *Seeing Things*. The necessity of reification and the longing for rarefication create a fresh duality in the verse.

In the parables in *The Haw Lantern*, for example, political reality is transmuted into the abstraction of its elements. However, the reality can still be made out. The sequence of moods in 'From the Canton of

Expectation' – optative/conditional to imperative – clearly grammaticizes the fortunes of Ulster Catholics before and during the Civil Rights movement: impotent desire/negotiation from weakness to educated demands. The parable ends with an imagined Lowellian figure who stands his ground in a third, resolving mood, 'in the indicative', who affirms but does not do so supinely 'from under', but – and Heaney calls up the 'male' imagery of *North* here – actively, with uncompromising self-belief.

Unlike the imagined David in a muddy compound this figure is ambiguously political and apolitical, 'whose boat will lift when the cloudburst happens'. (Civil war in Ulster, among other possible doomsdays in the world?) Here is a familiar ambivalence, Heaney torn between art amid life, poetry and polites, *but in a higher key*; now the ideal alternative to danger is purity, not the messier business or a relishable antiquity. Escape from politics and life is no longer declension and absorption; the imagined boat is buoyed up and floated free by the very force that has challenged it.

[. . .]

In the third and highest kind of poetry, the poet inhales in a commanding act the powers of the outer world. It is in turn a kind of knowing. In his first Oxford lecture (1989), Heaney approves of Auden's trinity of poetic faculties, making, judging and knowing, which strongly resembles Heaney's new tripartite understanding of poetry. In a poem first published as 'Quoting' but reprinted as poem xxxvii in 'Squarings' from *Seeing Things*, Heaney writes about the best poetry amid the inadequacy of merely writing about it:

> Talking about it isn't good enough
> But quoting from it at least demonstrates
> The virtue of an art that knows its mind.

The next stage is writing it, and one assumes 'Quoting' is only a blueprint, especially when we recall Heaney's formulation in his Oxford lecture: 'the best poetry will not only register the assault of the actual and the brunt of necessity; it will also embody the spirit's protest against all that'. It cannot, then, be truancy or mere jubilation, despite Heaney's resort to those words.

But it remains unclear whether the best poetry engages politics and society on their own terms, even tactically or provisionally. It is unclear how far the imagined boat-builder whose craft (vessel and art) lifts clear has actually met the challenge of the storm. In 'From the Frontier of Writing' (*The Haw Lantern*), freedom for poetry requires 'clearance' (i.e. permission to proceed) from some part of the poet's psyche corresponding to, and imaginable as, society in its starkest form, a soldier at a checkpoint of the kind with which inhabitants of Ulster are familiar. Since the psychic checkpoint may be necessary (it is unclear), then society's baffles in front of the artist and its permissions to proceed may too be necessary, or at least convertible to artistic profit.

The three psycho-social stages waymarked in this poem can be interpreted as alluding not only to composition but also to the three *kinds* of poetry I have discussed in this essay – of subjugation (and endurance); of conscience (protest or penitence); and of freedom. Freedom, however, seems to be passively won in this poem on the psychic and social levels.

In any event, here and elsewhere poetry is *figured as politics*. From early in his career, Heaney chose as his political allegory the troubled history of Ireland and, in greater detail, the history of Northern Ireland since his boyhood. He has employed this allegory even though poetry in its highest form is judged to have 'cleared' or surmounted politics. Before that, though, poetry is literally *challenged by politics* – a challenge the highest poetry in some unspecified way meets but without self-compromise. But even if politics is sublimated in the best poetry (hence the imagery of light, air, flight?), Heaney has always intended his poetry to be, and indeed it is, a political poetry of considerable if oblique power.

Despite the passivity of the writer in 'From the Frontier of Writing', Heaney nowadays discusses the best poetry in terms of 'command', 'mastery', 'authority'. His version of literary history is sparsely populated by 'exemplars' whose better poems create 'fields of force' and whose best poems are 'epoch-making'. The metaphors of democracy have given way to those of autocracy. Power in poems now 'spills over', the verse exerts itself in 'mighty heaves'. The metaphors of femininity have yielded pride of place to those of masculinity. It is as if Heaney in his imagination has raided the male side of the ledger and returned with useful vials of hormone; his re-evaluations of Kavanagh, Lowell, Mandelstam and the others are critical Steinach operations on those writers. Poetry is to be virilified and set free. Sympathy has gravitated from the possessed (and passively possessing) female, and from the thwarted self-possession of the conscientious male, towards a male whose self-possession (though exclusively poetic) is only imaginable in terms of masculine empery and which in the context of Heaney's *oeuvre* must be a kind of repossession of the female by her rightful mate and not the rhetorical colonialism of a Jonson, Hopkins or Yeats.

Clearly a kind of sexual redress has been under way in Heaney's enterprise from the beginning. Veneration of the female and the repeated return to the mother, accompanied by an under-estimation (or repressed over-estimation?) of the male, has lightly given way to a search for the father. Until *Seeing Things*, Heaney's father was the subject of few poems. The 1991 collection is in this regard another kind of redress. True, the father is dead and may 'never rise again' and in several poems is re-imagined, assumed, as at were, into the light of Heaney's vision. Perhaps the poet is engaged in a less personal search for poetic maleness that will not offend the female deities of his poetry (Ireland, the muse, the goddess of the fen). It could be, however, that certain poets, notably Lowell, fill the role of 'father' and exhibit paternal power.

The impersonality of the search leads to some confusion as to which set of imagery is primary: air, vacancy, trace (nominal images of neuter state beyond gender but in the beginning more female than male); or lift, heave, spill (verbal images of masculine exertion). But certainly the poems in *The Haw Lantern* redress the balance (and not always with poetic profit) between features that Heaney sexed in *Preoccupations*: design is now as important as verbal texture, statement as feeling, address as evocation, appeal to the mind as appeal to the senses. (But the mighty heave, one feels, has yet to come.)

Heaney's own painstaking and ingenious equations and correspondences make it impossible for us to separate clearly sexual from political redress. The search for a justifying (and justified) masculinity is the search for power which, in political form, Irish Catholics were deprived of for centuries, and Ulster Catholics for fifty recent years. In the beginning (to all intents) was the colonization of Ireland, the turning of the island into a possessed (and passively possessing) woman. The native desire for 'male' self-possession was the desire for self-government kept from total success, however, by the biddable nature of constitutional nationalism or the reasonable demands for mere civil rights inside the United Kingdom. Is the ideal re-possessing male not, then, the demanding republican who entertains, beyond redress, imperial designs of his own on his former oppressors? Might we even translate Heaney's stages of redress into all-Ireland terms and see a figurative passage from colony through Free State to the desired Republic?

The personal nature of the search for redress – personal because it is autobiographical in origin and part and parcel of Heaney's mission as a poet – gives a political dimension to the confusion between imageries. The nationalist chestnut tree that is later savoured in its absence is translated into a world above and beyond politics. Heaney's nostalgia for pre-colonial unity and his acceptance of 'constitutional nationalism' succeed, it seems, to a desired transcendence of the constitutional issue, though perhaps in a way that accommodates, by absorbing, the colonizing or would-be colonizing forces.

However, the imagery of male dominion unavoidably, in the light of Heaney's earlier verse, amounts to a potent revendication. The wish remains for a self-determination that seeks reparation for the past. Heaney has recently seemed to want to surmount his origins and tribal membership, and evade any possible imputations of regionalism or even nationalism. In one sense he has been both justified and successful in doing so. But in another, he is hampered by the very excellence under his belt. Whatever purity and aloofness his poetry achieves in future, it cannot but be seen as a kind of sovereignty wrested out of subjection or home rule, thereby implicating Irish politics and the empowering, the growing confidence, of Irish nationalist culture (in the largest sense of the phrase) in its relationship with Britain and Protestant Ulster.[19] □

BIBLIOGRAPHY

Works by Seamus Heaney

Death of a Naturalist. London & Boston: Faber, 1966.
Door into the Dark. London: Faber, 1969; New York: Oxford University Press, 1969.
Wintering Out. London: Faber, 1972; New York: Oxford University Press, 1973.
North. London & Boston: Faber, 1975; New York: Oxford University Press, 1976.
Field Work. London & Boston: Faber, 1979; New York: Farrar, Straus, Giroux, 1979.
Selected Poems 1965–1975. London & Boston: Faber, 1980; New York: Farrar, Straus, Giroux, 1980.
Preoccupations: Selected Prose 1968–1978. London & Boston: Faber, 1980; New York: Farrar, Straus, Giroux, 1980.
The Rattle Bag: An Anthology of Poetry, selected by Seamus Heaney and Ted Hughes. London & Boston: Faber, 1982.
Sweeney Astray. Derry: Field Day, 1983; London: Faber, 1984; New York: Farrar, Straus, Giroux, 1984.
Station Island. London: Faber, 1984; New York: Farrar, Straus, Giroux, 1984.
The Haw Lantern. London: Faber, 1987; New York: Farrar, Straus, Giroux, 1987.
The Government of the Tongue: The 1986 T.S. Eliot Memorial Lectures and Other Critical Writings. London & New York: Faber, 1988; New York: Farrar, Straus, Giroux, 1988.
The Cure at Troy: A Version of Sophocles' Philoctetes. London: Faber, 1990.
Seeing Things. London: Faber, 1991.
The Redress of Poetry: Oxford Lectures. London: Faber, 1995.
The Spirit Level. London & Boston: Faber, 1996.

Books on Seamus Heaney

Andrews, Elmer, *The Poetry of Seamus Heaney: All the Realms of Whisper*. London: Macmillan, 1988; New York: St Martin's Press, 1988.
Andrews, Elmer, ed., *Seamus Heaney: A Collection of Critical Essays*. London: Macmillan, 1992; New York: St Martin's Press, 1992.
Bloom, Harold, ed., *Seamus Heaney*. Hew Haven: Chelsea House, 1988.
Broadbridge, Edward, ed., *Seamus Heaney*. Copenhagen: Denmark Radio, 1977.
Buttel, Robert, *Seamus Heaney*. Lewisburg: Bucknell University Press, 1975.
Corcoran, Neil, *Seamus Heaney*. London: Faber, 1986.
Curtis, Tony, ed., *The Art of Seamus Heaney*. Bridgend: Poetry Wales, 1982. Revised edn. 1985, 3rd rev. edn, 1994; Chester Springs PA: Dufour Editions, 1985.
Foster, John Wilson Foster, *The Achievement of Seamus Heaney*. Dublin: Lilliput Press, 1995.
Foster, Thomas C., *Seamus Heaney*. Dublin: O'Brien Press, 1989; Boston: Twayne Publishers, 1989.
Genet, Jacqueline, *Studies on Seamus Heaney*. Caen: Centre de publications de l'Université de Caen, 1987.
Hart, Henry, *Seamus Heaney: Poet of Contrary Progressions*. New York: Syracuse University Press, 1992.
Maguire, Aisling, York *Notes on Selected Poems: Seamus Heaney*. Harlow: Longman, 1986.
McGuinn, Nicholas, *Seamus Heaney: A Student's Guide to the Selected Poems 1965–1975*. Leeds: Arnold-Wheaton, 1986.
Morrison, Blake, *Seamus Heaney*. London & New York: Methuen, 1982.

O'Donoghue, Bernard, *Seamus Heaney and the Language of Poetry*. Hemel
Hempstead & New York: Harvester Wheatsheaf, 1994.
Parker, Michael, *Seamus Heaney. The Making of a Poet*. Dublin: Gill and Macmillan,
1993.
Tamplin, Ronald, *Seamus Heaney*. Milton Keynes & Philadelphia: Open University
Press, 1990.

Articles and Reviews on Seamus Heaney

Agee, Chris, 'Heaney's Progress', *Books Ireland*, 126 (October 1988), pp. 164–65.
Allison, Jonathan, 'Acts of Union: Seamus Heaney's Tropes of Sex and Marriage',
in *Eire-Ireland*, 27, 4 (1992), pp. 106–21.
Alvarez, A. 'A Fine Way with the Language', *New York Review of Books*, 6 March
1980, pp. 16–17.
Bayley, John, 'Song and Suffering' *Poetry Review*, 78, 3 (Autumn 1988), pp. 46–47.
Bayley, John, 'Living In and Living Out: The Poet's Location for the Poetry',
Agenda, 27, 1 (Spring 1989), pp. 32–36.
Brandes, Rand, 'Secondary Sources: A Gloss on the Critical Reception of Seamus
Heaney 1965–1993', in *Colby Quarterly*, 30, 1 (March 1994), pp. 44–58.
Brown, Terence, *Northern Voices: Poets from Ulster* (Dublin: Gill and Macmillan, 1975)
Brown, Terence, 'The Witnessing Eye and the Speaking Tongue', in Elmer
Andrews (ed.), *Seamus Heaney: A Collection of Critical Essays* (London: Macmillan,
1992), pp. 182–92.
Byron Catherine, *Out of Step: Pursuing Seamus Heaney to Purgatory* (Bristol:
Loxwood Stoneleigh, 1992)
Cairns, David and Shaun Richards (eds.), *Writing Ireland: Colonialism, Nationalism
and Culture* (Manchester: Manchester University Press, 1988)
Carey, John, 'Poetry for the World We Live In', *Sunday Times*, 18 November 1979,
p. 40.
Carey, John, 'The Joy of Heaney', *Sunday Times*, 14 October 1984, p. 42.
Carey, John, 'The Stain of Words', *Sunday Times*, 21 June 1987, p. 56.
Carey, John, 'The Most Sensuous Poet to use English Since Keats', *Sunday Times*,
3 April 1988, G9
Carey, John, 'A Plea for Poetry in our Time' *Sunday Times*, 12 June 1988, pp. G1–2
Carey, John, 'Touching the Void', *Sunday Times*, 2 June 1991, Section 6, p. 1.
Carey, John, 'Brave New Worlds', *Sunday Times*, 28 April 1996, Books, pp. 1–2.
Carson, Ciaran, '"Escaped from the Massacre"?', in *The Honest Ulsterman*, 50 (Winter
1975), pp. 183–86.
Carson, Ciaran, 'Sweeneys Ancient and Modern', *The Honest Ulsterman*, 76
(Autumn 1984), pp. 73–79.
Coughlan, Patricia, '"Bog Queens": The Representation of Women in the Poetry
of John Montague and Seamus Heaney', in Toni O'Brien Johnson and David
Cairns (eds.), *Gender in Irish Writing* (Milton Keynes: Open University Press,
1991), pp. 89–111.
Crotty, Patrick, 'Vocal Visitations', in *The Irish Review*, 9 (Autumn 1990), pp. 102–04.
Cullingford, Elizabeth Butler, 'Thinking of Her . . . as . . . Ireland: Yeats, Pearse,
and Heaney', in *Textual Practice*, 4, 1 (Spring 1990).
Davies, Alistair, 'Seamus Heaney: From Revivalism to Postmodernism', in Gary
Day and Brian Docherty (eds.), *British Poetry from the 1950s to the 1990s: Politics and
Art* (Basingstoke: Macmillan, 1997), pp.103–17.
Deane, Seamus, 'Powers of Earth and Visions of Air', *Times Literary Supplement*,
16 March 1990, pp. 275–76.

Deane, Seamus, 'Seamus Heaney: The Timorous and the Bold', in *Celtic Revivals* (London: Faber, 1985), pp. 174–86.

Deane, Seamus, 'Unhappy and at Home', interview with Heaney, *The Crane Bag*, 1, 1 (1977) pp. 61–67.

Donoghue, Denis, 'The Literature of Trouble', in *We Irish* (Brighton: Harvester Press, 1996), pp. 182–94.

Fennell, Desmond, 'The Heaney Phenomenon', *Irish Times*, 30 March 1991, p. 5.

Fennell, Desmond, *Whatever You Say Say Nothing: Why Seamus Heaney is No. 1* (Dublin: ELO Publications, 1991).

Harmon, Maurice, '"We pine for ceremony": Ritual and Reality in the Poetry of Seamus Heaney', in Elmer Andrews, *Seamus Heaney: A Collection of Critical Essays*, pp. 67–86.

Hart, Henry, 'What is Heaney Seeing in *Seeing Things*?', in *Colby Quarterly*, 30, 1 (March 1984), pp. 32–42.

Hederman, Mark Patrick, 'Poetry and the Fifth Province' in *The Crane Bag*, 9, 1(1985), pp. 110–19.

Hederman, Mark Patrick, Seamus Heaney: The Reluctant Poet', *The Crane Bag*, 3, 2 (1979), pp. 61–70.

Jenkins, Nicholas, 'Walking on Air', *Times Literary Supplement*, 5 July 1996, pp. 10–12.

Kearney, Richard, *Transitions: Narratives in Modern Irish Culture* (Dublin: Wolfhound, 1988).

Kearney, Timothy, 'The Poetry of the North: A Post-modernist Perspective', *The Crane Bag*, 3, 2 (1979), pp. 45–53.

Kiberd, Declan, 'Heaney's magic', *Sunday Tribune*, 9 June 1991, pp. 21 and 36.

Lloyd, David, '"Pap for the Dispossessed": Seamus Heaney and the Poetics of Identity', *Boundary*, 2 (Winter 1985), pp. 319–42.

Longley, Edna, '"Inner Émigré" or "Artful Voyeur"? Seamus Heaney's *North*', in *Poetry and the Wars* (Newcastle-upon-Tyne: Bloodaxe, 1986), pp. 140–69.

Longley, Edna, 'Poetry and Politics in Northern Ireland', in *Poetry and the Wars*, pp. 185–210.

O'Brien, Conor Cruise, 'A Slow North-East Wind', *Listener*, 25 September 1975, pp. 404–05.

O'Brien, Conor Cruise, 'An Unhealthy Intersection', *New Review*, 2, 16 (July 1975), pp. 3–8.

Ricks, Christopher, 'Lasting Things', *Listener*, 26 June 1969, pp. 900–01.

Ricks, Christopher, 'The Mouth, the Meal, the Book', *London Review of Books*, 8 November 1979, pp. 4–5.

Smith, Stan, 'The Distance Between', in Neil Corcoran (ed.), *The Chosen Ground: Essays on the Contemporary Poetry of Northern Ireland* (Bridgend: Seren Books), pp. 35–64.

Vendler, Helen, 'A Nobel for the North', *New Yorker*, 23 October 1995, pp. 84–89.

Vendler, Helen, 'Seamus Heaney', in *The Music of What Happens* (Cambridge, Massachusets: Harvard University Press, 1988), pp. 149–65.

Waterman, Andrew, '"The best way out is always through"', in Elmer Andrews (ed.), *Seamus Heaney: A Collection of Critical Essays*, pp. 39–66.

Welch, Robert, '"A rich young man leaving everything he had": Poetic Freedom in Seamus Heaney', in Elmer Andrews (ed.), *Seamus Heaney: A Collection of Critical Essays*, pp. 150–181.

Wills, Clair, *Improprieties: Politics and Sexuality in Northern Irish Poetry* (Oxford: Oxford University Press, 1993).

Wilson, Robert McLiam, 'The Glittering Prize', *Fortnight*, November 1995, p. 6.

NOTES

INTRODUCTION

1 Helen Vendler, 'A Nobel for the North: Negotiating between the urgency of witness and the urgency of delight', *New Yorker*, 23 October 1995, p. 84.
2 Chris Agee, 'Heaney's Progress', *Books Ireland*, October 1988, p. 165.

CHAPTER ONE

1 Rand Brandes, 'Secondary Sources: A Gloss on the Critical Reception of Seamus Heaney 1965–1993', *Colby Quarterly*, 30, 1 (March 1994), p. 63.
2 John Carey, 'The Most Sensuous Poet to Use English since Keats', *Sunday Times*, 3 April 1988, p. G9.
3 Declan Kiberd, 'Heaney's Magic', *Sunday Tribune*, 9 June 1991, p. 22.
4 Robert McLiam Wilson, 'The Glittering Prize', *Fortnight*, November 1995, p. 6.
5 John Wilson Foster, *The Achievement of Seamus Heaney* (Dublin: Lilliput Press, 1995), p. 24.
6 Edna Longley, 'Poetry and Politics in Northern Ireland' in *Poetry in the Wars* (Newcastle-upon-Tyne: Bloodaxe, 1986), p. 200.
7 Chris Agee, 'Heaney's Progress', *Books Ireland*, October 1988, p. 164.
8 Helen Vendler, 'A Nobel for the North', *New Yorker*, 23 October 1995, p. 87.
9 Seamus Heaney, 'Frontiers of Writing', in *The Redress of Poetry* (London: Faber, 1995), p. 202.
10 John Carey, 'The Most Sensuous Poet to Use English Since Keats', *Sunday Times*, 3 April 1988, p. G9.
11 Christopher Ricks, 'Lasting Things', *Listener*, 26 June 1969, pp. 900–01.
12 Christopher Ricks, 'The Mouth, the Meal and the Book', *London Review of Books*, 8 November 1979, pp. 4–5.
13 A. Alvarez, 'A Fine Way with the Language', *New York Review of Books*, 6 March 1980, pp. 16–17.
14 Blake Morrison, *Seamus Heaney* (London: Methuen, 1982), pp. 12–13.

15 Morrison, p. 15.
16 Morrison, p. 19.
17 Blake Morrison and Andrew Motion, *The Penguin Book of Contemporary British Poetry* (Harmondsworth: Penguin, 1982), p. 13.
18 Morrison and Motion, p. 12.
19 Morrison and Motion, p. 12.
20 John Carey, 'The Stain of Words', *Sunday Times*, 21 June 1987, p. 56.
21 John Bayley, 'Living in and Living Out: The Poet's Location for the Poetry', *Agenda*, 27, 1 (Spring 1989), pp. 32–36.
22 Helen Vendler, *The Music of What Happens* (Cambridge, MA: Harvard University Press, 1988), p. 2.
23 Vendler, pp. 150–58.
24 Desmond Fennell, *Whatever You Say, Say Nothing: Why Seamus Heaney is No. 1* (Dublin: ELO Publications, 1991), p. 29.
25 Fennell, p. 31.
26 Fennell, pp. 33–34.
27 Fennell, p. 38.
28 Fennell, p. 39.
29 Vendler, p. 5.
30 Desmond Fennell, 'The Heaney Phenomenon', *Irish Times*, 30 March 1991, p. 5.

CHAPTER TWO

1 Seamus Heaney, 'Mossbawn', *Preoccupations: Selected Prose 1968–1978* (London: Faber, 1980), p. 17.
2 Seamus Heaney, 'Belfast', *Preoccupations*, p. 35.
3 Seamus Heaney, 'The Sense of Place', *Preoccupations*, p. 131.
4 David Lloyd, '"Pap for the Dispossessed": The Poetics of Identity', in *Seamus Heaney: A Collection of Critical Essays*, p. 94.
5 Lloyd, pp. 94–108.
6 Harold Bloom, 'The Voice of Kinship', *Times Literary Supplement*, 8 February 1980, pp. 137–38.
7 Seamus Heaney, 'Feeling into Words', *Preoccupations*, p. 41.
8 See Seamus Heaney's lines in 'The Ministry of Fear': 'Ulster was British, but with no rights on / The English lyric'.
9 Seamus Heaney in interview with

Seamus Deane, 'Unhappy and at Home', in *The Crane Bag*, 1, 1 (1977), p. 65.

10 Seamus Heaney, 'Belfast', *Preoccupations*, p. 36.

11 Heaney, p. 34.

12 Heaney, p. 34.

13 Seamus Heaney, 'The Sense of Place', *Preoccupations*, p. 132.

14 Seamus Heaney, 'Feeling into Words', *Preoccupations*, p. 57.

15 Heaney, p. 57.

16 Heaney, pp. 56–57.

17 Heaney, p. 56.

18 Clair Wills, *Improprieties: Politics and Sexuality in Northern Irish Poetry* (Oxford: Oxford University Press, 1993), p. 69.

19 Wills, p. 70.

20 Wills, p. 98–101.

21 Seamus Heaney, 'Feeling into Words', *Preoccupations*, p. 57.

22 See David Trotter, *The Making of the Reader: Language and Subjectivity in Modern American, English and Irish Poetry* (Basingstoke: Macmillan, 1984), p. 188.

23 Seamus Heaney, 'Feeling into Words', *Translations*, p. 41.

24 Terry Eagleton, 'Recent Poetry', review of Seamus Heaney, *Field Work*, in *Stand*, 23, 1 (1980), p. 77.

25 Terry Eagleton, 'New Poetry', review of John Montague, *The Dead Kingdom*, in *Stand*, 26, 2 (1985), p. 67.

26 Seamus Heaney, 'Mossbawn', *Preoccupations*, p. 101.

27 Clair Wills, *Improprieties*, p. 96.

28 Wills, blurb on bookcover.

29 Robert Welch, '"A rich young man leaving everything he had": Poetic Freedom in Seamus Heaney', in *Seamus Heaney: A Collection of Critical Essays*, ed. Elmer Andrews (London: Macmillan, 1992), p. 156.

30 Welch, p. 155.

31 Richard Kearney, *Transitions: Narratives in Modern Irish Culture* (Dublin: Wolfhound, 1988), p. 14.

32 Kearney, p. 14.

33 Kearney, p. 102.

34 Kearney, p. 15.

35 Kearney, pp. 101–12.

36 Seamus Heaney, 'Feeling into Words', *Preoccupations*, p. 52.

37 Seamus Heaney, 'Mossbawn', *Preoccupations*, p. 21.

38 Seamus Heaney, 'Feeling into Words', *Preoccupations*, p. 57.

39 Heaney, p. 58.

40 Seamus Heaney, 'Belfast', *Preoccupations*, p. 35.

41 Heaney, p. 37.

42 Jacques Lacan, *Ecrits*, 1966.

43 Seamus Heaney, 'The Makings of a Music', *Preoccupations*, p. 78.

44 Timothy Kearney, 'The Poetry of the North: A Post-Modernist Perspective', *The Crane Bag*, 3, 3 (1979), pp. 49–51 and 52–53.

45 See Terence Brown, who imputes passivity and indecision to Heaney in this regard in *Northern Voices* (Dublin: Gill and Macmillan, 1975), pp. 181–86.

46 Against this, Terence Brown argues that this 'poetry of problem' works against the attainment of a 'poetry of assured vision' in the case of these writers. See Terence Brown, *Northern Voices*, 2 pp. 15–16. Seamus Deane in his essay 'Irish Poetry and Irish Nationalism' pursues a similar line to the one presented in this excerpt. See *Two Decades of Irish Writing*, ed. Douglas Dunn (Cheadle: Carcanet Press, 1975), p. 21.

47 Richard Kearney, *Transitions*, p. 113.

48 Alistair Davies, 'Seamus Heaney: From Revivalism to Postmodernism', in *British Poetry from the 1950s to the 1990s: Politics and Art*, ed. Gary Day and Brian Docherty (Basingstoke: Macmillan, 1997), pp. 108–16.

49 Martin Heidegger, 'The Nature of Language', in *On the Way to Language*, trans. Peter D. Hertz (New York: Harper & Row, 1971), p. 62.

50 Helen Vendler, 'Echo Soundings, Searches, Probes', in *Seamus Heaney, Modern Critical Views*, Ed. Harold Bloom (New Haven, Connecticut: Chelsea, 1986), p. 178. This essay originally appeared in *The New Yorker*, 23 September 1985.

51 Felix Guattari, *Molecular Revolution: Psychiatry and Politics*, trans. Rosemary Sheed (Harmondsworth: Penguin, 1984), p. 36.

52 Roland Barthes, *Roland Barthes by Roland Barthes*, trans. Richard Howard (London: Macmillan, 1977), p.143.

53 Barthes, p.131.

54 Patrick Crotty, 'Vocal Visitations', in *The Irish Review*, 9 (Autumn 1990), p.103.

55 Stan Smith, 'The Distance Between', in *The Chosen Ground: Essays on the Contemporary Poetry of Northern Ireland*, ed. Neil Corcoran (Bridgend: Seren Books, 1992), p.46.

56 Smith, p.36.

57 Smith, pp.44–46.

58 Seamus Heaney, 'The Sense of Place', *Preoccupations*, p.145.

59 Seamus Heaney, *Place and Displacement* (Grasmere: Trustees of Dove Cottage, 1984), p.3.

60 Heaney, p.4.

61 Heaney, p.8.

62 Seamus Heaney, *Field Work*, pp.7, 9, 10.

63 Stan Smith, 'The Distance Between', in *The Chosen Ground*, p.53.

64 Smith p.60.

65 Neil Corcoran, *Seamus Heaney* (London: Faber, 1986), p.153.

66 Smith, 'The Distance Between', pp.60–61.

CHAPTER THREE

1 Robert McLiam Wilson, 'The Glittering Prize', *Fortnight*, November 1995, p.6.

2 Eoghan Harris, 'A Nice Poet Bogged Down in the Past', *Sunday Times*, 8 October 1995.

3 James Simmons, The Trouble with Seamus', in *Seamus Heaney: A Collection of Critical Essays*, ed. Elmer Andrews, p.60.

4 Conor Cruise O'Brien, 'An Unhealthy Intersection', *New Review*, 2, 16 (July 1975), p.7.

5 Conor Cruise O'Brien, 'A Slow North-East Wind', *The Listener*, 25 September 1976, pp.404–05.

6 Ciaran Carson, '"Escaped from the Massacre"?', *The Honest Ulsterman*, 50 (Winter 1975), pp.183–86.

7 Maurice Harmon, '"We pine for ceremony": Ritual and Reality in the Poetry of Seamus Heaney, 1965–75', in *Seamus Heaney: A Collection of Critical Essays*, ed. Elmer Andrews, p.76.

8 David Cairns and Shaun Richards, *Writing Ireland: Colonialism, Nationalism and Culture* (Manchester: Manchester University Press, 1988), p.144.

9 Denis Donoghue, 'The Literature of Trouble', in *We Irish: Selected Essays*, (Brighton: Harvester, 1986), pp.187–94.

10 Blake Morrison, *Seamus Heaney* (London: Methuen, 1982), pp.67–68.

11 John Carey, 'The Poet of the Bogs', *Sunday Times*, 1982.

12 Edna Longley, 'Poetry and Politics in Northern Ireland', in *The Crane Bag*, 9, 1 (1985), pp.26–41; reprinted in *Poetry in the Wars*, p.185.

13 Edna Longley, '"Inner Émigré" or "Artful Voyeur"? Seamus Heaney's *North*', in *Poetry in the Wars*, pp.150–69.

14 James Randall, interview with Seamus Heaney, *Ploughshares*, 5, 3 (1979), p.17.

15 Seamus Heaney, 'Feeling into Words', *Preoccupations*, pp.57–58.

16 John Haffenden, *Viewpoints: Poets in Conversation* (London: Faber, 1981), p.61.

17 Haffenden, pp.61, 66.

18 John Wilson Foster, *The Honest Ulsterman*, 50, p.184.

19 Haffenden, p.64.

20 Seamus Heaney, 'Englands of the Mind', *Preoccupations*, p.160.

22 Seamus Deane, 'Irish Poetry and Irish Nationalism', in *Two Decades of Irish Writing*, ed. Douglas Dunn (Carcanet, 1975), p.16.

23 Seamus Heaney, in interview with Seamus Deane, 'Unhappy and at Home', *The Crane Bag*, 1, 1 (1977), pp.67–8.

24 Heaney, p.67.

25 Heaney, p.69.

26 Heaney, p.69.

27 Mark Patrick Hederman, '*The Crane Bag* and the North of Ireland', *The Crane Bag*, 4, 2 (1980), pp.98–99.

28 Derek Mahon, *The Snow Party* (Oxford: Oxford University Press, 1975), p.10.

29 Mark Patrick Hederman, 'Poetry and

the Fifth Province', *The Crane Bag*, 9, 1 (1995), p.112.

30 Hederman, p.111.

31 Hederman, pp.114–16.

32 Hederman, p.118.

33 Hederman, p.118.

34 Edna Longley, 'A Reply', p.120.

35 Maurice Riordan, 'Eros and History: On Contemporary Irish Poetry', *The Crane Bag*, 9, 1 (1985), pp.49–56.

36 Riordan, p.55.

37 Richard Kearney, *Transitions*, p.296.

38 Kearney, p.275.

39 Edna Longley, 'Poetry and Politics in Northern Ireland', in *Poetry in the Wars*, p.201.

40 George Watson, 'The Narrow Ground: Northern Poets and the Northern Ireland Crisis', in *Irish Writers and Society at Large*, ed. Masaru Sekine (Gerards Cross: Cohn Smythe, 1985), p.210.

41 Watson, p.214.

42 Watson, p.223.

43 Watson, p.207.

44 Seamus Deane, 'The Timorous and the Bold', *Celtic Revivals*, pp.179–86.

45 Heaney, in interview with Seamus Deane, 'Unhappy and at Home', in *The Crane Bag*, 1 (1977), p.67.

46 Seamus Heaney, 'Belfast', *Preoccupations*, p.30.

47 Heaney, p.34.

48 Seamus Heaney, 'Feeling into Words', *Preoccupations*, p.56.

49 John Carey, 'A Plea for Poetry in our time', *Sunday Times*, 12 June 1988, Books Section, pp.1 and 2.

50 Seamus Heaney, 'The Government of the Tongue', in *The Government of the Tongue* (London: Faber, 1988), p.108.

51 Seamus Heaney, 'The Redress of Poetry', in *The Redress of Poetry* (London: Faber, 1995), p.5.

CHAPTER FOUR

1 Seamus Heaney, 'Mossbawn', *Preoccupations*, p.19.

2 Seamus Heaney, 'Belfast', *Preoccupations*, p.37.

3 Heaney, p.34.

4 Seamus Heaney, 'The Sense of Place', *Preoccupations*, p.132.

5 Heaney, p.131.

6 Seamus Deane, 'The Timorous and the Bold', in *Celtic Revivals*, pp.175–76.

7 Deane, p.186.

8 Jonathan Allison, 'Acts of Union: Seamus Heaney's Tropes of Sex and Marriage', *Eire-Ireland*, 27, 4 (1992), pp.106–08.

9 Allison, pp.110–111.

10 Allison, p.120.

11 Allison, p.111.

12 David Cairns and Shaun Richards, *Writing Ireland*, p.145.

13 Seamus Heaney, 'Mossbawn', *Preoccupations*, p.19.

14 Seamus Heaney, 'Mother Ireland', *Listener*, 27 November 1972, p.790.

15 Seamus Heaney, 'Feeling into Words', *Preoccupations*, p.57.

16 Elizabeth Butler Cullingford, '"Thinking of Her . . . as . . . Ireland": Yeats, Pearse, and Heaney', *Textual Practice*, 4, 1 (Spring 1990).

17 Patricia Coughlan, '"Bog Queens": The Representation of Women in the Poetry of John Montague and Seamus Heaney', *Gender in Irish Writing*, eds. Toni O'Brien Johnson and David Cairns (Milton Keynes: Open University Press), p.99.

18 Coughlan, p.89.

19 Coughlan, p.89.

20 Coughlan, p.90.

21 Coughlan, pp.99–108.

22 Catherine Byron, *Out of Step: Pursuing Seamus Heaney to Purgatory* (Bristol: Loxwood Stoneleigh, 1992), p.234.

23 Byron, p.218.

24 Byron, pp.122–28.

CHAPTER FIVE

1 'An Interview with Seamus Heaney' (James Randall), in *Ploughshares*, 5, 3 (1979), p.21.

2 Clair Wills, *Improprieties: Politics and Sexuality in Northern Irish Poetry*, p.68.

3 Seamus Heaney, 'The Indefatigable Hoof-taps: Sylvia Plath', in *The Government of the Tongue*, p.158.

4 Seamus Heaney, 'Nero, Chekhov's Cognac and a Knocker', in *The Government of the Tongue*, p. xxii.

5 Andrew Waterman, 'The best way out is always through', in *Seamus Heaney: A Collection of Critical Essays*, ed. Elmer Andrews, pp. 11–38.

6 Mark Patrick Hederman, 'Seamus Heaney, The Reluctant Poet', *The Crane Bag*, 3, 2, (1979), p. 61.

7 Hederman, p. 66.

8 Hederman, p. 66.

9 Ciaran Carson, 'Sweeneys Ancient and Modern', *The Honest Ulsterman*, 76 (Autumn 1984), pp. 73–79.

10 Seamus Deane, 'Powers of Earth and Visions of Air', *Times Literary Supplement*, 16 March 1990, pp. 275–76.

11 Terence Brown, The Witnessing Eye And the Speaking Tongue', in *Seamus Heaney: A Collection of Critical Essays*, ed. Elmer Andrews, p. 187.

12 Brown, p. 190.

13 Seamus Heaney, 'The Government of the Tongue', in *The Government of the Tongue*, p. 108.

14 'Seamus Famous: Time to be Dazzled', Seamus Heaney interview with Blake Morrison, *Independent on Sunday*, 19 May 1991.

15 Henry Hart, 'What is Heaney Seeing in *Seeing Things?*', *Colby Quarterly*, 30, 1 (March 1994), pp. 33–42.

16 Nicholas Jenkins, 'Walking on Air', *Times Literary Supplement*, 5 July 1996, pp. 10–12.

17 John Wilson Foster, *The Achievement of Seamus Heaney* (Dublin: Lilliput Press, 1995), p. 43.

18 Richard Kearney, *Transitions*, pp. 14–15.

19 John Wilson Foster, *The Achievement of Seamus Heaney*, pp. 44–55.

ACKNOWLEDGEMENTS

The editor and publishers wish to thank the following for their permission to reprint copyright material: Bloodaxe Books (for material from *Poetry in the Wars*); *London Review of Books* (for material from 'The Mouth, the Meal and the Book'); *New York Review of Books* (for material from 'A Fine Way With the Language'); Harvard University Press (for material from *The Music of What Happens*); Macmillan (for material from *Seamus Heaney: A Collection of Critical Essays*); Oxford University Press (for material from *Improprieties: Politics and Sexuality in Northern Irish Poetry*); Wolfhound (for material from *Transitions: Narratives in Modern Irish Culture*); *The Crane Bag* (for material from 'The Poetry of the North: A Post-Modernist Perspective' and 'Poetry and the Fifth Province'); Macmillan (for material from *British Poetry from the 1950s to the 1990s*); *The Honest Ulsterman* (for material from '"Escaped the Massacre"?'); Harvester Press (for material from *We Irish: Selected Essays*); Faber and Faber (for material from *Celtic Revivals*); *Eire-Ireland* (for material from 'Acts of Union: Seamus Heaney's Tropes of Sex and Marriage'); Open University Press (for material from *Gender in Irish Writing*); Loxwood Stoneleigh (for material from *Out of Step: Pursuing Seamus Heaney to Purgatory*).

Every effort has been made to contact the holders of any copyrights applying to the material quoted in this book. The publishers would be grateful if any such copyright holders whom they have not been able to contact, would write to them.

Elmer Andrews is Senior Lecturer in English at the University of Ulster at Coleraine. His books include *The Poetry of Seamus Heaney: All the Realms of Whisper* (London: Macmillan, 1988), *Seamus Heaney: A Collection of Critical Essays* (London: Macmillan, 1992), *Contemporary Irish Poetry: A Collection of Critical Essays* (London: Macmillan, 1992) and *The Art of Brian Friel* (London: Macmillan, 1995). He has also published essays on American and Irish writers in various books and journals.

INDEX

Index compiled by Valerie Lewis Chandler, BA ALAA

THE ICON *CRITICAL GUIDES* SERIES

Virginia Woolf
To the Lighthouse, The Waves
Edited by Jane Goldman
ISBN 1 874166 70 6

James Joyce
*Ulysses, A Portrait of the Artist
as a Young Man*
Edited by John Coyle
ISBN 1 874166 68 4

D.H. Lawrence
The Rainbow, Women in Love
Edited by Richard Beynon
ISBN 1 874166 69 2

Shakespeare
King Lear
Edited by Susan Bruce
ISBN 1 874166 71 4

F. Scott Fitzgerald
The Great Gatsby
Edited by Nicolas Tredell
ISBN 1 874166 67 6

Toni Morrison
Beloved
Edited by Carl Plasa
ISBN 1 874166 73 0

Herman Melville
Moby-Dick
Edited by Nick Selby
ISBN 1 874166 75 7

Seamus Heaney
The Poetry of Seamus Heaney
Edited by Elmer Andrews
ISBN 1 84046 017 2

Mark Twain
Tom Sawyer, Huckleberry Finn
Edited by Stuart Hutchinson
ISBN 1 874166 76 5

Shakespeare
Richard II
Edited by Martin Coyle
ISBN 1 874166 72 2

NEW TITLES FOR AUTUMN 1998

Joseph Conrad
Heart of Darkness
Edited by Nicolas Tredell
ISBN 1 84046 019 9

Charles Dickens
Great Expectations
Edited by Nicolas Tredell
ISBN 1 84046 020 2

Emily Brontë
Wuthering Heights
Edited by Patsy Stoneman
ISBN 1 84046 021 0

E.M. Forster
A Passage to India
Edited by Betty Jay
ISBN 1 84046 027 X

Edith Wharton
*The House of Mirth,
The Age of Innocence,
The Custom of the Country*
Edited by Stuart Hutchinson
ISBN 1 84046 023 7